The Best of Friends,
The Worst of Enemies

Also by Eva Margolies:

Sensual Pleasure: A Woman's Guide

The Best of Friends, The Worst of Enemies

WOMEN'S HIDDEN POWER OVER WOMEN

Eva Margolies

The Dial Press
DOUBLEDAY & COMPANY, INC.
GARDEN CITY, NEW YORK
1985

Library of Congress Cataloging in Publication Data
Margolies, Eva.
The best of friends, the worst of enemies.
1. Women—Psychology. 2. Friendship. 3. Women—
Employment—Social aspects. I. Title.
HQ1206.M343 1985   305.4   84-26066
ISBN 0-385-27872-1
Published by The Dial Press
Copyright © 1985 by Eva Margolies

To my mother and my father

CONTENTS

ACKNOWLEDGMENTS

THIS BOOK in many ways has been a collaborative effort. I am first indebted to Dr. Jane Flax and Angela Fox. Their willingness to share their expertise with me paved the way for many of the ideas discussed in this work.

Dr. Flax received her Ph.D. at Yale and has extensive training in psychotherapy and psychoanalysis. She is presently an assistant professor at Howard University in Washington, D.C., and has a private psychoanalytic practice. Dr. Flax also has published numerous articles on psychoanalytic, feminist, and political theory. Angela Fox is a psychoanalyst who received her training at the Guild for Psychoanalysis. Her private practice in psychotherapy and psychoanalysis is located in New York City. The voices of these two women are heard throughout this book, and I want to thank them both for their time and effort.

I would also like to thank my editor, Frances McCullough, for her sharp eye, her wit, and her patience as the volume went through its numerous drafts. Roberta Hackel, Joyce Ferman, and my sister, Caryn Margolies, who read various chapters of the book, also had invaluable comments. I am especially grateful to my mother, Ruth Margolies, and my close friend, K. M., who both stayed up long hours with me offering their comments and ideas.

Support of another kind came from my children, David and Melissa, who gave their patience, their interest, and their stories about their own friendships. And to my husband, Louis Genevie, my greatest thanks—

for his creative and editorial help, for his organizational perceptiveness, and for his support and love.

Finally, I would like to express my gratitude to the many women who shared their stories with me and who offered leads to other women for me to interview. They are, in many ways, the true authors of this book.

*The Best of Friends,
The Worst of Enemies*

Chapter 1

COMFORT AND CONFLICT

I vividly remember the first time that I made the connection between women's friendships with one another and their relationships with their mothers. A friend of mine whom I had not seen in nearly two years had recently moved back from California and invited me to spend a week in her mountaintop cabin. I had just completed a sketch for a possible magazine article about women's friendships and had shown it to my mother, who had responded typically, "You'll never pull it off." The fact that my husband had liked the idea didn't count; I always expected him to be supportive. Besides, he was not a woman—what did he really know about the psychological nuances of women's lives? I packed the handwritten pages in my valise, kissed my husband and children goodbye, and made the four-hour trek to the country, looking forward to the reunion. And to get a reversal of my mother's opinion.

Despite the blizzard which nearly doubled the driving time, my spirits were high. Vanessa, whom I had known since college, had always been a kind of mentor to me. Bright, talented, and seemingly far more independent than I, I had come to look up to her and had turned to her frequently for support. And from what I remembered, that support had always been forthcoming, no matter how cockamamie my ideas were.

When I told her I had opened my own counseling center, she applauded my independence and initiative. When I shared with her a secret wish to become a writer, she said, "You'll never know unless you try." And when I was feeling down in the dumps, she was always there for me, although she, in turn, rarely seemed to need a shoulder to cry on. It never occurred to me that Vanessa's support was propelled as much by her own need to be the "mothering" figure in our friendship. Nor did it dawn on me that if she had been staunchly behind me up to that point, it might be because I in no way posed any threat to her.

When I arrived at the cottage, I was shocked. The beautiful girl I had known looked haggard. She had cut off the long chestnut hair which had hung to her waist, and the pounds she had gained since I had last seen her made her look frumpy. I knew something must be terribly wrong.

Something was. Crying hysterically, she confessed she was miserably unhappy. She was thirty-four years old, and had no better idea of who she was now than she had during her college days. She was working at a low-paying job which she kept because she still hadn't figured out what she wanted to do professionally. She was desperate to find a husband and have kids, but no good prospects were in sight. Although she had never been very religious, she had done a complete about-face, joining the ranks of born-again Christians. It was her way, she told me, of trying to find a direction for herself. And meeting a man who was willing to make the old-fashioned commitment of marriage.

For the next three days she was depressed, and while I certainly did not enjoy seeing her so distraught, I soon realized that our friendship had taken a major step forward, that we were no longer locked into this mother-child sort of bond but were relating as equals. I felt needed and trusted, and was not at all threatened by her vulnerability—in part because I had just finished my first book and was feeling pretty good about myself; and also in part because it was comforting to know that I wasn't the only one that needed mothering. It seemed to me that we were closer than we had ever been. It was only later I learned that Vanessa had different feelings about the new twist in our relationship.

The fourth morning of my visit, Vanessa woke up in good spirits and apologized profusely for having "dumped all of her problems" on me. "I don't know what came over me," she said, squeezing fresh orange juice.

"You were feeling rotten, and I'm your friend," I told her.

"Let's just forget it, huh?" she answered in an almost undetectable snarl. "Let's talk about you."

I mentioned the friendship article, still in its embryonic stage, and how I felt I was onto something; I would really like her to read it and let me know what she thought. I left out the part about my mother's opinion.

As she walked into the bedroom with the ten sheets of paper on which I had scribbled my ideas, I felt, in some strange way, that she had my life in her hands. Why was it that I so desperately needed her approval? Later I realized that I had unconsciously imbued her with the power of a mother superior, that I expected from her the support my own mother could not give to me.

Thirty minutes later Vanessa emerged from the bedroom, her face a blank. I decided to take the constructive-criticism approach.

"Any suggestions?" I meekly ventured.

She sat down next to me on the couch. "Yeah. Can't you find something more original to write about? This stuff stinks."

"This . . . stuff . . . stinks." The words seemed to glare in front of my face, flashing on and off like neon signs. I saw red. My palms became clammy and beads of perspiration covered my brow. I ran to the door in dire need of air.

Vanessa was out on the porch in a flash, soothing me with a damp cloth. My first thought about it was, "How wonderful to have such a nurturing friend."

At the same time, there was something unnerving about all of this, and as I lay in bed while Vanessa went to work, other incidents with Vanessa that I had relegated to the interior of my memory crept into consciousness. I flashed back to my wedding day, when Vanessa, off gallivanting in Europe, had not even taken the time to send a card or telegram. And I remembered how she had seemed to become less enthusiastic about my counseling center as it became increasingly successful. There were other things, too—such as the time I had sent her a copy of my first book and she did not even bother to comment on it. How had I forgotten all of these things? And why had I forgotten them? Then it hit me like a ton of bricks—Vanessa had always, on some level, seemed more comfortable with me when I needed her, when she was the one in charge. And I had suppressed this knowledge because my mother had always preferred me when I was sick and helpless, too.

Drawing on my experience as a therapist and my knowledge of Vanessa's relationship with her mother, I began to piece together her side of the story. Raised by a strong woman who had always dominated her father, Vanessa had often confessed how she had always felt overshadowed by her mother. And her mother had held the reins on her daughter with an iron grip. It occurred to me that I (and, I suspect, other friends of Vanessa's) was bearing the brunt of Vanessa's feelings of powerlessness in relationship to her mother; that given her history, she couldn't allow herself to be in a relationship in which she wasn't the one "on top." That would explain why she seemed so uncomfortable when I had assumed the caretaking role those past three days. It also explained why she had the unconscious need to put my work down.

The psychological reverberations of Vanessa's rejection, however, did not emerge until a few weeks later. Despite the fact that I intellectually understood what had happened, I found that in the weeks after my visit with Vanessa my writing was completely blocked. I had experienced writer's block before, but this was something else. It was as if the combined opinion of my mother and Vanessa was more than I could overcome, despite the fact that my husband had liked the idea for the article from the very start. His opinion counted, of course, but it didn't seem to have as much psychic weight as the opinions of the two women who had rejected me, who had told me, "Don't waste your time."

I sometimes wonder if I would have been stuck on that article forever had it not been for my friend Brenda. About a month after I had visited Vanessa, during which I had produced absolutely nothing on the friendship article, my family and I were invited to spend the week with some friends who owned a home in New Hampshire. He was an attorney; she, a successful marketing manager. It had been months since we had seen one another, and my girlfriend and I exchanged gossip as I unpacked my suitcase. When I put away my last sweater, she noticed a bundle of crumpled-up papers at the bottom of the valise—the long-lost magazine sketch, which I had left there, I suppose, for posterity.

"What's that?" Brenda inquired.

"Oh, it's nothing—just some ideas I had for an article," I said with a distinct air of self-loathing.

"Well, let's *see* it," she said in a way that let me know she would not take no for an answer.

"Oh, God," I thought, "not again," when she returned from the porch straight-faced twenty minutes later.

Suddenly, Brenda broke into a grin. "This is terrific! I think women are just dying to know more about their friendships!"

The next morning as we sipped our coffee, watching our husbands through a window as they slammed a tennis ball, and the kids who were playing tag close by, Brenda said, "You know, I've been thinking about what I read yesterday, and I think you're wasting your time on an article."

"Oh no," I thought, "yesterday she was just trying to be kind. . . . Here comes the real truth . . . brace yourself."

"I think you should turn it into a book."

"You think I should what?" I asked her, having heard the words without registering the message.

"A book, Eva, why don't you write a book!"

The prospect at once exhilarated and frightened me. I recounted what my mother and Vanessa had told me about women not really being interested in the subject matter.

"Oh, they're just jealous," Brenda said reassuringly. "I have faith in you. And while you're at it," she said, scrambling some eggs, "you might want to consider why you go around choosing friends like Vanessa to begin with."

Suddenly, amazingly, the block of the past month lifted and ideas started coming in a mile a minute. On the surface all that had happened was that I had gotten an opinion which was more encouraging—the kind of affirmation that all but the most self-assured writers need to keep going. Deep down, however, I knew that far more had taken place. It was as if my relationship with Vanessa was an unconscious repetition of my relationship with my mother, which was why her rejection had hit home so hard. Brenda, on the other hand, was like the compensatory "good" mother—by giving me the approval I didn't get from my own mother, I could now move on.

When I returned home that Sunday, I wrote a proposal for a book on women's friendships in record time. It was about mothers and women friends, and the threads that linked one to the other. I sent it to my agent and within ten days had an offer from a publisher. Both Brenda and my husband were ecstatic, although my husband could not resist asking, "Why was it that when *I* said you had a great idea, that wasn't enough?" By that time I knew that it was because it was in my relationship with other women that the real need for validation and approval, that the real power rested.

PIECES OF A PUZZLE

The real work, of course, had just begun. The book proposal, while containing many ideas, only scratched the surface when it came to really understanding what went on between women friends. It was as if I were immersed in a gigantic psychic jigsaw puzzle: the pieces, while all there, still did not quite fit.

I turned to Freud, who had been the first one to say that the problems in women's relationships were a direct offshoot of conflicts in the mother-daughter dyad. In fact, the whole psychoanalytic school seemed to affirm the idea that we unconsciously recreate our relationship with our mothers through "significant others" during the course of our lifetimes. That, in and of itself, explained a lot: why a woman, time and time again, would tell me that she expected her friends to be better friends to her than she was to *her* friends; why she frequently complained about friends when that acceptance was anything short of unconditional.

Old problems with dependence and separation also were at the fore in many interviews: "She wanted too much of me." "I asked too much of her." "Sometimes I feel as if she's suffocating me." And always, the mention of the underground competition.

But these observations seemed to tell only half of the story. True, I could see women repeating some of the less healthy aspects of their relationships with their mothers through their friends, in the same way that I had unconsciously chosen a friend like Vanessa who would reject me when I felt strong and independent. But what about friends like Brenda? Friends who personified the kind of mother women wanted, who seemed to undo mother's dirty work by providing the kind of support that women need? Other women, I quickly learned, had similar stories: Yes, they had less than idyllic relationships with their mothers, but at the same time they reported having terrific relationships with women friends. If friendships were purportedly these endless repetitions of vicious mother-daughter scenarios, then where did friends like Brenda fit?

Skimming the literature for validation of what seemed to be almost a healing of old wounds that took place in many women's friendships, I hit a brick wall. Most of the research on friendship, I quickly learned, had been done by men, about men. And the few times women's friendships were broached, the portrait that was painted was about as bleak as a winter's day in downtown Pittsburgh.

Then a friend of mine who knew about the project sent me an article by a Dr. Jane Flax. It was entitled "The Conflict Between Nurturance and Autonomy in Mother-Daughter Relationships and Within Feminism." I knew the moment I read it that her ideas would form a central organizing theme for the book. The thesis, which I later discussed with Dr. Flax at length, was stunning in its simplicity. All children, she says, have two basic needs: the need to be loved and the need to be independent. Boys, whose mothers love them for their ability to achieve and to master their environment, have both needs met. Girls, who tend to get approval for clutching at mother's apron strings, do not. What results is a kind of schism in our development, with most of us growing up to believe that either we can be loved, or independent, but not both; that nurturance and autonomy are each at the expense of the other.

The problem, says Dr. Flax, starts with our mothers. But the same conflict gets transferred to our women friends with whom "our sense of self is bound up . . . in an intensity and depth not present in relations with men,"[1] throughout our lives. One of two outcomes is possible. Either we can repeat the old conflicts with our mothers through our friends, or we can turn those conflicts around by being better friends to each other than our mothers were to us. The idea is that whatever our earliest experiences may have been with our mothers, they can be reversed if our experiences with other women go against the early grain. It's what psychologists refer to as the importance of "successive life events."[2]

Which is why our relationships with one another have so much power to help.

And to hurt.

I was excited by Jane Flax's insights, although she was the first one to caution: "Not everything can be traced to general mother-daughter issues." But what other links were there? "Keep digging," she told me, "you'll find them."

The "digging," which took nearly two years, during which time I interviewed close to two hundred women of all ages across the country and read hundreds of books and research articles, led me to three primary goals for this book. The first was to discover the way mother-daughter relationships were interwoven in the tapestry of our friendships with one another. There are certain predictable conflicts that arise between mothers and daughters, such as difficulties with separation, that get replayed in our friendships later on. But each of us also carries our own individual scripts, in addition to certain "common denominators." Some of us, for example, had mothers who worked and encouraged us to achieve, while others had mothers who wanted us to follow in more traditional footsteps. Some of us were locked in perpetual mother-daughter conflict and hostility, while others had reasonably positive relationships. It intrigued me to learn how these differences explained our feelings about women later on, how our friends were the mothers we chose.

The second objective was to discover how living in a society that is largely run by men affected women's feelings about each other. It quickly became obvious that women who said they had reasonably good relationships with their mothers still felt, on some level, that relationships with men were a step above those with women—a fact of life that continually influences our relationships, especially in the work environment. On the one side there were women who had become "more male than male" in order to function in what they viewed as a man's world. On the flip side there were women who found themselves stuck at certain levels because they refused to adopt any of the male rules at all.

The other context which became important in explaining women's friendships had to do with what stage of the life cycle women were in. Each phase of development poses us its unique tasks: It's difficult to talk about women's relationships without such reference points. During adolescence, for example, when there is a strong need to establish our own identities, intense friendships between girls are the wave of the day. Friendships between single women are often infused with a kind of tenuousness that has to do with the search for a husband, while relationships between married women often depend on the kind of relationship a woman has with her husband, and whether or not she works. And certain crises, such as divorce, often trigger conflicting feelings, which have a way of sorting themselves out in our friendships.

WOMEN AND INDEPENDENCE: WILL THE REAL CULPRIT PLEASE STAND UP?

Throughout these themes one common pattern reverberated with stunning consistency: When it comes to liberating ourselves, our friends both push us forward and hold us back. While many of us have put the blame on men for keeping women down, we have been barking up the wrong tree.

Though it is commonly believed that what a woman needs most is a man, the truth is that our real reliance, the dependency that touches us most significantly, has never been on men, but on women. Women have always been the ones to whom we turn for approval.

That is not to say that men play no part in the saga that prevents women from actualizing themselves; their own insecurities and needs for omnipotence do contribute to our fear of independence. But to point the finger at the opposite sex is skirting the issues that lie closer to home. It is out of our emotional ties and identification with Mother that our basic conflict with independence and autonomy is born. And it is within our friendships with each other that this conflict is nurtured, cultivated, perpetuated.

How it happens is what this book is all about.

While my ultimate goal was to report objectively, some of the material in this book will seem biased. In particular, I suspect that some of what I have to say about friendships between women who opt for dependency will be, at best, controversial, at worst, offensive. The bias is not mine: While the stories are reported by me, they were written by the women themselves.

At times it may also appear that women's friendships are more neurotic than healthy, that while women experience difficulties in their friendships with other women, they haven't made many steps to resolve them. That's largely because many women have a tremendous amount of difficulty in expressing conflict and anger in their relationships with other women. If certain aspects of women's friendships appear unresolved, it's because that's the way they are.

Finally, there are a number of issues that are not covered in this volume. The number of minority women in my sample is small, and the problems of relationships between women of color are not discussed. Female homosexuality is only alluded to. Nor is friendship between women in old age specifically addressed. The exclusion of these topics by no means suggests that they are less important than the issues included in this book. To the contrary, each subject deserves its own exclusive volume.

In all cases, the names and other identifying characteristics of the women in the stories have been changed, largely because almost every woman, including my closest friends, opted for anonymity. In fact, most of them insisted on it, refusing to be interviewed at all unless they were made unrecognizable to their friends. For some, particularly women I interviewed regarding their work relationships, it was a matter of professionalism. For most the fear was having their friends find out what they *really* thought about them, with the stuff that friendships are made of being so volatile that many requested anonymity more than once. (Three women actually wrote panicky letters months after I had interviewed them, requesting that I remove their stories from the text.) Complying with that request was easy: the stories, in one form or another, were stories I had heard time and time again.

The request to be a name without a face was also a tip-off to how much difficulty women have confronting conflict in their relationships. An interview that I conducted with a group of suburban housewives in Pennsylvania is a good example. The first interview, which lasted four hours and included five women who called themselves close friends, largely focused on the camaraderie and support they received from one another in the absence of husbands who spent the majority of their waking hours away from home. What came out when I spoke to them individually at a later date was another story—one which was filled with conflict that they were not willing to bring into the open. Again and again in the individual interviews I was to hear: "I feel terribly guilty telling you this, but. . . ." Most were aware that openly discussing their feelings with their friends might do some good. Nevertheless, most were unwilling to do so.

I understood their position completely. It was with much deliberation and great pains that I was able to ask my own friends certain obviously leading questions which tapped into some of the conflicts in our own relationships. How I reacted to what I both wanted and was afraid to hear, naturally, depended on their answers. Being able to ask a good friend who is climbing up the professional ladder what she most disliked in women, and having her tell me it was the inability of many women to understand that she really didn't have time for friendships right now, opened the door for dealing with her anger at me for being too demanding and mine at her for being so inaccessible. Not so easy to swallow was learning that the woman I considered my best friend had two other "best friends" whom she put ahead of me. Nor was it easy to place a call to a woman in California whose friendship with me ended badly, and to not have it returned.

Generally, the discussion I had with friends did not open a Pandora's box but the door to greater understanding and acceptance. By taking the first step of opening up, we not only cleared the air, but often found new and better ways of dealing with the conflicts between us. I found myself telling friends things that had long disturbed me about them, and they me. Sometimes it hurt to hear those things. And to say them. Almost always it enabled us to grow. And accept one another not just as women, but as people. Best of all, my relationship with my mother is better than it has ever been.

The only case in which talking it out led to the demise of the relationship was with Vanessa. While she later admitted that perhaps she had been envious after all, it was a feeling she could not overcome. During the course of this project, I found myself looking to her for support that never came. So after much thought I told her that I was finding it increasingly difficult to deal with her, adding that at any time she felt she had resolved her feelings, I would be here for her. That was over a year ago. I have not heard from her since.

Chapter 2

Early Dramas

AFTER glaring out the window intently for an hour at the moving van that was parked across the street, my nine-year-old daughter, Melissa, began jumping up and down. "They have girls," she said, clapping her hands in delight. Our block, up to that point, had been dominated by a young group of ruffians who seemed to get pleasure out of giving Melissa and her best friend Audrey a hard time. "I'm going to Audrey's to see if she wants to come with me to the new neighbor's house and say hello."

An hour later she returned with a big grin planted on her pixie face. "One's eleven but the other one's nine just like me. And you know what? She's going to be in my class next year."

"What's her name?"

"Denise, and she's really nice."

For the next few weeks before the school year resumed, the triumvirate was inseparable. Three, they quickly learned, had a lot more clout than two, especially when it came to dealing with the boys. And they all seemed to get along so well.

"They're sure enjoying themselves," said Audrey's mother when I met her. "And it's so nice to have another girl on the block."

She could not know then that it wouldn't be long before she'd have different feelings about it.

About a month into the school year there was a knock on my door. It was eight-fifteen and my daughter had left the house a quarter of an hour before.

"Do you know where Melissa is?" asked Audrey with a distressed look.

I was stunned. "I thought she was with you and Denise. She left the house fifteen minutes ago."

"Well, she's probably with Denise then," said Audrey on the verge of tears.

I began to get the picture.

"Didn't Melissa call for you this morning?"

"Oh no. She hasn't called for me for the past two weeks. Ever since then she's been walking alone with Denise."

That night at the dinner table I confronted my daughter.

"Audrey says you haven't been walking to school with her."

"So?"

"So, you've walked to school with Audrey for the past two years. I thought she was your best friend."

Silence. "She's not. She's not even my friend anymore. We don't like her."

"*We?*"

"Me and Denise. Audrey's dumb and says stupid things and we don't want to play with her."

And so ended one best-friend tryst and began another. As Audrey and Melissa had been, Denise and Melissa became the dynamic duo, with Denise's house becoming a sanctuary for Melissa and vice versa. And when Audrey's mother asked me what happened, I had little solace to offer. "I guess girls are just fickle," I told her, knowing full well how upset I would have been had my daughter been in her girl's position.

Denise had a profound influence on my daughter for the next year. In fact, every other word out of her mouth seemed to be, "Denise said this," or "Denise did that," or when we'd have an argument, "Well, Denise told me such and such so it must be true." They dressed alike, and for a while Melissa even begged for a perm so that her baby-fine hair would be curly like her friend's. And while Denise opened the doors to a new level of companionship for my daughter, she also closed the doors to other friendships. Take, for example, Melissa's ninth birthday party.

"I want to have nine girls at my swimming party," she insisted.

"Our car can fit only eight."

"Well, somebody can sit on a lap."

I gave in. But the day of the party only eight girls showed up.

"What happened to Laurie?" I asked.

"Oh, I uninvited her."

Fury. "You did *what?*"

"Well, Denise said she didn't like Laurie and if I invited her, she'd get all the other girls not to come. So what else could I do?"

"You could have told Denise to go to hell," I thought to myself.

When, at the beginning of fifth grade we moved to Vermont for six months, Melissa was inconsolable. She cried every night and wrote Denise almost daily. The feeling was apparently reciprocal. "I sneaked a look at Denise's diary," her mother confessed, "and all over the pages it said, 'I love Melissa, I love Melissa.' "

When the six-month separation ended and the two girls were reunited, they were in a state of bliss. "Denise and I exchanged friendship rings today," she said, "and we swore we would be best friends for at least the next twenty years," Melissa told me. It lasted all of twenty days.

Eight-fifteen. A knock on the door.

"Do you know where Melissa is?" asked Denise.

"I thought she was with you."

"Oh no, Melissa hasn't called for me all week. She's been walking to school with Audrey."

"Here we go again," I thought, waiting for the showdown that night.

"Denise came to call for you this morning. She said you haven't walked to school with her all week."

"Denise isn't my friend anymore."

Silence.

"Denise is a big boss. The whole class hates her. She gets mad when she doesn't get her way. Besides, none of the other girls will be friends with me if I'm Denise's friend."

"But how do you think Denise feels being dropped like that?" I shouted, half angry at my daughter's ability to betray, half portending the aggravation I would have to go through when her turn to be excluded came around.

GIRLS' FRIENDSHIPS are not unlike the old cliché about girls themselves: "When she was good she was very, very good; but when she was bad she was horrid." If little girls can be sugar and spice, they also can be little monsters.

My own best recollection of my earliest friendships is of the summer that I was eleven and my best friend Suzanne and I went to summer camp together. On the bus ride up we pricked our index fingers with safety pins, dipping our fingers in the other's blood and mixing it with our own. We pledged eternal devotion to one another as blood sisters forever.

When we arrived at the campsite, our bunkmates were ready and waiting. "We're the Lady Bugs and if you want to be part of our group, you have to go through initiation," squealed a tall, lanky redhead. "What do we have to do?" Suzanne and I asked, clutching each other's hands for support. "You have to tell what the word 'whore' means," said the redhead. Suzanne knew. I didn't. For the rest of the summer the bunk cheer was, "Eva is a who-ore, Eva is a who-ore," with Suzanne leading the chorus.

The next year I switched camps. Once again I and one other girl named Roberta were the newcomers and the scapegoating began within minutes after I unpacked my trunk.

"What's a frizz bomb," said a cherubic-looking brunette, referring to my curly hair—my nemesis until curls became the height of chic. But by this time I was wise to the ploy, and had come armed.

"Yeah," I said, laughing along with her, "my friends call me Brillohead."

The girl stared at me for what seemed like an eternity and then burst into a smile. "Welcome to the clan," she said, putting her arms around me.

The next morning when the group decided to initiate Roberta by squirting shaving cream between her breasts while pinning her to the bed, I was the first one in line.

These patterns of behavior, I later discovered—the intense best friendships often followed by equally intense rejection; the jealousy among three little girls that leads to stunning viciousness; the name calling and the vendettas—are specific to little girls' friendships. And what is too painful to remember ourselves, we see in our own daughters.

From a mother who has sent her daughter to sleep-away camp for the first time, for example: "The first week Jean was away I got this postcard saying, 'Camp's great. I have lots of friends.' The second week she wrote, 'Camp is horrible. All the girls hate me. I want to come home.' I was ready to go and get her until a friend suggested I wait for the next postcard. Sure enough, camp was great again; she was having a terrific time. My guess," she added, "is that there was probably another little girl who had written her mother that week about how awful camp was."

A mother receiving such a letter understands her daughter's devastation. She has been there herself. But experience tells her there is little she can do to assuage her girl's misery. With a sigh, a shrug of the shoulders, she offers her the same caveat her own mother offered her: That's how girls are.

If you have a son, chances are you're muttering to yourself that little boys can be merciless, too. And you wouldn't be wrong: all children feel insignificant, and the easiest way to feel more powerful is to make another child feel small. But virtually every research on the subject indicates that while boys can be nasty, they aren't nearly as vicious to one another as girls.

The catch is, neither are they as close.

GIRLS WILL BE GIRLS

When researchers compare the friendships of boys to girls, one finding pops up again and again: girls not only have a much stronger need for friendship than boys, but demand an intensity in those friendships that boys seem to prefer living without.[1] All children, of course, need friends, but that need shows up much earlier in girls than in boys.[2] Even as preschoolers, girls exhibit a strong leaning toward close, exclusive friendships which boys don't seem to need. To the contrary, little boys prefer playing on teams, comfortably interacting with four or five friends at once.[3] The ebb and flow for girls tells another tale. As most mothers of daughters discover, even three little girls have a hard time playing peacefully together.

On the bright side, these early best-girlfriend relationships often have a maturity not to be found in boys' friendships. Girls, one study found, have a greater appreciation of the nature of friendship, and are much more concerned with the quality of emotional interchange than the "who's the leader, who's the follower" of boys' friendships.[4] Girls also empathize with each other more readily and have a "higher aptitude for nurturance and emotional expression."[5]

But if girls have a stronger capacity to care, they are also less accepting. Consider, for example, the following excerpt from the Detroit *Free Press:*

TEST SHOWS LITTLE GIRLS ARE NOT AS NICE AS BOYS

If you think that little girls are made of "sugar and spice," you're mistaken.

So says Los Angeles research psychologist Norma Feshback who has just finished a behavior study of little girls and boys.

Dr. Feshback, a 39-year-old mother of three, including an 8-year-old girl, organized 84 first graders into two-member "clubs" with special names and badges. One club's members were all boys and the other girls.

Then she introduced a child from another classroom to each of the clubs.

Boys, it turned out, were much nicer to the newcomer.

"The initial response of girls to a new member . . . was more likely to be one of exclusion and rejection," reported Dr. Feshback.[6]

A girl's capacity to go straight for the jugular is another quality found among girlfriends that is mysteriously missing among boys. That's not to say that boys don't fight—in fact, boys are noted for quarreling often, physically lashing out at each other. Girls do not kick and bite, but the verbal slings and arrows they hurl at one another and their merciless vendettas are often far more piercing.[7] We do not give each other black eyes, but we do give each other broken hearts.

Moreover, when boys reject other boys, it's usually for a specific reason—Johnny doesn't like football, Stanley doesn't have a good bike. Girls' rejections are much more complete—"Susie is funny looking," or "I don't like her because she's just a creep." As psychologist Judith Bardwick puts it, "Girls' covert aggression leads, ultimately, to rejection. . . . Unlike boys, who may not be chosen first for the baseball team because they cannot hit but may be chosen third because they can run, girls are rejected for themselves, for their total selves."[8]

In a nutshell, our friendships are much more a battle of extremes. They are more intimate and emotional, but boys' friendships tend to be more stable and long-lasting.[9] We get more love, but oh, what a price we must pay!

The question is, why?

For a long time the only answer that behavioral scientists could point to was the discrepancy in sex-role training of the two genders. If boys are taught to be aggressive and girls to be relational, then naturally you'd expect girls to need their friends more. Boys, they said, are also trained to play games like baseball and hockey which require more than one friend. And, of course, you'd also expect girls to express their hostility toward each other less overtly because direct aggression is not sanctioned for females.

But this is only part of the story, and more recently psychologists have begun to pinpoint the origins of these differences to deeper roots: the unique relationship between a mother and daughter which puts us in the confusing situation of having to break away from the person we're most expected to be like.

THE MOTHER-DAUGHTER CONNECTION

In recent years a lot has been written about women's difficulty with separation and independence, with Mother usually being seen as the source of the problem. Mothers we've been told, don't want their daughters to be independent. They don't want them to have lives of their own. And so they encourage their girls early on to become dependent.

This is only a partial truth. Even if a little girl has a mother who pushes her to become independent, to be her own person, the task of breaking away from her mother is monumental. That's because while we may have to leave mother to become independent, we also have to be like her to become "feminine."

All children begin life with a strong attachment to their mothers which they eventually must give up. But for boys the task is much more clear-cut. From the outset a little boy recognizes by the way he is treated, by looking at his own body, by almost everything around him, that he is different from Mom. When he asks himself "Whom am I like?" the finger points directly to Dad. And even though it may be initially painful for him to break away from his mother, who for all intents and purposes is almost every child's first love, the break is only temporary. When he grows up and marries, he can once again claim a "mommy" of his own. He never really has to give Mom up at all.

For girls the task is much more complicated. We, too, must leave mother's arms, but unlike boys, it's a leaving wrought out of more than the need to grow up and separate. Sure, girls need to grow up, but growing up for females means attaching herself to a male. When we give Mom up as our first love, we give her up literally and symbolically forever.

All of which wouldn't be so confusing if at the same time we weren't expected to be like Mom, too. How can we totally break away from something we're supposed to mimic? "The girl's situation is really a dilemma," says Angela Fox, who is a psychoanalyst in private practice in New York City. "She's supposed to break away from her mother, but she never really can because she has to identify with her, too. It's like telling someone to swim the English Channel while at the same time telling them they'll drown if they don't keep at least one foot on land. The girl's supposed to swim away from her mother in the name of separation, but if she leaves her completely, she'll have no anchor for her femininity. So even if she wants to swim, she's already got an inbuilt fear of drowning."

Our struggle between wanting to remain attached and wanting to test the waters is complicated by a mother's difficulty in letting her daughter go. From the start, her son's biological differences signal that he is separate from her. As intense as her early attachment to her little boy might be, it's not as intense as with a daughter, who is made in her own image, who is herself in miniature.[10]

The fact that a mother sees herself in her daughter also paves the way for stronger feelings of rejection when her little girl begins expressing the need to break away. Every step in the opposite direction is seen as a slap in the face and reads psychologically something like this: If you leave me, that must mean that you don't want to be like me, and if you don't want to be like me, how could you possibly love me?

"A friend of mine who's also an analyst sees this kind of thing in her relationship with her daughter all the time," Angela Fox told me. "She sees her daughter's wanting to be like her as evidence of her daughter's wanting to be close to her. And she sees her daughter's moving away from her as an indication that her daughter doesn't love her." The result, not surprisingly, is that mothers try to keep their little girls from separating. "As knowledgeable as this woman is, she knows there's a part of her that becomes rejecting when her daughter tries to go too far off on her own." That is not the case, she admits, with her son.

Where does this leave a daughter? In a kind of mutual song and dance with her mother in which she needs to have an intense relationship with her but needs to let go of her at the same time. In which she wants to be independent but finds that getting mother's love all too often means staying attached to her. In which she wants to be both merged and separate.

It is these conflicts that are the taproot of our relationships with the other girls.

FROM MOM'S LAP INTO THE OTHER GIRLS' ARMS

Evidence of the underlying turmoil hits the fan the minute we enter school. Learning to stand on our own two feet, to get along without Mom there every step of the way to guide us, is a necessary task in development. But unlike boys, who have by this time taken many healthy steps away from Mom, a girl, even as old as nine or ten, is almost as psychologically attached to her mother as when she was two.[11]

Is it any wonder that we run to our friends at the beginning of third grade with a passion and neediness that only another little girl can understand?

"The easiest device of the young girl in prepuberty is to attach herself directly to another girl in order to feel more secure," writes Dr. Helene Deutsch. "Despite her noisy self-assurance, she is aware of her inadequacy and needs someone as insignificant as herself in order to feel stronger, doubled as it were. She wants someone who not only shares with her the pleasure and burdens of secrecy and curiosity, but who also resembles her and who, like herself, is undergoing the suffering of feeling insignificant. . . .

"This relationship is 'monogamous,'" continues Dr. Deutsch. "Faithfulness and exclusiveness are demanded of the friend and, above all, complete partnership in common secrets. The partners must tell each other everything and exclude all others, particularly the grownups, from their confidences."[12]

"If there's anything I remember about the other girls at that age, it's having a best friend or not having one, and how important that was," one young woman tells me. "There was also a vicious competition to be best friends with certain popular girls. There was this one girl that everybody liked and we would fight over her like a pack of wolves."

"The girls in my group used to have private dates," another woman says. "Let's say Wednesday was my private date with one girl. Then every Wednesday we'd play and no one else was allowed to play with us. That girl was your best friend for that day. Every day of the week was taken up with these dates. I was completely dependent on my friends."

"Oh, God," says a third, "if you didn't have a best friend, that was it! It didn't even matter if you liked the girl or not. My best friend was this girl who lived in my apartment building, and she wasn't too bright. We didn't have much in common. But she was better than being alone."

In many ways these friendships are a toboggan slide back to the intense relationships we had with our mothers. It's the old dependency with a new face. Our need to be merged has not gone away but simply has been redirected toward a safer target.

At the same time, there are a lot of positive qualities to these early best-friend relationships, elements of compassion and empathy that are direct offshoots of the more positive aspects of girls' relationships with their mothers. True, the kind of fused mother-daughter state of affairs doesn't do much for independence, but while boys are out there competing for dear life and collecting other valuable skills necessary for achievement in the working world, girls are giving each other practice in intimately relating to people, a skill that many boys never acquire. Our intense connection with Mom, which gives us a feeling of being interwoven with the rest of the world, may be something of a liability in terms of developing a separate identity, but it does give us a woman's sensitivity and sensibility, which some theorists are beginning to recognize as an asset at least equal to the ability to become number one. As Dr. Nancy Chodorow writes, the fact that a little girl's identity is intertwined with her attachments to others "does not mean that women have 'weaker' ego boundaries than men," but that girls leave their early relationship with their mothers with "a basis for 'empathy' built into their primary definition of self in a way that boys do not."[13] And if it's true that "what the world needs now is love, sweet love," we might all be better off if boys were a little more like girls.

The problem is that our ability to feel for the other girls also gives us the ability to go straight for the jugular. And because girls both want the intensity of an exclusive relationship and fear it at the same time, the viciousness can be stunning. So what starts out as an exercise in gaining love and security often ends up as a battle for the survival of the fittest.

And the meek definitely do not inherit the earth.

LEARNING NOT TO TRUST

"I loved my friend in fourth grade so desperately that there was nothing I wouldn't do for her," one woman tells me. "But I also remember that I didn't want to share her with anybody; I wanted her all to myself. I hated all of Gloria's other friends—absolutely hated them. I can remember that she started becoming friendly with this girl who moved down the block and how threatened I felt. The girl started hanging around with us all the time and I couldn't stand it. So I started this rumor in school that the girl's parents weren't married, that she was illegitimate. It was a horrible thing to do, but it was the only way I could think of getting Gloria back."

It is not viciousness but need that's being expressed in these kinds of betrayals. Still attached to Mom in a primitive kind of way, fighting to the death for her best friend is a girl's way of guaranteeing nurturance. And who can blame her? Deep down, she knows that the other girls are just as needy.

To top it all off, as much as she's lured to that intense love, she also fears it at the same time. Being close is great, but being too close means she won't be able to separate. And so emerges the great I'm-your-friend-I'm-not-your-friend syndrome, a pattern psychologist Judith Bardwick suggests is specific to little girls.

"Two girls are best friends. After a while another girl joins this dyad and it becomes a triad. Then one girl is rejected and again there are two best friends, but now there is also one who was repudiated. This pattern of compelling intimacy and the mutual deliciousness of being 'best friends,' along with the potential for feeling devastated or replaced by someone else, is very different from the typical play patterns of boys. Of course, boys can also have a 'best friend,' but this relationship rarely seems as passionate and crucial to boys as it is to girls."[14]

If they are more crucial, they are also more frightening. "The patterns of going from one friend to another and the rejection of other girls is often a defense against fusion at a time when the girl is trying to separate, in the same way that having lots of different lovers can be a defense against the fear of intimacy," Jane Flax told me in an interview. "That's why relationships between young girls are monogamous but often don't last that long. It is similar to the woman who has a multitude of monogamous flings that don't last for a long time. It's very intense and fused for a while, and then total panic. You get the nurturance, the feeling of fusion you need, but you flee from it before it takes you over, before you really get stuck."

The irony, says Dr. Flax, is that the push-pull between wanting to be attached and wanting to be independent precludes girls giving each other the love they need. "A girl's feelings about needing the other girls so desperately is so ambivalent, in the same way that her needs for her mother are, that what you get is a girl who needs a close one-to-one relationship but can't be depended on to give it. So she goes from one girl to the next looking for what she needs, using whatever tactics she needs to get it, including rejection of the other girls. The result is that she doesn't trust herself, or the other girls."

Of course, we don't understand these unconscious motives. What does register is that our position with the other girls is as precarious as the next little girl who moves onto the block. How can we not be leery? One day our best friend says, "You can tell me anything, cross my heart and hope to die, I won't tell a soul." The next day she trades our secret for a chance to play with the girl next door. Is it any wonder we feel betrayed? Our need to establish an intimate relationship similar to the one we had with Mother is suffused with the knowledge that we may not be chosen or may end up the outsider—a situation that makes us act in ways that are safest, that will make us popular.

The feeling is: I'd better go along with the crowd, or else.

LESSONS IN CONFORMITY

"I had this friend in elementary school who was a real bitchy little thing," recalls one thirty-year-old woman. "Thinking back, I wonder why I remained friends with her at all. She was always teasing me about one thing or another, and I remember feeling a lot of the time that I hated her. There was also this other girl that we played with sometimes who was a real easy one to get on. She'd cry at the drop of a hat. Sometimes my friend would say, 'Let's get on Harriet's back,' and the two of us would torment her relentlessly until she broke down. I knew how bad she felt; I had been the victim, too. But I guess I was afraid if I didn't go along with my friend, she'd be even meaner to me."

How many girls go along with the scapegoating of an innocent victim because they dread the idea of being a victim themselves? There is only one thing worse than empathizing with another girl who is the target of such cruelty. It is being the target of that cruelty herself.

Another woman tells me that at the start of every school year she gives her daughter money to select her wardrobe. But within two weeks the girl is wearing the same thing almost every day. "My daughter says she doesn't like her clothing, but that's hard to believe since she's the one who picks it out," says the mother. "She wouldn't talk to me about it, so I decided to have a long talk with her good friend. Her friend told me that the girls were jealous of my daughter's new clothes, that they made fun of her. If she'd wear a cute T-shirt with a picture of a scrambled egg on the front, the girls would ask her why she was wearing her breakfast. If she wore a long skirt, they'd say she looked like a gypsy. My daughter is insecure, so piece by piece her things got stashed away until she was down to a pair of designer jeans and two sweaters. She doesn't even *like* jeans; she says they're uncomfortable. I've tried telling her that what she thinks is most important, that the other girls are just jealous, but apparently, she can't stand up to the criticism."

If girls are dishearteningly effective in keeping each other in line, it's because they are well practiced in the art; it is the same threat that keeps her attached to her mother. "Don't worry about what the other girls think," Mother says out of one side of her mouth. "Be like me," she implies out of the other. How can we be like her and be ourselves? we question, already knowing that our attempts at becoming independent make her anxious, rejecting. From the other girls, who are supposed to be our saviors, we get the same innuendo, playing on our deepest insecurities, using the most effective weapon they have. The deal is that if we do as we're told, our friend will be there for us. If not, she threatens to abandon us. "If you're Mary's friend, I won't be your friend," says our playmate. "You look ugly in that dress," chides our best friend. We give up Mary and the dress with the same abruptness, fearing the repercussions if we do not. With our mothers our dependence on her forces us to forgo our autonomy for nurturance. Once again we are in that same place.

THE COST OF WINNING

Our need to keep our relationships on an even keel not only coerces us into conformity, but forces us to put a lid on our competitive impulses. Consider, for example, the girl-boy competition gap. Despite the women's movement, boys still thrive on competitive endeavors while girls opt for games like "A My Name Is Alice," or jacks, where one girl's success does not necessarily dictate another girl's failure. Girls' games also tend to end a lot sooner than boys', usually at the point there's some dispute about the rules.[15] "You're supposed to put all the money in the middle for Free Parking," we yell in a heated contest of Monopoly. "You are not, you are not," retorts our friend. "Aw, let's forget it and play something else" is the typical upshot. Girls prefer to end the game rather than argue. Too afraid to contradict each other, they squelch their competitive feelings. Why gamble with rejection just to win a "stupid" game? Unable to tolerate being loser or victor, we cast the game aside and bring the battle to safer grounds, convincing ourselves it's more fun to trade secrets.

In recent years some experts have given another interpretation to these findings. Girls' propensity to drop the rules, to avoid hand-to-hand combat with each other, is a sign of their greater maturity, they say. It is an indication that girls have "a heightened perception of the 'other side' of competitive success, that is, the great emotional costs at which success achieved through competition is often gained—an understanding which, though confused, indicates some underlying sense that something is rotten in the state in which success is defined as having better grades than everyone else."[16]

The argument certainly has its appeal except for one small fact. When girls compete with boys, they don't seem to have any problems. For example, one study conducted at Tulane University compared the levels of competitiveness of both girls and boys between the ages of seven and nine when competing against same-sex and opposite-sex opponents in a board game. The results showed that boys were highly competitive under all conditions. The girls were another story. Girls playing with boys showed much higher levels of competition than girls playing against girls.[17] In other words, something happens to girls when they vie with one another to quell their rivalrous urges. What we call tolerance for the rules is really a coverup for our inability to express anger, our struggle with assertiveness, our fear of being rejected.

THE VOLCANO ERUPTS

With no channels for feelings of aggression to be released directly, our hostile, competitive impulses are forced underground, seeping out in malevolent ways. When boys get angry at one another, when they disagree, they have it out face-to-face. But overt aggression is not encouraged in girls; besides, it's too risky, needing each other as we do. That's why so much of little girls' hostile behavior emerges in more subtle ways: not inviting a friend to a party, not choosing a girl to be on a team, excluding another girl from a secret club.

"Any kind of aggression that is limited to such constricted channels is bound to arise in malevolent ways," says Jane Flax. "There's not much you can do with aggression as a girl. A girl has few outlets for her aggressive feelings—even in sports she's supposed to be ladylike. Her aggression has to be relational, centered on the female sphere. It's not as if she can go out and kick a football and have that reinforce her identity." Another problem, she tells me, is that when a girl expresses aggression toward another girl, she is also expressing aggression symbolically toward her mother, and by definition toward herself. "That gives it a kind of edge that can be really vicious."

"You want to know whether the other little girls ever did nasty things to me?" asks one woman with a smirk that barely hides the pain underneath. "Where do you want me to start? How about the time that I got my period in fifth grade, and one little girl who saw the stain on my dress passed around a note to the whole class? Or how about camp—that was the best of all—having my bra hung up on the flagpole, finding shampoo in my mouthwash bottle, being tied up to the bed?" The woman pauses for a moment, reflecting on her diatribe. "You know, when we started speaking, you asked how I felt about women, and I told you that I never really trusted them, that I always preferred men. Maybe this is where it all got started."

Angela Fox warns me about making a causal connection between a woman's early relationships with other girls and her feelings about women later on. "A woman may feel that her mistrust of other women goes back to her early childhood friendships, but chances are such a woman also had a negative relationship with her mother. That will make her acutely sensitive to the rejection of the other girls; it reinforces her feelings of not being loved that were planted in her relationship with her mom." I agree. But who of us can say she has received the kind of strength it would take to dismiss such merciless cruelty?

Ironically, the closer the mother-daughter bond, the more vicious a girl is likely to be. That's because girls who have tight relationships with their mothers are the same girls who will have the most difficulty separating from them. She's also bound to have the most trouble expressing anger toward her mother. "Her dire need to break away, coupled with her own bottled-up anger that she's been harboring toward her mother, may get unleashed in one heartfelt swoop," says Angela Fox. "And if you tell mothers like these that their girls are little beasts, they can't believe it because at home they seem to be such angels."

Whatever kind of mother we had, knowing and identifying with each other as we do, little girls have the capacity to hit where it hurts most. Gossiping, teasing, rejecting, we have little trouble bringing another little girl to tears within a matter of seconds. I think the names are the worst. Two stick in my mind the most: lak-fats, (a variation on the old fatso theme), and ninipa, a made-up word that meant "vagina." Other women have their own fond remembrances: lesi, chubs, horseface, hooker—I could go on. And if the scars last so long, it's because the sword stabs so deep.

"When I was nine, I was obese," an attractive, lithe college professor told me. "I took up one and one half seats on the school bus. The tormenting from the other girls was horrible; I used to come home crying almost every day because some girl had said something mean. When I was fourteen, my mother sent me to one of those fat farms and I took off a lot of weight. But you know, I never quite got over feeling ugly; I still think of myself that way. I'm so uptight about the way women see me that on the night I began going into labor with my son, I insisted on polishing my toenails before going to the hospital."

Teasing another girl about her body is one of the most devastating things that a girl can do to another girl since women's identities are so much bound up in how they look. Jane Flax told me about an experience in a women's consciousness-raising group where the women were dealing with their negative feelings about their bodies. They decided to take off their clothes to check their self-perceptions. What they discovered was that even the women that everyone else in the group thought were the most beautiful, the most perfect, had negative feelings about their bodies. "There was not one woman there who did not have some negative feelings about her body," she told me. "Girls pick this up early; they know that one sure malicious way to hurt another girl is to draw attention to something that differentiates them from the female norm of beauty—it's like saying you're not good enough, you're not worthy of esteem, you're not lovable."

PLANTED SEEDS

Not surprisingly, little girls leave childhood with conflicted feelings about other girls which often lead to countless problems with other women later on. Needing the intimacy, but never having been sure of when rejection might show itself, we continue to be acutely sensitive to what other women think of us, altering our behavior so that we'll be liked and thus avoid rejection. Eons after the wounds, we sit in front of our mirrors, magnifying every blemish, wrinkle, and flaw in our figures, spending millions of dollars to cover our glaring imperfections to make ourselves acceptable to one another. Virtually every study that's ever been done on makeup has concluded that most men are against it; painting our faces, apparently, is something we do for other women's approval.

Having been jostled between intimacy and rejection, we also continue to feel possessive of our friends throughout adulthood. Many women have told me that they make it a point not to introduce their close friends to each other for fear that the two women may like each other too much, leaving the first woman out in the cold.

Finally, as women we continue to have trouble expressing our anger toward each other directly.[18] As when we were young, the anger often emerges in more malevolent ways—stealing lovers, gossiping about each other, ending relationships abruptly because we do not have the courage to tell the other what she has done.

At the same time, neither do we forget that wonderful feeling of having been someone's "best" friend, the love and warmth that comes out of being another woman's number-one choice. And throughout our lives we continue to search for that feeling, still.

Chapter 3

BEST OF FRIENDS

IT had been four years since my relationship with Helena had ended, four years during which we had not exchanged a word although we had gone to the same high school and now attended the same college. It had never occurred to me that Helena would be at this year's personal-awareness conference. Nor did it cross my mind that seeing her at the conference would make me uncomfortable. My feelings toward Helena had long since been resolved.

Or so I thought. Midafternoon of the first day I saw Helena standing with a friend across the large front lawn of the dorm complex. Her presence shot through me like an electric shock. As I turned away to return to the sanctuary of my room, I prayed she had not seen me, and felt eternally thankful that I had been spared the harrowing experience of having been placed in the same group as hers. We had not communicated since we were fifteen, and now was no time to start.

I spent most of the next day successfully managing to avoid her. But, of course, I knew that something was going on. I was shaken, agitated to the point of distraction. That afternoon, while daydreaming in a group session from which I felt detached and disinterested, my real feelings came into focus. I was yearning for her in a frantic, desperate sort of way I had never experienced with anyone else, man or woman. I wanted to have contact with her; to break the iron wall that had stood between us for so many years. After all this time, a lifetime of new experiences in which Helena had played no part, I still felt attached to her.

As luck would have it, I met the professor who was Helena's group leader. He offered to act as an intermediary, and later that day informed me that he had set up a meeting between us. The next few hours were spent in a state of anxious anticipation. What would we say to each other? Had she, too, felt the pain of the icy uneasiness between us all of these years, or did she dismiss all thoughts about me after our relationship had ended? Underneath all these questions loomed the real question that despite my supposedly enlightened self I could not allow myself to ask: What had our friendship meant to her? Had she ever cared about me the way I knew I had cared about her?

Actually, it was not Helena, but I, who had cruelly and without warning terminated our relationship. During ninth grade, we were virtually inseparable. We walked to school together, sat next to one another in almost every class, did our homework together. In the evenings, seemingly unable to tolerate any separation, we filled the gap with marathon phone calls. I learned to tweeze my eyebrows and shave my legs in her bathroom, and we slapped each other on the back as we choked down our first cigarette in mine. When I was failing algebra, Helena tutored me through the late night hours, and let me copy her answers when it became clear that all the tutoring in the world wasn't going to help. I loved her—was perhaps even a bit in love with her.

That's not to say I had no interest in boys. To the contrary, I looked and acted the part of what we have come to think of as the typical adolescent girl. I can remember the countless hours sitting in Helena's kitchen, daydreaming about Jason Rubovsky to the beat of "He's So Fine." We constructed "checklists" of all the boys in our class, rating them on such critical attributes as eye color and whether or not they had suede patches on the elbows of their sweaters. And certainly, we would have been Van Cliburns if the time we devoted to rummaging through Helena's older sister's makeup case or posing in front of the mirror had been spent preparing for our piano lessons.

But whatever I felt about boys or my fantasy crushes paled next to what I felt about Helena. Boys were still an odd and distant species. Helena was real, and very special. We could discuss everything from boys to philosophy and shared a penchant for intellectual endeavors. Helena was everything I could have wanted from a friend, and from a mother, too.

Then, without warning, my feelings for Helena underwent a change. I began to feel uncomfortable about the intensity of our relationship. Despite the fact that our expressions of affection were limited to occasional pecks on the cheek, there was no doubt that my feelings were stronger for her than the innocent attachment of one girl to another, a depth of feeling that was obvious to everyone including my then-eight-year-old sister. "There was a spark, an electricity between you," she recently told me. "You just couldn't miss it."

On some level I didn't miss it, and the message reverberated with terrifying psychological resonance. That summer in camp I became obsessed with boys, no matter how gawky, no matter how much my lips bled from the gnashing of their braces against my mouth. Receiving a letter from Helena in which she announced she, too, had a boyfriend only stepped up my quest for a leading man in my life. It was not, I realized looking back, just a matter of competition that spurred me on, but jealousy. As much as I wanted a boyfriend, I couldn't help but feel that they interfered with my relationship with Helena. And on some level I wanted her all to myself. Distancing myself from Helena first was my way of softening the blow.

But there was something else affecting our relationship, too. Helena was brilliant, to be sure, but she was not, as the expression goes, "with it." That didn't seem to bother Helena at all, who at a very young age seemed above the pressures of others. But it did leave its mark on me. For example, when Helena ran up to receive her reward for scholastic excellence at our junior high school graduation, the two girls sitting to my right giggled.

"Look at that hairstyle," one said to the other.

"Yeah, what a fag."

"Don't you dare talk about my best friend that way," I had wanted to shout. Instead, I said nothing. Deep down, I knew that to defend her would be an automatic indictment of myself. And I hated the thought that I might be viewed as "faggy," even if it meant giving up Helena.

High school offered me the chance to escape from potential "fagdom"—my first opportunity, actually, to be in with the in crowd. Through ninth grade I had been a short, stout girl with frizzy hair that betrayed me every time the weather was humid—the kind of girl that the more stylish girls made fun of. But during that summer I lost weight, shot up three inches, and discovered hair straightener. If still not a raving beauty, I was obviously a far cry from the "chubbo" I had been only a few months before, because I was almost immediately be-friended by an absolutely stunning girl named Jacqueline who was in my homeroom class. Before I knew it, I was introduced to her friends who were bright but not intellectual, who all seemed confident when it came to boys, and most of all, who accepted me with open arms. It was then that I learned the power of the statement "It's not who you know but who knows you"—within months of my association with these girls, my social standing increased dramatically. In fact, the clique was one of the most popular in the school, which made me popular via association, too. It was a lure baited with honey.

Helena, on the other hand, started becoming friendly with a group known as the "bookworms," and during tenth grade we saw less and less of each other. By the following summer, I decided to end our relationship once and for all. I wrote her a long letter, spelling out the details of my male conquests, on the envelope adding a deadly slight in code: I.Y.B.S.T.Y.O.—translated: "Is your boyfriend still twelve years old?" referring to the fact that the summer before, Helena's boyfriend had been younger than she. (This atrocity was something I conveniently forgot until Helena reminded me of it when I interviewed her.) Helena was no fool, and in order to preserve her own pride, she wrote back a scathing letter of her own, saying her mother forbid her to be friends with me anymore. I remember getting that letter. I laughed.

There was, I learned, ultimately a price for this. Being popular was wonderful, but there were a number of accommodations I had to make in order to "fit." The first was to tone down my intellectual zeal. Even in my circle, being smart was acceptable so long as it didn't overshadow what was supposedly the real important thing, which, naturally, was boys. And, of course, to get the right boy, you had to spend endless hours obsessing with looks, and in my junior year I headed straight for the plastic surgeon to have a small bump in my nose exorcised. My metamorphosis had already made me suspect that "personality" was less of an asset than beauty; after my face had been remodeled, I was entirely convinced of it. Suddenly, I not only associated with the best-looking girls, but was one of them, with a dashing and handsome older boyfriend to show off. Instead of being on the outside, I became a social pivot, a constant supplier of blind dates for my friends who found the high school selection limited and immature. Sounds wonderful? It was. Except for the fact that I've been somewhat obsessed with my looks ever since. And that I was turning into the kind of person I knew, in my heart of hearts, I really was not.

My "split self," as I later thought of it, became evident to me in all sorts of ways. Although I enjoyed my group of new friends, I never really felt I could let down my hair around them with the kind of spontaneity I had with Helena; they were friends, but somehow I felt they were rivals, too. And while our regular conversations and debates about "over the bra" or "under the bra" certainly helped us alleviate our apprehensions about sex,[1] talking about boys all the time got pretty dreary. Most of all, I found myself hiding my ambitiousness and desire to achieve academically, boasting, as did the others, that I had hardly studied for this or that exam. (Miraculously, we all had excellent grades —I later learned from Jacqueline that she and the others had also studied ferociously, although we had all publicly denied it.)

If I had modified my behavior with my girlfriends, I did a complete Jekyll and Hyde with my boyfriend. If a certan amount of healthy assertiveness had been my trademark, you'd never have known it.

"Let's spend the whole summer on a boat fishing," he'd say.

I hated fish and worms even more. "That sounds terrific."

"I think people overestimated JFK."

"You're right," I said, even though I idolized the President.

"I need to, uh, expand my sexual horizons, you know, see other girls."

"Sure, I understand," I answered, fighting back the tears, waiting until he had a change of heart, at which point I would welcome him back unequivocally.

The biggest price of all, of course, was my relationship with Helena. I didn't feel it immediately, but over time I began missing her, the intensity we'd had, the twosome which had been replaced by the "group." I began yearning for the feeling that comes from being with someone who understands you and accepts you for your true self—a feeling I had neither with my other friends or with my boyfriend. And each time I passed Helena in the hall and her eyes turned away, I felt a stab of guilt for what I had done to her. And remorse for what I had done to myself.

These feelings simmered until our fated reunion during our third year of college.

Now after years of silence Helena and I were standing face-to-face. I was overcome by the intensity of the experience. Looking at her, she seemed much more a woman than I, exuding quiet confidence from every pore. I was shaken by my feelings of admiration for who she had become and a sense of loss for not having been there to grow up with her.

As we fumbled over our initial awkwardness, laughing nervously, feebly attempting to give each other the sketchy details of our lives over the past five years—neither of us were still virgins; no, I didn't have a boyfriend right now; yes, she had a steady; yes, I was into the field of communications; she was into science and research. As our inhibitions were slowly sidestepped in the spirit of the conference, we floated back and forth between the past, the present, the future: the state of the world, the state of our lives, the state of our relationship. Though we had not spoken for years, in our own ways we had each followed the existence of the other, maintaining a strange sense of interest and connectedness, despite the feelings that had torn us apart. I confessed my guilt, which I had carried around with me since the beginning of high school when I had betrayed our friendship. She confessed her jealousy as she watched from the back of the college auditorium as I ran to the stage to receive a prize for a contest I had won. We were a heap of emotions, vacillating between openness and remoteness, the facade of strength and the vulnerability of tears, a sense of closeness and one of complete strangeness.

Then the showdown.

"What made you do it?" she asked, looking me squarely in the eye.

Freeze. What could I say? That I had loved her both too much and not enough to forfeit my social ambitions? That while I loved her as I had loved no other friend, my own insecurity made me need the approval of the other girls more?

"I don't know," I answered finally, breaking into tears. "I guess I just lost myself."

"Don't feel so bad," she told me. "That was years ago, and while it hurt a lot then, I've gotten over it."

It was at that moment that I became aware of the real reason I had asked for this reunion. While Helena might have gotten over it, I hadn't; more than anything else in the world, I wanted that kind of feeling, that kind of friendship again.

Helena did not share my sentiments. In part, it was because her life had gone on just fine without me. She had met the man she was eventually to marry and seemed to have plenty of friends. And, she admitted as tactfully as she could, she had become disillusioned by the way I had ended our relationship. When we had met, her attraction to me was based on the fact that I had been different, "creative," as she put it. But I had disappointed her, had become, well, just like the "other" girls.

I wanted to tell her that I had changed, that I really wasn't that way at all, that something beyond my own control had propelled me to hurt her so badly. But as we sat holding hands on the bus ride home together, I sadly acknowledged that it was too late; that the naive bliss of our friendship was lost forever.

What I have not lost was the sense of powerful attachment and love that can grow between two girls, a feeling which has pervaded my relationships with women ever since. Nor have I forgotten how much we give up in the name of becoming "feminine."

Ever since there have been theories about adolescent development, the assumption has been that puberty is a period of tremendous growth and expansion. This is only a half-truth.

True, adolescence starts out with a great push toward self discovery. But by mid-puberty, a far more pressing task intervenes, takes over, and stops the drive for independence dead in its tracks. What begins as a search for our individuality often ends up as a step back to dependence. And what starts out as friendships which help us find ourselves often ends up as relationships in which our identity is lost to peer group conformity.

What is the imperative that lies at the root of this stagnation? A time span of five to six years during which girls have to make one of the most difficult transitions of their lives: the switch from girls to boys.

WHAT'S A NICE GIRL LIKE YOU DOING WITH A FRIEND LIKE THAT?

Of course, you'd never suspect the struggles that lay ahead by looking at girls who are at the initial stages of adolescence. To the contrary, most girlfriends, like Helena and I, are all but inseparable, hanging onto each other for dear life as they cultivate the seeds of separation from mother which is the hallmark of the teenage years. That's because every girl feels the need to grow up, which in large part means breaking the fetters of her dependence on her mother. But every girl is also more dependent on Mom than she'd like to admit.[2] That's where friends come in, allowing us to begin reckoning with the unknown, giving us the security of the arms we just left. As Mother once was, she's there every day for us—at school, on the weekends, on the phone—a protector, soothsayer, confidante all rolled in one. We are in cahoots; two fugitives escaping the clutches of the same captors.

The trust and exclusivity of young adolescent girls' friendships[3] is the cushion that enables us to begin sowing our own oats. For Helena and I the rebellion was relatively benign—smoking, shaving our legs, stealing a few sips of wine from our parents' liquor cabinets. For others, the transformation can be an almost complete about face triggered by a desire to be as "other" from Mom as possible.[4] For example, I recently bumped into a girl who used to be friendly with my daughter in my old neighborhood—or more accurately, I walked past her until she stopped me to say hello. Aside from her high-pitched voice, she was unrecognizable from the well-polished twelve-year-old with the penny loafers and long black ponytail I had known only a year ago. Having traded in her more conservative attire for black boots, black sweat pants, and a too tight black sweater, the only polish to be seen was psychedelic purple and coating her two-inch-long fingernails. Her long black curls, now loose, looked as if she'd stuck her finger into an electric socket.

"Well," I said, gaining my composure, "I must say, I hardly recognize you."

"Yeah," she said with delight. "I learned all about dressing from my friend Adeline. She's great. She really helped me find myself."

I gulped at the thought of what "self" that might be.

As far out as a girl may seem to go, and as disconcerting to the parents on the receiving end, most psychologists agree that finding these "alter egos" is a critical step in learning about who we are, particularly for girls, whose identity is less clearly defined than boys' to begin with. The intimacy girls share provides a sounding board against which we can project our fears and uncertainties. In fact, some experts believe that a girl who does not have a close friend at this stage may remain overly dependent on her mother; if she doesn't break away from Mom now, she may never do so.[5]

Of course, girls also bring with them their own unique psychological agendas. Some girls who either had less than terrific relationships with their mothers or less than satisfying friendships when they were younger, may seek out intense, romantic friendships. Other girls find themselves latching on to older girls in search of a role model.[6] Still others care less about the girl per se than how much her mother will disapprove, partaking in the forbidden fruit with an extra ounce of zeal and flavor. "My mother absolutely despises my friend Elaine," one fifteen-year-old told me. "She thinks she's a tramp because she wears lots of makeup. Elaine is really a pretty decent kid, a prude, actually, but I don't let my mother know that. I guess I like the idea that she doesn't like her and that there's little she can do to stop me from seeing her."

Whatever the modus operandi, one thread runs throughout: friends are replacements for the mothers we just left. They are our Rocks of Gibraltar. In them we find security and support; from them we demand exclusivity and loyalty.[7]

They are, I think, a girl's first true love.

HIDDEN DANGERS

But the bliss does not last.

As soon as we get into the ebb and flow of separating from our mothers vis-à-vis our friends, girls are hit with another more urgent developmental imperative: the consolidation of our heterosexuality.

The first clue that it's time to begin moving on to boys is most obviously reflected in the heightened sexual tension that almost suddenly infuses our friendships. While only one out of ten girls reports having any overt sexual encounter with her friends during adolescence,[8] there's no doubt that combing one another's hair, giggling hysterically under the covers as we read our parent's porno books, the long, torrid conversations into the wee hours of the morning, are all reflective of the increasing sensations being ignited in our loins. And what might be considered innocent child's play at ten or eleven, is not so innocent at fourteen or fifteen, particularly when the spillover into eroticism is more concrete. "When we were twelve and thirteen my best friend and I used to read *True Confessions* and act out the parts with each other," one woman told me. "It felt great and for a long time it didn't bother me—we'd say that we were rehearsing for the real thing. But when we hit fourteen or so—*shazaam*—it stopped just like that. Somehow, we both knew it wasn't right to do that after a certain age. Besides," she added, "we were already starting to go out with boys."

"Seeing the light," so to speak, is exactly what experts count on. Given the fact that our hormones are pumping at record speed at a time we're not quite ready for boys, these kinds of encounters are generally considered well within the range of normal behavior in the early teens. In fact, psychologists warn that boy craziness at too green an age is something to be much more concerned about than these passionate same-sex trysts.[9] That's because they assume that falling in love with another girl, sexual overtones and all, is a passing phase, something that, given time, most girls simply outgrow.

But normal feminine development is trickier than it sounds because heterosexuality has two sides: the sexual and the emotional. And while turning to boys sexually for most girls poses little problem, giving boys number-one billing in our hearts is far more difficult.

THE HETEROSEXUAL LOOP

Psychologists have known for some time that it isn't easy for girls to develop an emotional attachment to boys, but only recently have they tuned in to the reason why: The first one a girl loves is her mother, who, of course, is another woman. And on some level, we never rid ourselves of the desire to return to that love.

This one "small" fact of life makes a girl's development a convoluted affair. In order for her to be well adjusted, she has to give up her primary attachment to her mother in favor of men. But why should she? Her mother's the one she's been most intimate with, in whose arms she's been cradled. To add to the problem, becoming "normal" also means learning what it means to be feminine. So while she's supposed to reject mother, and later other girls, she's still expected to be like them.

Schizoid as these dual imperatives might seem, that's exactly what we have to do. And not surprisingly, there is trouble from the start. It first becomes apparent when we're about five, when we first become aware of our sexuality. It used to be believed that this shift to Dad was as easy as pie—after all, Dad's so much more powerful and alluring, who wouldn't rather be associated with him? Today we know that things don't go so smoothly: Dad may be wonderful, but all our real nitty-gritty interactions have been with Mom. How, then, do girls make the switch?[10]

There have been volumes written on the subject, each offering a different explanation. Some analysts claim that a girl becomes so enraged at her mother for not giving her a penis that she automatically rejects her right off the bat. Others say that a girl's turn to her father arises because Dad offers her a way of breaking away from Mom's stronghold. Still others posit the view that the sexual attraction between the sexes is biologically determined and that turning to Dad is a way of expressing our innate sex drives.

As varied as these interpretations might be, almost all of them share an important argument: that while a girl does tend to turn toward her father during the classic "oedipal" stage, she never gives up her primary attachment to her mother. To the contrary, she usually strikes an unconscious compromise that goes something like this: Okay, I'll focus my erotic attention on Daddy, but I'll keep Mom number one in my heart.

I recently saw that resolution being played out with my friend's four-year-old daughter. My friend was dressing to go out for the evening when her husband walked in holding a lollipop in the shape of a heart in his hand.

"How's my beautiful girl," he said to his daughter in a way that was flattering, flirtatious, and fatherly at the same time.

"Hi, Daddy," said the girl, rushing to throw her arms around him.

A few minutes later my friend announced she was ready to leave.

"Where are you going?" demanded her daughter.

"I told you, honey, I'm meeting a friend of mine for dinner."

"But who's going to make dinner for us?"

"I am," said her dad. "How does spaghetti and meatballs sound?"

The girl expressed her sentiments with a hefty "Ugh."

"I thought you liked spaghetti and meatballs," said her father with a twinge of hurt in his voice.

"I like *you* to bring me candy," she replied, "but I like *Mommy* to make spaghetti and meatballs."

This Mommy-Daddy-Me triangle works fine until we reach puberty. No one minds if we cling to Mom and the other girls when we're ten or eleven. But by fourteen or fifteen, people begin wondering about us if we aren't making a definite statement that the opposite sex is *numero uno* in our minds. Even if there's no evidence of any inherent sexuality, girls who seem too close are susceptible to ostracism, as two Palo Alto, California, high school students discovered.

As an experiment, for three weeks the girls playacted at being best friends—sometimes walking arm in arm, pecking each other on the cheek occasionally after class—expressing affection as close friends would. Their express purpose was to give the impression that their feelings were in no way sexual. The reaction of their classmates told a different story. At the end of three weeks the boys started calling them names. The girls were even more outraged and threatened to beat them up.[11]

If there were no sexual overtures between the two, why were their classmates so incensed? For the same reason that I became increasingly uneasy about my relationship with Helena: Same-sex relationships stand in the way of what's considered normal development, which, of course, means having a primary sexual *and* emotional attachment to a male. And for girls that's something that does not come naturally.

AFFAIRS OF THE HEART

Thus emerges the great female dilemma. We're supposed to switch our allegiance to boys, but emotionally, there isn't any good reason to do so. Then again, being overly involved with a girlfriend at sixteen is unacceptable. How do we satisfy both our emotional needs and the social demands of the culture?

The answer is that most of us continue to rely on the old know-how from when we were five—we find ourselves a boyfriend to latch on to for the sake of appearing normal, while keeping our girlfriends in the forefront of our emotional lives. Some girls continue to rely on their one and only best friend. Others, as I did, find that having one best friend is too narrow and emotionally intense, and trade in exclusivity for the safety of numbers. Either way, the outcome is virtually identical: What looks like a grand obsession with boys is often a way of binding girls together.

One night at my son's parent-teacher conference, for example, I over-heard two pretty girls, about sixteen, who were involved in an intense and very secret discussion. The blonde was filling in the brunette about the details of last night's hot and heavy date. "He wants me to 'do it' with him," she related.

"You mean all the way?"

Nod. "But I don't like the way he kisses. . . . He has a cyst on his tongue."

Hysterical giggles.

"Why don't you tell him you have herpes or something," suggested the brunette.

"Stop making me crack up. I can't tell him that. Besides, I need someone to take me to the basketball game on Saturday."

The brunette scrunched her nose. "Why don't you come with Johnny and me, and then I can keep an eye on you. And you can sleep at my house. I'll also tell my mother to say we have to be home *real* early."

"But what will Johnny say about that?" protested the blonde half-heartedly.

"Who cares? He's not such a great kisser either."

The scene, with variations, is familiar to most of us. Necking and petting are fun, but if we're honest with ourselves, the real fun comes from telling our friends all about it. We fix each other up with dates half out of generosity, half out of knowing that we have a better time when our friends come along—to say nothing of the protection they provide against roaming hands. For the teenage girl who is more emotionally and physically mature than boys of the same age, and whose relation-ships with other girls are emotionally richer, the real story is this: Boys may serve a social function, but not much of an emotional one.[12] They're something akin to high-heeled shoes—they make us feel more grown-up, but goodness knows we can't wait to take them off and step into our slippers.

What boys *do* do for girls is provide them with the developmental seal of approval. The simple fact of having a boyfriend is enough assur-ance that we're normal after all. It is a circumvention that serves us well, but it is also very tricky.

Girls' involvement with boys is a double-edged sword. On the plus side, boys allow us to maintain strong allegiances to one another while simultaneously preparing us for marriage. The darker side is that to be successful with boys often requires certain codes of behavior that end up pitting us against one another.

To say nothing of what learning to be "feminine" does to our sense of independence.

A POPULAR GIRL IS . . .

Boys like girls who are pretty.

And who aren't as smart as they are.

A good date is cheerful, a good listener, and never grouchy.

Or a girl who puts out.

The "best" girl is the girl who gets the "best" boy.

The dating personality,[13] as it's often been called, is largely defined by the culture and the prejudices of boys (and later men). It's promulgated by teen magazines and columns that tell girls how they can dress more enticingly or whiten their teeth or how they can act in a way that will be attractive to the opposite sex. By the time most girls are ten, they are well aware of it. By fourteen or fifteen, it's difficult not to fall prey to it.

The rules of the game create all sorts of conflicts for a girl. On the one hand, we want to be loyal to our girlfriends. Yet we need the attention of the boys to satisfy our cravings for social approval. We want to grow and expand, but we get the message that boys are more interested in the more external, superficial aspects of our selves. It's a message that's hard to slough off—the whole culture supports it—and it's one that often divides the girl both against herself and her friends.

POWER IN NUMBERS

Somewhere around mid-adolescence almost every girl can expect to trade in her intense one-to-one relationships for the more amorphous safety of the group. That's because the group provides both the safety of numbers as well as a larger base from which to form liaisons with the boys.

"During adolescence, popularity and friendliness become intertwined," writes sociologist Robert Bell. "But friendliness does not have the exclusiveness friendships had. Adolescents quickly learn that the closer and more intimate the friendship the fewer the number of friends."[14]

The irony is that while group life may feel exciting, deep down most girls would rather have the close, best-friend variety. In fact, according to one researcher, while the group may imply that girls are obsessed with popularity and with boys, the fact is that most girls turn to the group as a way of providing them with more options for choosing and finding a best friend.[15]

THE PRETTY AND THE NOT-SO-PRETTY

Then, of course, there's the question of what group? It's here we first become attuned to the Great Divide among teenage girls: beauty.

Janis Ian may have learned the truth at seventeen, but for most of us the message comes a lot earlier: As far as most boys are concerned, beauty really is only skin-deep. When popularity with the boys wasn't so pressing, the size of our bust or the shape of our noses made no difference in terms of our friends. Now suddenly, we are faced with the hard-hitting truth that an unattractive girlfriend can be a social liability.

"I've been going with this boy for more than a year," a sixteen-year-old tells me, "and we really get along great except when it comes to my friend Mary Ellen. She's not very good-looking, and he calls her Dog-face. He refuses to fix her up with any of his friends. It makes me mad because she's really funny and has a great personality. And it's very embarrassing because her mother keeps asking me why I don't get her a date. I feel really bad about it; I don't want to hurt her feelings. So I've kind of let the friendship drop. I don't know what else to do."

She could, of course, break up with the boy, or tell the girl's mother the truth. Two unlikely prospects.

And if a girl's lucky enough to have friends that do stick beside her? The dilemma is often as painful. About now she begins to notice that when the boys come over to talk, they all but ignore her. Or that she's becoming a pseudo Ann Landers—giving advice about things she couldn't possibly have experienced. Or that while she's included, she always seems to feel like extra baggage, tolerated more than really accepted.

From the other side of the fence, the girl with the peaches-and-cream complexion has her fair share of flak to deal with. Being pretty baits both the boys and the other girls, but to be too beautiful often leads to envy and rejection by her peers. And if, heaven forbid, she's also got a good head on her shoulders, she may be in for real trouble. "I was the dumb blonde," one magnificent woman explained. "I wasn't dumb, but it was very hard for me to shake that image. It was as if some of the girls had to find something wrong with me to keep me in my place."

Actually, this woman was more fortunate than others. Viewing her good looks as a potential trap, she began cultivating her intellectual assets—today she is a successful engineer. Other girls, believing that life at sixteen is the way life is, period, integrate the "beauty is better than brains" message as life's strategy, only to find the rug pulled out from underneath them the minute the wrinkles start showing.

Either way, the adolescent girl gets duped. At a time when she's most likely to feel insecure about her looks, the not-so-pretty girl feels almost exclusively judged by them. The beautiful girl gives up meaningful friendships for the sake of social success, or comes to believe that she can ride the crest of the wave with her Ivory Snow smile.

It is ironic that at a time when the urge to expand and the need for self-definition are pressing, girls are coerced into becoming obsessed with the most superficial aspects of themselves. Some girls, says psychologist Elizabeth Douvan, outgrow it. But others "lose track entirely of the inner self under the pressure to attract affection and attention."[16]

LEARNING TO BE A LADY

While the importance of looks is being played up, the importance of intelligence and achievement is being played down.

Adolescence begins the great female academic decline. Up until eleven or twelve, girls' zeal for doing well in school puts boys to shame. But when puberty hits, the situation begins turning on itself, with boys being the ones to make the grade as girls increasingly slip farther and farther behind. Even girls who continue to do well in school have their future vocational plans much less concretely defined than their male counterparts.[17]

And so begins the push to become ladylike, a kind of collective endeavor supported by society, mothers, and the other girls. Deep down, a girl may find shopping boring as hell, or spending hours in front of the mirror painting her face a waste of time, but as she sees, so she does. Even among friends who want to achieve, a girl is likely to find that getting good grades doesn't seem to have as much clout as wearing Joe's ID bracelet.

She begins noticing that the same friend who only last night was rattling off algebraic equations has a vacuous look when she's around the captain of the basketball team. Or that she becomes a giggling hyena, agreeing with everything the boys say. Suddenly, it occurs to her that she and her friends act differently with the boys; that she has two selves—her "real" self and her "dating" self.[18]

"Double-dating is kind of strange," one girl confessed. "When you're just with your friends, you can talk about all sorts of things, you can be yourself. But when we go out together with boys, it's like we become different people."

It is ironic that at a time when a girl is trying to get a handle on her identity, what her friends teach her is that a girl's "self" must be fragmented.

COMPETITION UNLEASHED

As the social pressures gather thunder, and the arena in which girls are allowed to compete narrows, getting the boy increasingly becomes the name of the contest, and love the battlefield.

Adolescent girls will often say, "You should never tell a girl if you like a certain boy because she'll try to get that boy, too." Most girls don't steal their friend's boyfriends, but even the one or two cases she knows about are enough to make her feel insecure. Even if she doesn't see it in her friends, she can't escape seeing the competitive impulses in herself. "I'm going out with this counselor named Stu," said the letter a friend wrote to me long ago. "I think he's the cutest boy in camp. The best part about it was that he was first going with this other girl, and he *broke up with her for me!* Poor girl. (Ha, ha, what a fakeout.)" In her postscript she wrote: "There's also this other counselor that I like, too, but I'm keeping it a secret. You never know what some girls will do to get a boy. . . ."

Deep down, she probably suspects some girls would do anything. "When I was in high school, we used to go on what were called 'late dates,' which meant you'd climb out of the window late at night and go hang out with a boy in his car for a while," said a forty-year-old woman. "Anyway, I had this late date with a guy named Brent. No one knew about it. And we were sitting in his car when a song came on and he said, 'That will be our song from now on.' A week later I came to school and my best friend at the time was wearing his ring and humming the song that had been ours. I saw stars. To this day when she sees me on the street, she crosses to the other side. I think she's afraid I might hit her."

"Maybe," I speculated, "it was the boy who was at the heart of the betrayal."

Her eyes opened in astonishment. "You know, I never even considered that possibility. And to think that that one incident has made me leery of women ever since." At the ripe old age of sixteen, girls already are concluding that when it comes to the opposite sex, girls can't be trusted as far as they can be thrown.

Theories that try to explain girls' competition for boys range from the idea that girls are trying to resolve old competitive issues with their mothers to the notion that the competition for boys is really a repressed drive to win and achieve. It's all well and good for psychologists to suggest that what girls are really doing is expressing their "skills in winning and maintaining love,"[19] or acting out their rivalrous urges toward their mothers, but have you ever tried convincing a fifteen-year-old who's just lost her boyfriend to a rival that there's no malice intended?

Total trust and security is the cement that brings adolescent girls together. Now our best friend suddenly also becomes a rival. And we can't afford to give up every friend who's competitive, or chances are we'd have no friends left.

More detrimental in the long run is that we begin to perceive that the quest for men is the primary arena in which competitive feelings between girls and later women can be expressed.

It is ironic that during a time that we're supposed to be expanding and developing our unique capabilities, our outlets to "win" are confined to such a narrow sphere.

GIRLS ARE NICE, BUT BOYS ARE BETTER

As our glimpses into the turn to boys become everyday realities, the full weight of the impact begins to register: It's not who you are that counts, but what boy you have.

About now we begin to notice that even during school hours our friends would rather hang out with boys. Or when we do get together, the new love of her life always seems to be tagging along.

Then, of course, there's the notorious "Let's go to the movies on Saturday night unless something better happens to come up" routine. "My best friend and I do everything together," one fifteen-year-old told me. "We're like a team. The only fights we ever have are about boys. We'll plan, say, to do something on a Friday night, and then a boy will call up and she'll break her date with me. Sometimes she's done that as late as twenty minutes before we're supposed to meet. It makes me really mad, but she expects me to understand. She explains it by saying we're only girlfriends."

"Only" girlfriends. Not exactly a bolster to our self-esteem, to say nothing of our feelings about being female.

The reverberation, says Angela Fox, is about as deadly as they come. "Passing on the idea that boys are intrinsically more valuable than girls is about the worst thing that teenage girls do to each other. It's not only a slight to her individuality but to her self-esteem. Society's told her all along that boys were more valued, and it's probably a feeling she picked up from her mother, too. Now she and her friends are communicating the same thing."

Where does that leave her? Even more dependent on her attachments with the opposite sex. "It's as if her whole identity becomes obliterated, and she begins to think that the only way she can be a complete person is by linking up with a male."

One girl was able to articulate the emotional upheaval of these messages in a poem she had written for an English class:

What is a friend?
It all depends when.
At fourteen you ask?
Ah, how you bask in loyalty and solidarity and knowing
For sure
Where you stand.
At fifteen, you say?
The boys start coming around and suddenly you don't know
If you can count on her or not
It's part of the plot, this
Now-I-love-you-best, now-I-do-not
By seventeen you waiver no more
You have a pretty good overview
When she cancels a date and doesn't say boo
That he's number one and you're number two.

It is ironic that at a time when we are trying to find ourselves, we get the message that it's more important to find someone else.

THE BIG FAKE

The real paradox of all this is that our supposed obsession with boys is more facade than truth. Every girl wants to grow up, most want to marry—and having a boyfriend is a definite testimonial that we are headed in the right direction. Wearing Stanley's ring also gives us a sense of elevated status via association: We, too, become members of the more valued caste. But while boys signify our desire to become women, when it comes to meeting our emotional needs, girls turn to their girlfriends almost every time. While it doesn't always look that way, the fact is that girls rate the importance of their friendships with girlfriends as more important than relationships with the boys *during the entire adolescent period.* [20] Even our supposed preoccupation with sex is largely a myth. When Dr. Aaron Hass interviewed more than three hundred girls in the suburbs of Los Angeles, "having a sexual relationship" lagged far behind not only girls' interest in having girlfriends, but their concerns with things like sports and athletics. [21]

"I call it the great female collusion," said Jane Flax. "Girls are complicit in this game 'boys come first.' They're playing it all together, saying, 'Let's pretend we're more interested in boys, that we care about this stuff above our relationships with each other.' In my own adolescence, none of my friends were particularly interested in boys. But there was that incredible pressure that came from our mothers and each other to start dating, to have a boyfriend. It's sort of a mutual agreement, a way in which we keep each other in line in terms of the demands of the culture. Girls are very effective in doing that with each other."

The problem is that while the obsession with boys may begin as pretense, by the time we're through the Sturm und Drang of adolescence, our allegiance to our girlfriends often becomes so muddled that we may feel it isn't there. Together we mutually encourage each other to make our forays into the male orbit. But our efforts are so convincing that before we know it, our best friend has left us stranded at a party, or doesn't call as often. We've been beaten by our own game. As the lyric from the song "I Whistle a Happy Tune" suggests:

> Make believe you're brave and the trick will take you far;
> You may be as brave as you make believe you are.

If there's any real paradox to girls' friendships in adolescence, it is that while they help us grow up in one way, they also work to the detriment of development in another. The tremendous energy we expend in attaching ourselves to a male thrusts us from mother's lap right back into the female sphere. For the teenage girl, autonomy is like a treadmill: one step forward, two steps back.

FINDING THE WAY OUT

Which leaves one question hanging: If finding a boyfriend is both a necessary and desirable step in terms of development, aren't the conflicts inherent in the switch to boys inevitable? I don't think so. If girls were raised to derive their feelings of self-esteem through their accomplishments as opposed to attaching themselves to others, we might be more concerned with what we do than how we look. If we had other outlets than success in the social arena in which to direct our competitive impulses, we might not feel so driven to beat the other girls out in terms of men. Most of all, if we could accept the fact that our strong emotional attachments to the other girls, and later to women, are as important as our emotional bonds with men, if not more important, we might not have to bend over backward in proving this is not so.

Chapter 4

SINGLES: COMPANIONS, OR COMPANIONS IN LONELINESS?

THE popular notion of friendships between single women has all the attraction of a tussle with a boa constrictor. We're all familiar with the hallmarks: women who scratch each other's eyes out when it comes to a man; the inherent mistrust; the banality of ever present gossip. Everyone knows that most single women have about as much interest in other women as William F. Buckley has in dining with Bella Abzug. Right?

Wrong. Contrary to the myth, single women these days place tremendous value on their relationships with other women, hailing them as a primary life-support system—friend, confidante, therapist, mother—all wrapped into one. College-aged women, one study found, are even beginning to say that, all in all, they prefer the company of women to men.[1] Nor do all relationships between single women inevitably boil down to a regurgitation of one's love life, many women citing a richness in their friendships, with discussions ranging from philosophy to business to the latest fad in hairstyles to the prevention of nuclear war. You might also be surprised to learn, as I was, that friendships between single women rarely end over competition for a man.[2]

"There is a certain healthy humility I get from women that I don't find with men," said one thirty-year-old. "It's a gentleness, a concern, a questioning of self—a lack of this self-righteousness that I find in even the best men. Men are less capable of stepping outside themselves. The women I like can laugh at themselves. I know very few men who can do that."

"When you're a single woman, friends serve very much the same purpose as a mate," another woman told me. "They're your sounding board, your emotional backbone. If I've had a rough day or something is troubling me, the first thing I do when I get home is call a friend and air it. Even when it's a crisis over a man and I am boringly repetitive, my good friends still listen and console me. To tell you the truth, I think I'd be in better emotional shape having friends and no man than if I had a man and no women friends."

One twenty-four-year-old summarized the feelings of many women I spoke to with one deft stroke: "A married woman's life revolves around her husband. A single woman's life revolves around her women friends."

Ironically, despite testimonials like these, some women, experts included,[3] still cling to the old stereotype. Women are innately competitive for men, they say. While admitting that the conditioning and socialization which teaches women that men are intrinsically more valuable are in part to blame, the caveat among these women remains unchanged:

Single women cannot be trusted.

From my own interviews, if there's any inherent mistrust between single women, it has less to do with the competition for men than with the temporary nature of their single status. Even in the staunchest of friendships, where man stealing would be completely out of the question, a single woman can't be trusted to put her friends first when there's a man in her life. That's because if there is any truism about single women, it is this: Most wish they weren't. And most won't be forever.

THE SINGLE FACTS OF LIFE

A real estate broker admitted that she had all but given up trying to sell houses or co-ops to unattached women. "At first, these women seem very excited about wanting to buy. They're well informed and generally are in a relatively high income bracket. But almost without fail, whatever I find for them ends up being unsatisfactory—too big, too small, too expensive. 'I guess I'm not really ready to make that commitment,' is the way it usually ends up. What I think they're really saying is that they don't want to do anything that's too permanent until they're married."

This woman is right on target. While the definition of what it means to be a woman has undergone a complete facelift over the past few decades, the fact is that most of us do not feel complete until we've become wives (and mothers). The "old maid" ideology may be passé and the stigma on voluntary childlessness lifted, but the push to marry and bear forges on. Magazines are replete with articles about successful career women who, in their mid-thirties, suddenly feel the "biological pull," run off and get married, and structure their careers around their new babies, sometimes to the point of becoming full-time Moms. In fact, there are so many babies being born to women over thirty that the trend has often been referred to as the new baby boom. While the singles life may be advertised as second only to the Great American Dream, most single women would gladly trade in their supposed freedom for the bliss of matrimony any day. When Virginia Slims took a poll in 1980, only 2 percent of the women interviewed said they preferred the advantages of permanent single living over those of marriage.[4]

How is it that despite alternative models most women still seem to need the old conventions of marriage and motherhood? According to psychologist Erik Erikson, it's all part of the developmental railroad, with the roles of mother and wife being at the core of women's identity.[5] It's not until we fulfill these developmental prescriptions, he claims, that we feel complete, whole as women. And while it can be argued that a woman can have a meaningful relationship with a man without marrying him, and creative people are often known for viewing their art as their "babies" (someone once told me that Simone de Beauvoir had publicly admitted that all the books she had written could never take the place of the child she never had), for most women the rewards of fame and fortune do not compensate for the rewards of having a family. As one high-powered thirty-year-old executive put it: "Everyone thinks of me as a 'successful woman,' and professionally that's true. But you want to know what really defines me? It's having a man in my life—

someone to have a child with, someone to love. Sure, it's great to pull off a multimillion-dollar deal. But can you put your arms around it at night?"

If being single doesn't do much for a woman's identity, it does even less for her health. Compared to their married counterparts, single women and men smoke and drink more, traipse to the doctor's more often, are involved in more car accidents, are more likely to develop cancer of the digestive system, and have much higher rates of admission to the psychiatric wards.[6] Even the idea that living on one's own is good for autonomy is largely false. If anything, concluded one study, singles tend to be more dependent than marrieds or those in living-together arrangements. "The biggest hurdle for the majority of unattached singles that I interviewed was learning to be emotionally self-reliant, and how to build that self-reliance into a satisfying relationship without becoming overly dependent," wrote the author. The proclivity to lean on someone else, she noted, was so extreme in some cases that some singles, afraid of showing their real colors, opted for permanent solitude.[7]

Given all the forces which push women in the direction of coupling, it's little wonder that most women see singlehood as a hallway and not a destination. And on some level single women have a kind of unspoken agreement that their ultimate purpose is to find a suitable mate. It's reflected in women's conversations about men, in the generosity of fixing a friend up with a man she might fall in love with, in the tidbits of advice that are easily shared and traded.

At the same time, the tacit understanding that finding a husband is a raison d'être is also filled with ambivalence. Behind the facade of the most sophisticated lady is often a girl who's clamoring for undivided attention, who does not want to feel she comes in second.

It's the voice of the child who wants her friends to be there as she wanted her mother to be—unconditionally.

EMOTIONAL FLIP-FLOPS

If there is any common plaint among single women about their friends, it is this: The friendship undergoes a dramatic change with the entrance of a man.

There is little doubt that most single women share the understanding that ultimately they are looking to form a life around a man. At the same time, when a woman's closest friend announces that she is now "we," or when a woman finds herself outside of that special intimacy now shared with someone else, the emotional upheaval can be disquieting. "There is this devastating repetitive pattern among single women friends," one woman told me. "You're close friends with someone; you spend a lot of your free time together. Then, enter the man; that's your exit call. Of course, if her Prince Charming turns out to be a royal dud, she runs back and asks your forgiveness. Naturally, you take her back, but you never completely forgive. It's like being pulled through an emotional wringer—on again, off again, on again, off again."

The older a woman gets, the more iffy her friends' availability becomes. While a young woman may find a constant supply of companions, the older woman discovers she's losing her single compatriots by virtue of attrition—a decline that even the increasing number of newly divorced does not compensate for. She also notices, correctly, that among the friends she retains even after they've crossed the threshold, which is estimated at two out of every ten,[8] get-togethers now include the new man in her friend's life. Most of all, she finds herself slipping into an ever decreasing minority. In the sweet freedom of being young and out on her own, surrounded by hoards of women like her, she rarely contemplated being left out in the cold. But now, each wedding, every pregnancy or birth, signals that she's being left behind in the shuffle.

The facts are these: By the time a woman is thirty-five, 90 percent of the women she knows will have been married at least once.[9] By the age of forty, this figure jumps to 94 percent.[10]

Under these circumstances, what's the normal or "mature" way to feel? And just what's reasonable to expect of a friend who's involved with a man? A recurring theme among the women I interviewed was a schism between the way they thought they were supposed to react to this emotional flip-flop and the way they felt in their heart of hearts. Intellectually, almost every woman understood that in the heat of a romance, the man would take priority. But these same women often said that deep down they felt differently about it:

"When a friend of mine has a man and I don't, and we go from seeing each other two or three times a week to once every three weeks, I feel abandoned."

"I've never been totally 'dropped' by a woman for a man, but to tell you the truth, it's difficult to tell the difference between the attenuation of a friendship and a betrayal."

"This may sound ridiculous, but on some level I expect my friends to put me on equal footing with the men they're seeing. The irony is that when I'm involved with someone, I seem to need to be with my friends less, too."

It stands to reason that when you're close to someone, and suddenly that person isn't there in the same sense as they once were, there is going to be a feeling of loss. To say nothing of the potential jealousy that can flare up when you're feeling lonely and your closest friend isn't. But the words women use—"abandoned" and "betrayed"—speak to something much deeper: the split between the adult in us that accepts the interference of men as a fact of life during the single years and the child in us that's still looking for the available mother. The conscious and less conscious sides sound something like this:

ADULT: It's perfectly normal for a man to take the forefront. Of course I understand.

CHILD: Why the hell aren't my needs being met? Where is she when I need her?

ADULT: When a woman finds a man she loves, the mature thing to do is to support her and be happy for her.

CHILD: What kind of friend are you anyway? We hardly see each other anymore!

The flip side of the coin can be heard from the woman who's bearing the brunt of her friend's "demands." When a woman declares, "I really get furious when my friends complain that I don't have as much time for them as before I met Joe," or "My friends sound like my mother, complaining that I don't call them enough," they are speaking to the other side of the available-mother syndrome. "A good mother means two things to a child," says Angela Fox: "You should be there whenever I need you, and when I don't want you around, you should vanish. You see it in kids all the time. They can get very upset if their mothers aren't there when they expect them to be, but they also assume that she's supposed to do a disappearing act when they want to be alone. The same thing happens between women. When neither woman has a man, it's fine for both of them to expect the other to be there. But when one finds a man before the other does, the child part of her expects her friend to gracefully take the backseat, to disappear when she wants her to and to reappear when she wants."

The woman who's involved in a relationship often has a fair amount of guilt to deal with as well, says Ms. Fox, which is why she may feel defensive when her friends accuse her of disloyalty. "A friend's love to a woman, like a mother's love, is supposed to be true-blue and last forever. So while putting the man first may feel right, it also smacks of disloyalty. So a woman may withdraw when a friend criticizes her to avoid feeling guilty."

Part of the dilemma is that single women are more dependent on one another than they like to admit. Single women frequently refer to their friends as their "substitute family," found one study. More to the point, the only women who could function without strong ties to women friends were those who maintained close ties with kin, particularly with sisters and mothers.[11]

At this point you might be saying to yourself, "Don't I live far away from home? Aren't I supporting myself? Isn't that what independence means?" Not always, says Jane Flax. "It's easy to confuse physical separation from psychological separation. I've seen lots of women who have virtually no contact with their mothers. But quite often they're extremely dependent on their friends. They'll get very upset, for example, when the women they know aren't committed to the friendship above all else. They turn to their friends with all their problems and expect them to come through for them unequivocally. What they've done is simply surround themselves with other versions of the old symbiosis."

While intense one-to-one friendships that are akin to best friendships in adolescence are most prone to these disturbances, few single women are immune to them. Not surprisingly, single women take out a number of emotional insurance policies. Single women, reported one study, share the intimate details of their lives with other women less than they do when they are adolescents or when they are married.[12] It's not that they don't inherently trust each other, but they are leery about the tenuousness of their own and their friends' single status. As one woman put it, "Why invest totally in something you know you might lose?"

Keeping some emotional distance is not the only device by which single women protect themselves. Trading in the dyad of earlier years, most women have a bevy of friends, opting for the safety of threes or the larger network.[13] Men also become increasingly important to fill out a woman's friendship circle. Man or woman, the message is clear: Having lots of friends is a shield against potential loss or the simple problem of having no one to go to the movies with on Saturday night.

While these multileveled relationships are the solution to one problem, however, they are also at the root of others.

IS SHE OR ISN'T SHE MY FRIEND?

Waiting in front of their respective racketball courts, two women glanced nervously at their watches.

Brrnnnggg.

"Damn," said Lisa, stamping her foot. "I've been stood up."

"I think I have, too," said the other woman whose name was Evelyn.

"Wanna play?" the two said simultaneously.

And so began a great racketball partnership. Evelyn looked forward to her regular Thursday night bout with Lisa, with whom she was perfectly matched, to their discussions about work, the men who were or weren't in their lives, their feelings about themselves, as they unwound in the sauna. And occasionally after working up a sweat, the two women would take in a movie, having found they shared a penchant for old Katharine Hepburn films. Their acquaintanceship, at least that's how Evelyn viewed it, went on beautifully for two months. "Lisa was a welcome addition in my life," Evelyn told me. "I had a couple of very close friends that I had gone to college with, a few men that I was dating, but no one I knew liked racketball. And most of them would take E.T. over Katharine Hepburn any day."

One night after Evelyn had walloped her usually competitive partner, Lisa broke down in the locker room. "I'm really feeling depressed. I'm having lots of trouble with this guy I've been seeing; he's doing a number on me. Would you mind coming over tonight and spending some time with me?"

Evelyn did mind. Thursday night was her time to relax, her time for herself. So many hours during the week were spent in intense conversations with her close friends, in playing the caretaker or being taken care of, that the last thing she wanted was another person in her life that she felt some heavy-duty responsibility to.

Then again, Lisa seemed so upset.

"Of course I will," Evelyn told her.

But when Lisa made a similar request a few weeks later, Evelyn felt increasingly uncomfortable. It didn't take her long to realize that Lisa wanted more from the relationship than she did. Even after warding off Lisa's invitations and putting on her phone machine when she was home in order to screen her calls, she couldn't shake the feeling that Lisa was becoming a "leech." Evelyn's solution was to begin cutting down on their squash games from once a week to once every two weeks, and finally to once a month. During the other weeks she found other partners and played at a court on the other side of town. "I've really been hard-pressed at work," she explained to Lisa.

It was on one of those Thursdays, exhilarated from a fine match, that Evelyn heard a knock on her racketball court door. "The bell's not working—your period is up," said the woman on the other side. Where had Evelyn heard that voice before?

Opening the door, there stood Lisa.

"Hi," said Evelyn, red with embarrassment.

"You know her?" asked Lisa's partner as Evelyn scurried down the hall to the locker room.

"Yeah," she heard Lisa reply, "at least I thought I knew her. I used to think she was a friend of mine."

While the specifics vary and not all cases are this extreme, this type of hurt and confusion is very common among single women. That's because for women the line between a true friendship and an acquaintanceship or casual friendship is as thin as a split hair. And given women's propensity to relate to each other emotionally, it's difficult to tell which side of the line you're on.

The multileveled nature of single women's friendships was the subject of a doctoral dissertation by J. L. Barkas. Her findings shed a lot of light on the source of Evelyn and Lisa's difficulties.

Tracing the friendship patterns of women on New York's Upper West Side, Dr. Barkas found that almost every woman had at least one close friend of the tried-and-true variety, a friend that could be counted on for almost anything. These friendships took, on the average, three years to develop, were maintained because both women valued the characteristics of, and exchanges with, the other, and had enough holding glue to withstand the structural changes of marriage or a move. At the time the friendships were initiated, the overwhelming majority of women had the same marital status. But when Dr. Barkas interviewed the women years later, only two thirds were still matched on marital status. That's not to say that marriage or a move to another state had no impact on the relationship. While some of these friendships were active, with women going out of their way to visit one another, others were carried out long-distance, the women getting together only rarely. Whatever the case, all the women felt that faraway or close by, they had a true friend.

Although these friendships provided a sense of emotional security and well-being, Dr. Barkas found that one or two close friends were insufficient for a healthy social life—especially if those friends lived halfway across the country or were involved in the trials and tribulations of raising a family. Friends like these were lanterns in the dark when it came to really needing someone, but they didn't do much for filling up the empty evenings. For that purpose, women developed more convenient, utilitarian friendships, relationships that were initiated because of proximity or the desire to have someone to do things with. These "friends for all seasons," concluded Dr. Barkas, were essential to the single woman's mental health. At the same time, they were also much more likely to end when the relationship was no longer as convenient as it once was.[14]

All of which would be rosy if women could readily accept the limited nature of these relationships as men do. In fact, "instrumental" relationships tend to be the norm for most men throughout their adult lives —the drinking buddy; the tennis partner; the business associate. Nor do most men have any great expectations of these relationships, which is why they are so rarely disappointed.

"Would I feel bad if a guy I played tennis with found a partner he thought was more on his level?" responded one man to my questioning. "Sure, it might be a hassle to find another partner, or I might feel bad if

I really enjoyed playing tennis with him. But my feelings wouldn't last very long."

But, I wondered, wouldn't he also feel a bit "used"?

"Of course," he answered without a bit of resentment in his voice. "Men use each other like that all the time; I don't mean in a manipulative sense, necessarily, but I have lots of friends that I 'use' for a specific purpose just as they 'use' me."

The problem is that while it may be easy for men to decipher the difference between a close and casual friend, for women the line between the two is more blurred. That's because almost all female-female relationships, even cursory ones, are based on some kind of emotional interchange. Therein lies the rub. While the emotional content of women's exchanges allows for an almost instantaneous connection, it also engenders certain expectations. Evelyn may have been very clear in her own mind about the level of intimacy she wanted with Lisa, but when she confided in Lisa about her personal problems, how was Lisa supposed to know where that intimacy stopped? Evelyn could, of course, have steered clear of any self-disclosure at all, but while that's the best way to set limits on the relationship, it's also the best way to run the risk of appearing cold.

An even subtler coercion is often at work for the woman in Evelyn's position: her own guilt. Deep down she knows that she's not really committed to a relationship with Lisa—that she is "using" her for an express purpose. And while the man who takes care of himself first hardly raises an eyebrow, "nice" women aren't supposed to do things like that. It's a slap in the face to their femininity. The fact also begins to register that if anyone's going to be hurt in the relationship, it's the other party. Bingo—off goes the guilt button. "Well," she tells herself, "if I can't offer her true friendship, at the very least I can give her some intimate details about myself" . . . an offering of sorts.

The woman on the receiving end has her own demons at work. Looking for more closeness and unconsciously expecting that all women will be devoted and loyal, she chooses not to read the handwriting on the wall, to see only what she wants to see. And, quite legitimately, she views the intimate conversations as a signal that her desire for the other woman's friendship is reciprocated. All of this leads women like Lisa to expect more than they're going to get, and ultimately to be hurt.

If women are uncertain of what it means to be a friend, or what exactly the commitment to a casual friend should be, what would we expect in terms of their relationships with men?

Here is a woman of twenty-three. A medical student who has always valued her friendships with other women, she recently found herself being challenged on that commitment. "There was this woman that I had known for about a year or so with whom I'd spent some time. I liked her, although I did not consider her a close friend. So when she broke up with this guy she was seeing and he asked me out, I didn't have any guilty feelings about it. But this woman blew her stack when she found out. She called me all sorts of names. She said I had no regard for women. That's not true at all. I would have never gone out with the guy if he had been seeing a close friend of mine. But I didn't know this woman very well and I didn't feel that kind of commitment to her or the relationship. Apparently, she thought that I should have."

It's situations like these that give life to the idea that women can't be trusted. Most women told me that they religiously abided by the dictum "Thou shalt not steal thy friend's lover." Then again, if the woman was only a casual acquaintance, or if she did not perceive the friendship as significant, that was a different story. After all, women said, if they felt obliged to be loyal to every woman they knew, there would never be any men in their lives given the structure of their friendship networks. And as far as the other woman was concerned, if she got upset, well, that was her problem.

In some ways Angela Fox agrees it is. "Women who expect every woman they know to be true-blue have unrealistic expectations. It's as if they're expecting every woman to be a good mother to them. Sure, that would be nice, but it's unreasonable." At the same time, she admits that incursions like these cause difficulties. "Given women's history with their mothers in terms of the competition for Dad, it's difficult for women to accept losing out to another woman no matter how casual the relationship might be. So what happens is that women often develop a leeriness about, if not their close friends, then other women more generally."

USEFUL OR EXPLOITATIVE?

Still, one question remains: Are these less than tried-and-true relationships exploitative or not? Is it wrong to "use" other women in this way? The key, Angela Fox told me, has to do with whether both women understand the parameters of the friendship. If both women are useful to each other, but still have regard for each other as people, then relationships like this can be very positive. "Women often feel that either they have to have a close relationship with a woman or no relationship at all. That's because women experience themselves as either fused or separate. But it can be very productive when women can find some kind of meeting ground in between. There's a lot they can learn from each other without necessarily having the strong obligations of a friendship."

Which isn't to say that some relationships aren't exploitative. "Some women make a habit of using other women. It's not a give-and-take situation—just a take. They don't have any regard for the other woman or her feelings. They just keep the relationship going until they don't need it anymore. For instance, a patient of mine had a really hard time breaking off a relationship with a woman she had known for a long time. She no longer got any pleasure from this woman, but still she couldn't end it. That's because this woman contributed greatly to her social life, and she didn't want to lose that element. There are some women who engage in that kind of behavior all the time."

What accounts for the difference between these two "types"?

Women who exploited other women, I found, generally were desperate to get married, to find a man to take care of them. Men were the light at the end of the tunnel, and women only temporary companions along the way to their ultimate destination. Not surprisingly, they had little or no compunction about breaking a date when a man came along, or about stealing a woman's lover if they thought they could get away with it. They were the epitome of the feline stereotype.

Other women told a different tale. Often they were interested in getting married, too, but the whole of their identity did not rest on finding a husband. In fact, it was just as important that they develop an identity based on their own unique capabilities. Friends supported them in this struggle, they said, and while different from an intimate relationship with a man, their relationships with women were every bit as valuable.

On the following pages, let's trace the stories of both types.

RUSH-TO-THE-ALTAR GIRLS

Bridal showers, babies, and a gorgeous house in the suburbs—these are the dreams of a woman who wants nothing more during the single years than to find a suitable mate. And while we might like to think that things have changed, the pattern of what is called the "unambivalent feminine girl" is still very common.[15]

If she would have had it her way, she wouldn't still be single. Coming from a working-class background, her wish would have been to run off with her high school sweetheart. If she's of middle-class origins, she may appear a little more savvy about the whole affair, going to college to expand her horizons, which, of course, means enlarging the potential pool in which to discover the right man. Chances are she joined the "best" sorority, which, as one study suggested, is less a "sisterhood" than a conspiracy for finding good husbands.[16]

What goes into the makings of such a woman? Ironically, it is often a friendly, positive relationship with a traditional mother. Too friendly, in fact, which is why these women often don't develop much of a desire for independence. While a close relationship with Mom might feel emotionally nourishing, as a rule, the better relationship with a Mom who's a housewife, the less separated the girl.[17]

Because women like these perceive themselves as dependent, their whole modus operandi is to find a husband who will take care of them. And if they're successful, they'll have married by the time they finish their schooling.

But what happens to the rush-to-the-altar girl who hasn't found a mate, who's single not out of choice but because she hasn't been chosen?

AT FIRST GLANCE, the woman who greeted me at the door didn't seem to be the type who was preoccupied with finding a husband at all. Tall and imposing, she fit the image of the up-and-coming Wall Street executive, dressed in a dark silk suit which flatteringly covered her ample hips, and stylish black pumps. An attaché case leaned against her umbrella rack. She seemed cordial and sophisticated.

"Sorry I took so long to answer the bell," she apologized, "but I was on the phone with a friend."

We began the interview informally, with Lottie giving me a little background information. She was twenty-five, had never been married, and before landing this job in a Madison Avenue advertising firm, had had a host of "professions"—from waitress, to jazz singer, to graduate student. What initially sounded like a full, exciting life, however, quickly showed itself as a cover-up for Lottie's lack of commitment to any one thing long enough to make it work. And if nothing worked, it was because deep down she didn't want to work at all. "The excitement of going out there and making it on your own has really worn thin," she explained. "Frankly, I'd give it up tomorrow if the right man came along." Obviously, up to this point he had not.

I began the formal interview with a question that for most other women had been quickly and easily answered. "How much time during an average week do you spend with your friends?" Devoid of emotionalism, it had generally been useful as an icebreaker—nothing more. In this case, however, it tapped more precisely into the dynamics between single women such as Lottie more than almost any other.

Lottie heard my question, chuckled, and got up to get her appointment book. "I think you'll find what you're looking for in here," she said, opening to the appropriate page. If I hadn't known better, I would have thought it was the calendar of a presidential aide. Every free hour after work from six to eleven every night was booked with different names, with the exception of Thursday, (Thursday was her yoga class). Joan and Lucinda on Monday; Elena and Deirdre on Tuesday; "the group" in Chinatown Wednesday; our interview followed drinks with Sara on Friday. Saturday and Sunday had other women's names down with question marks next to them. Seeing my puzzlement, Lottie explained that she did not yet know whether the man she was seeing would be back from his business trip, and she wanted to keep all bases covered. Occasionally, she admitted, she even overbooked, scheduling more than one person for the same evening and then determining, often at the last minute, which friend and which activity most suited the fancy of her mood.

Her friends, I learned, who covered the gamut from gay to straight, men to women, young to not so young, had been "accumulated" in a number of ways. Some were old professional colleagues; others were discovered at parties or brunches; a few were from her present job.* One woman had even been "picked up" waiting in line to see a movie.

"I felt sorry for her. She was French, and new to the city and didn't know anyone." At this point, however, the girl was getting to be a pain, "a real leech," as Lottie put it. She was going to have to find a way to gently get rid of her.

I was about to comment that she was certainly never lonely, when the phone rang. It was, not surprisingly, another friend inviting her to go hear some music the next evening (Saturday). Lottie politely told her that she wasn't sure of her plans, that she would have to let her know.

"Sorry," she said, returning to the couch. Her apology was to be repeated at least eight more times during the two hours we spent together—her phone, it seemed, rang incessantly.

As if reading my mind, she responded to the question I had been about to ask before we had been interrupted.

"Right now I'm in this cycle where I have more friends than I know what to do with. I am a major friend to a number of people, but they are just one of many to me. So I end up having to juggle them. It's like making the rounds. Sometimes it gets pretty exhausting."

The situation, however, was not without its benefits. "I'm not big on being alone. I'd much rather be married. Having lots of friends is a way of getting by until I find the right guy. Some women say they like being single. For me it's just a passing phase."

Most of her friends, she added, shared the same sentiments, making them equally unreliable. "There are one or two good friends that I really have deep feelings for. But with the rest—well—I hate to say this, but in a way, they're expedient—people to do things with, to shoot the bull with, to pick you up when you're not feeling so hot. It's kind of Machiavellian. You can tell because the minute a guy shows up, the friendship pretty much goes out the window. You go from seeing a friend maybe once or twice a week to getting a phone call from her once every six weeks. That is," she added, "until they break up."

How did Lottie feel about being "used"?

*Barkas found single women frequently made friends at their jobs. For the problems this creates, see the chapter "Office Hours."

She shrugged her shoulders. "Sometimes I don't like it, but mostly I accept it. I do the same thing myself. I think it's built into the species."

The longer we spoke, the clearer it became that the main function of women friends for Lottie was as a way of helping her bide her time until she tied the knot. That is not to say that she had no feelings for the close friends she had made, but there was no doubt in her mind that they were second best to the real thing. "I just don't feel that I can really appreciate women until I have the man thing settled, until that's out of the way," she told me. Which was why, she admitted, that she preferred having friends who were beautiful. "Going to a party with my friend Elsie is like going with a man magnet."

Near the close of the interview the phone rang once again. It was a woman friend informing Lottie of an exciting opportunity: A friend of hers had just flown in from L.A. on business and he brought a very attractive (and rich) friend with him. Would Lottie like to join them for drinks?

"I'll be ready in fifteen minutes," she said, undoing the buttons of her dress as she talked.

"Tah-dah," she said, making her entrance in a black jumpsuit and shocking red boots five minutes later. "Hold on a minute and I'll walk you to the subway."

Half out the door, Lottie stopped short. "Oh, Jesus, I forgot."

Scurrying to the phone, she dialed Sara's number. "Hi, Sara, this is Lottie," she said in a slow, hushed voice that reeked of mock exhaustion. "Look, I'm not going to make it over tonight. Remember that interview I told you about? Well, it wiped me out. I'm going to bed early." Silence. "Thanks for understanding. Speak to you soon."

"Okay," she said, effervescing once again and checking her appearance in the mirror, "I'm all set."

If women like Lottie sound so unappealing it's because they have little regard for other women. They consider most of their single women friends as expendable because they view their single years as a period in their lives that will be over as soon as the opportunity presents itself. They do not invest in their relationships with women because they are reserving their energy for the *man,* who of course, is their primary concern.

Ultimately, what they are really reflecting is a lack of regard for themselves. Studies consistently show that women consider "masculine" abilities like assertiveness and independence as far more valuable than more traditionally feminine traits like passivity and dependence.[18] Yet women like Lottie are, by their own admission, very dependent: "I feel like a nothing when there's not a man in my life," Lottie confessed. With feelings like these about herself, how can we expect her to feel about other women?

On the positive side women like Lottie do not necessarily end up as lobotomized hausfraus fifteen years later. In fact, the security of marriage often precipitates the move to greater autonomy. The idea is that once we have certain critical needs met, we are free to step out and explore other sides of ourselves. While Lottie feels, at the moment, that she could spend the rest of her life riding on the coattails of her husband's success, there is a good chance that once she finds the right guy, she'll eventually return to work. She may even decide she wants a career. "I see this kind of thing in women all the time," Dr. Flax tells me. "Some women who suffer from terrible depression about being single, who can't make a commitment to work or friends, go through a complete metamorphosis after marrying. The reason is that many women feel their lives, their identities as women, are tenuous until they do that." The research suggests similar findings. Judith Bardwick, for example, observed that female graduate students who were married tended to sustain much higher levels of academic performance than those who were unattached. The reason, explains Dr. Bardwick, is that "she has achieved an acknowledged love relationship; she has a settled sense of identity in terms of the man she married, and he has accepted her abilities and ambitions."[19]

It's too bad that the cost of this "achievement" is the trust of other women.

A NEW SORORITY

Fortunately, for every woman I interviewed like Lottie, there was another woman who did not see her women friends as fill-ins until her white knight landed on the doorstep.

If a man calls her up for a date on the same evening she has made plans to dine with a friend, she does not cancel her plans with her friend, but politely tells him she is busy. She does not even feel torn. If that same man suggests that her appointment is less important than an evening with him, chances are she asks him not to call her again. Should she find a man with whom she would like a relationship, she does not relegate her friends to the backburners of her life, but juggles her schedule to make sure they remain an integral focus. Women who are part of this new sorority are women who attempt to balance their love lives with a heartfelt commitment to friends, and who persistently work to overcome any imprinting that makes it difficult for them to do so.

A profile of these women appears in J. L. Barkas' *Singles in America.* Almost all of these women eventually wanted to marry. At the same time, they did not live to marry, nor did their lives feel lonely and incomplete. Two blunt conclusions were made about this group. First, because they were autonomous, they felt relatively good about themselves and were relatively content with their lives. As a result, they had a number of good friends and kept themselves busy. While enjoying company, however, they were also happy to be by themselves. They were willing to eat out alone, or to venture to dinner parties where they might be the odd woman out. Most importantly, "friends are not abandoned—or appointments canceled—because a romantic prospect suddenly appears. Contented singles are sure of what they want, they are not afraid of being alone . . . they are autonomous."[20]

What is it that separates the rush-to-the-altar girl from the independent, contented single woman? For one thing, the latter has a strong investment in defining herself outside of the little golden band. She is interested in becoming a Somebody as opposed to a Mrs. Somebody. Many women like these have mothers who worked.[21] At the very least, there is usually a father who encouraged independence.

Because women like these tend to feel good about themselves, they also tend to have high regard for other women. While wanting the intimacy with a man, they value their relationships with women in an equal albeit different way. One tip-off to a woman who falls into this pattern is the way she spins out her stories about her women friends. "My friends and I relate on all kinds of levels," she will say, "work, politics, culture." Only later does she mention that they of course talk about men, too.

But while there are an increasing number of women who have a stake in being independent, the word "content" is the key, because a woman who is unhappy with her life cannot offer the same kind of friendship as the woman who feels satisfied with her single status. There's the hitch. While many aspiring women in their twenties are happy being single, the same woman only a decade later might have very different feelings about it. These "transitional singles" are content with their single status because they're young and can still look forward to the golden land of opportunity.[22] Their underlying sentiments read something like this: Being single is dandy as long as it's temporary.

What happens when this woman hits her thirties and there's still no prospect of marriage on the horizon? When she reaches that apostrophe in time when suddenly more of her friends are married than not? When the biological clock seems to be ticking away?

A relatively successful woman in her thirties who until recently had no qualms about her single status admitted: "It was a shock for me to wake up one day and realize that this might be it—that I might be single forever. And I very much want to settle down and have kids. So these days if it's a choice between doing something with a woman friend or doing something to get what I want out of life, I'm going to choose the latter, which means the man. It's as ugly as that."

Fortunately, if a woman still hasn't found the man of her dreams by her forties, she usually learns to come to terms with her singleness, to accept it, to be reasonably content with it. The thought of living alone is no longer so frightening because by now she knows that having a husband is not the answer to all her problems. So while the woman in her twenties may feel totally committed to her women friends, that commitment may temporarily waver in her thirties, only to be renewed with vigor later on once she has come to accept her single status as permanent.

THIS PATTERN WAS demonstrated by a woman I shall call Lorraine.

About the last thing Lorraine was interested in in her early twenties was getting married. Recently transplanted from the plains of Iowa, where the people spent their days "watching the corn grow," to the flash of L.A. neon, she felt she had a lifetime of living to make up for. As far as missing her parents who lived clear across the country and who carried on when Lorraine packed her bags and headed for the Greyhound station, Lorraine said with little compunction, "I couldn't have been far enough away."

As far back as she could remember, Lorraine and her Mom saw eye to eye on almost nothing. But what really got her goat was what she viewed as her mother's succoring behavior, deferring to her dad's every wish. If Dad wanted dinner at six, dinner at six it was. If he didn't like a dress his wife had bought, it was immediately boxed and corded and returned, no questions asked. Some girls, she knew, would have taken from all of this certain lessons about a woman's "place." What Lorraine took from it was a resolve never to end up the way her mother had.

And so, after a heated argument about Lorraine's decision to break up with a country boy she had been going steady with for three years, she packed her bags and headed for the star-studded shores of California. Her parents, of course, had wanted her to go to secretarial school. But Lorraine wanted to be a graphic artist. So during the day she worked as a receptionist for a small electronics firm, and the nights, which other single women used to pursue a social life, were filled up with art classes.

It was there that she met Beth and Amy, women who, like herself, had a fierce pride in wanting to be more than a mother and wife, despite the pleas of their mothers who simply could not relate to such crazy ambitions. And after six months of going back and forth between each other's makeshift apartments that were furnished in early Salvation Army, the three women decided to pool their resources and move in together.

"Those were the best years of my life," Lorraine said, recalling their five-year liaison. "Sure, we had squabbles about cleaning up and things like that, but mostly we got along terrifically. We were like sisters. And never, not once, did we let each other down because of a man in our lives."

Amy and Beth became the family she had left behind. One night, for example, Lorraine awoke with a searing pain in her abdomen. Looking at the bed sheets, she screamed—they were drenched with blood. The problem had been caused by her IUD. Her roommates called an ambulance and rushed her to the hospital. And they took care of her during the three weeks of ordered bed rest after she returned home.

"They did everything for me—the shopping, the cooking, and they kept me company and tried to keep my spirits up. They brought me books and made me laugh and let me know they would be there as long as I needed them. I will never forget that feeling of love."

As far as their attitudes toward men were concerned, the women were mixed. They wanted to marry someday, but not yet—there was too much to do, too much fun and growing up before they were tied down. Besides, men often were too much trouble—fickle, often unreliable, and most of all, seemingly more desirous of finding women with excellent culinary skills than women intent on having careers—no matter what they might have said. A recent study found that male-female relationships in which the woman does not at least pretend to be traditionally oriented tend to break up much more quickly than relationships in which women were more deferent.[23] Lorraine and her roommates' experience fit that pattern to a tee.

"None of us wanted that kind of relationship," Lorraine said, "and yet a lot of the men we met, even though they said they wanted women who were their own persons, still were looking for the kind of girl who had the silver pattern all picked out." Their mothers, of course, saw things differently. "I'm glad you're enjoying your classes," one or the other would write, "but I wish you'd just find a man and settle down."

The women became a constant source of reassurance and support for one another. "To reject Mother's life is frequently experienced as treachery toward her, for which the ultimate price is rejection," Jane Flax told me. Bonded in unity, without consciously knowing it, Lorraine, Beth, and Amy were helping each other ward off the fear that if they reached for the stars, a little woman would pull the ladder out from underneath them. They became watchdogs for each other, giving perspective lovers the once-over. Only the stamp of approval was different than what their own mothers would have supported—what mattered was not if he was rich or successful, but whether the potential candidate would allow the woman in his life equal footing. And if he didn't, he was out.

"Hey, baby, how about getting me a beer," said one of Lorraine's new loves, sprawling on the living-room couch as if he owned the place.

"You'd better cross that one off," Beth and Amy told her later that night. Lorraine didn't see him again.

"The group's word became sort of a gospel," she explained, "and if they disapproved, well, that was pretty much the end of that."

The women lived together for the next five years, during which time they all made progress in their careers. And when Lorraine received a sizable salary increment, after much thought she decided to get an apartment of her own. "I loved my roommates but I felt that I needed some solitude to really experience who I was, how I went about living when I had no one to account for but myself." Her roommates, saddened by the move, nevertheless gave her their blessings.

Another five years passed during which Lorraine maintained her close ties with her friends, continued to climb the career ladder, and dated a host of men that more often than not resulted in a host of problems. In fact, she was beginning to give up on the male species altogether when Beth gave her a call.

"I want you to come over and meet someone," she said, still abiding by the old need for approval from years earlier.

"Well," said Beth insistently after her suitor had left. "What do you think?"

Lorraine hugged her friend with genuine happiness. "He's terrific, just perfect. Don't let go of that one."

A year later Lorraine was maid of honor at the wedding. Six months later Amy also joined the ranks of the newly married. In fact, almost overnight, it seemed, most of the women Lorraine knew seemed to be heading for the altar en masse, or boasting large protruding bellies.

For the first time her single status made her antsy. "At first I was thrilled when a friend got married. But after a while, weddings would depress me. I was reaching a point in my life where I wanted to get married and settle down, and I was beginning to wonder if that would ever happen for me."

At the time, Lorraine was thirty-one.

For the next four years her attitudes about friendship did a complete about-face. She stayed close with Beth and Amy, whose marriages were models on which she wanted to base her own, but she began seeing other single women more as vehicles for meeting men than important in and of themselves. If she thought a man she liked might call, she avoided making plans with anyone else. She began staying home, "waiting, like an idiot, for the damn phone to ring." And deep down, she began to see women who were still unmarried as "losers" like herself.

"It was as if every ounce of independence I thought I had went right down the tubes. I don't know what happened."

What happened was that Lorraine's contentment with the single life in her twenties had given way, in her thirties, to a dire fear of being single forever. Studies show, in fact, that the same women who hail freedom and mobility as great virtues in their twenties would gladly trade in such privileges for a little down-home security a decade later.[24] She's also likely to be seized by anxiety as she feels her biological clock ticking away. "My God," she thinks to herself, eyeing what at her advanced age appear to be adolescent nymphets wheeling baby carriages, "if I don't find a husband soon, I'll be an old lady when my kid's just an adolescent."

The panic is exacerbated by the fact that the older a woman gets, the worse her prospects for marrying become. In the single population as a whole, there is already a dearth of men, with 135 single women to every 100 eligible men. With age the proportions get gloomier; the figures jump to 147 women to 100 men in the 30-to-35 bracket and 160 women to 100 men for those between the ages of 40 and 44. All this before you take into account the number of confirmed bachelors and gays. Running the statistics this way, the balance is 290 women to every 100 men! Given these grim numbers, it's not surprising that women like Lorraine begin to worry.

Lorraine's life seemed to be on a downhill slide when what looked like love at long last came into her life. He was handsome and successful. So what if he insisted that she use his name when they got married? "Sterling" was much nicer than "Mole" anyway.

One night Lorraine announced to her fiancé that she was offered another promotion. The money was terrific. The only drawback was that she would have to travel out of the country on the average of once every two months.

"Not on your life," he told her. "I'm not having some wife of mine gallivanting around the world." Then the bombshell. "I thought that when we got married you'd forget about this career stuff, that we'd have kids and you'd stay home."

Lorraine called Beth and Amy in despair. They confirmed what she already knew. Lorraine decided to go along with the marriage anyway.

"You'll see," she told her friends defensively, "he'll change and the marriage will last forty years."

It lasted all of fourteen months.

Lorraine was on her own once again. But it was different this time—harder—as if all the years she had spent taking care of herself hadn't existed. That's because being married, even a short marriage, accustoms people to having someone else to lean on. And while living alone can be lonely, it is a loneliness wrought of being without someone as opposed to being without one's "other half."[25]

Lorraine dulled her anxiety about being on her own again by popping Valium every four hours. She sank into a deep depression. And while

Beth and Amy were initially sympathetic and supportive, after a year of the clinging-vine routine, they suggested she seek outside help.

"I'm thirty-seven, I have no husband, no children, no nothing," she wailed to her shrink. "And my nights are so lonely sometimes I think I'm going to jump out of the window."

"But surely," said the therapist, "you must have friends."

Lorraine didn't. Other than Beth and Amy, the other women in her life had been jettisoned long ago.

"Well, then," suggested the therapist, "it would do you well to go out and make some."

She did. Five years later Lorraine is still not married, and the women she's close to are at the center of her life. Since her failed marriage, there have been other men, other promises of love gone awry. And each time, Lorraine has survived a little better, a little surer of herself, a little less frightened at the prospect of living life without a mate, alone. Well, not alone, exactly, because these days Lorraine has women friends to whom she feels totally committed, whom she considers as more important than any man who might come and go in her life.

It hasn't always been easy, she'll admit. Women are, after all, reared on intimate attachment, and it's difficult for even the most self-reliant woman not to want that kind of intimacy. At forty-two, Lorraine still thinks about finding Mr. Right. At the same time, she can also feel that her life is rich and rewarding should she not. And a lot of that feeling comes from having close women friends.

"To tell you the truth, the women that I'm close to are generally more interesting than the men I've been meeting. And even when I meet a man that I fall in love with for a while, I've come to realize that marriage isn't the be-all and end-all of life, and having close women friends is not something to be taken for granted. Men can be there and then not be there. Your close friends are forever."

"Well," she admits, speaking with the voice of experience, "almost forever."

A WOMAN LIKE Lorraine, who feels a strong commitment to other women in her life, who does not automatically assume that a man is the most important thing, is a woman in process. And she is a woman up against great odds. Even if she has a solid sense of herself, everything from childhood on has rehearsed her for a life based on living with a man. She has been groomed for an environment in which the male of the species is still the more valued. In which the only recognized attachment is between a man and a woman. In which close friendships with women do not entirely alleviate the loneliness because women's relationships are undermined. In which not to feel part of a couple is to feel undesirable. Even in this day and age, women who are unattached tend to complain of loneliness despite the many friends they may have. In an article in *New York Magazine,* single women indicated that making friends was not a problem for them. What they really wanted to know was, "Where are the *men?*"[26]

Finding a man who wants an autonomous woman is also difficult, and gets more problematic the older a woman becomes. The men that independent women are likely to be attracted to given the propensity of women to marry "up"—educated or professional men—are the least available. These men marry earlier and tend to remain married longer. The reverse is true for professional women: They marry later and divorce more frequently. The result is a kind of mismatch, with the men who are the most available being the least educated and women most in search being the best educated. As sociologist Jessie Bernard put it, in the singles pool "the men are the 'bottom of the barrel' and the women are the 'cream of the crop.' "[27]

It is against these obstacles that women are working. And as those like Lorraine attest, they are becoming increasingly successful. But old vestiges of the past nevertheless remain. One study reported that single women, despite the stated importance of women friends in their lives, still tend to drop or at least attenuate their relationships with women when they find a man.[28] The difference is that once having done so, they are beginning to think twice about it.

HOW MUCH DO WOMEN REALLY *NEED MEN?*

It is not only the cultural scenarios that work against friendships between single women, even single women who are self-reliant. Even the fervent sisterhood increasingly found among women today does not change one basic fact of life: Unless she is a lesbian, the closeness between any two women can only go so far.

Ironically, a significant number of women I spoke to said that, all in all, given the choice, they enjoyed the company of their women friends over the company of men. Some went so far as to say that their overall attitude toward men was that they were at worst, idiots, at best, far less interesting and integrated than women. Some of these women had had serious disappointments by the men in their lives. Others said that men simply weren't all they had been cracked up to be. All said that they often had the feeling that while needing men, they could actually do just fine without them.

Interestingly, none of the women to whom I am referring were lesbians. To the contrary, these were women who, while sometimes admitting to occasional sexual tension in their friendships, generally felt no physical attraction to the women in their lives. In fact, their main concern with men was getting their sexual needs satisfied. In a nutshell, the sentiments of these women ran something like this: Other than for sex, what do I need men for?

Paradoxically, the problem in terms of friendships with other women was not the interference of men in their lives, but the absence of that interference. Although these women generally enjoyed sex with men, they couldn't help but wonder if something was wrong with them. It didn't seem to matter that they had little physical attraction to members of their own sex—their emotional preference was enough to scare them. So much so that at some point many of these women panicked and got married.

One such woman was Susan Ritter. While the dynamics of her relationships with women are similar to those of other women I have spoken to, there is another variable which could possibly account for her strong attachment to women: a less than adequate relationship with her mother. But while her story has a possible underlying psychological component, her friendships with women are representative of many women who, unlike Susan, did have mothers who loved them enough.

A PRODUCT OF THE DEPRESSION, Marilyn Swanson Ritter vowed, much like Scarlett O'Hara, that she would never be poor again. Unlike the fictitious Southern beauty, however, she was going to make it by her own devices. Marrying a doctor was not enough. By the time she was thirty, she had received her doctorate in anthropology. But what was a major accomplishment to most was a mere pittance to Marilyn. At thirty-five, six months after the birth of her first and only child, she entered medical school. Nothing was going to stop her, including her daughter, Susan.

Susan remembers always thinking of herself as "an accident." Not that Mom was so direct, of course—she simply wasn't around much. Even when she was there in body, her mind was drifting off, preoccupied with some new technology or exotic disease, indifferent to the growing emotional starvation of her daughter. Susan desperately wanted a dog, "something to love," but Mom refused. "Dogs make a mess and I won't have this house looking like a ghetto," she told her. Dad wasn't much better. If he was less critical, it was because he was home even less than Mom.

Susan might have felt less lonely if she had had some friends, but her parents' restrictiveness precluded even that. "Every time I'd meet someone in school and want to go over to their house, my mother would make this big ordeal, interrogating the girl's parents as if this were the Inquisition. It was very embarrassing." Eventually, Susan gave up looking for friends and retreated into books. She graduated second in her high school class.

Her first sense of freedom came when she entered college. An exclusive all-girls school in the Boston suburbs, it nevertheless seemed as liberating as an orgy compared to the restrictions she had had at home. Makeup, or "war paint," as her mother had called it, was frowned upon, and Susan did not own her first lipstick until she was eighteen years old. Seeing one boy for more than two dates was, in mother's mind, close to blasphemy, and her interaction with members of the opposite sex up until that time had largely been restricted to chaperoned group affairs. Susan was already rejecting the subtle push her parents were making to find a suitable husband. "No way, José," she told herself, well aware of the fact that college was, for many of her dorm mates, a way of sating wedding-bell fever. Susan had her own agenda—to study hard and to have fun.

Susan's self-image at eighteen was of a caged lioness, an adventuress at heart; her explorer instinct had been nipped in the bud by her family. A wildness flickered inside her, excitement beating inside like a tomtom. Her freshman year, filled with fraternity parties that sometimes turned into drunken brawls, did little to appease it. The men she met, and there were many, seemed callow and bland as a pair of Bass Weejuns. Their idea of having a good time was drinking themselves into a stupor or until they threw up—whichever came first. Their pulse on philosophy, the larger scheme of things, consisted of little more than figuring out how they were going to make this or that girl.

Her first roommate was no less disappointing. A tall, willowy blonde from Denver, her interests were in tandem with the fraternity men. "She was the type who gets into college on Daddy's pull, well endowed in the chest department but vacuous upstairs." Needless to say, the two had little in common.

It was during an acting class in summer school that Darla came into her life. Darla was a theater major, a woman with a fey personality who had a wonderful sense of the absurd. To Susan the most wonderful thing about Darla was her ability to laugh at herself. "You take yourself too seriously," she told Susan, who was sullen-faced after blowing a long, rehearsed monologue. She encouraged Susan to loosen up, and the two practiced their "ooooooommmmmmmsssss" in the center of campus. "We look ridiculous," Susan commented, sneaking peeks at the looks from passersby who were staring at the two grunting swamis. "Who the hell cares," said Darla, "I'm not laughing at you."

They lived together for the next three years, during which time they were almost inseparable. Susan would read lines for Darla, rehearsing her through the scenes, in return for Darla's relentless drilling in anatomy, which was Susan's nemesis. There were men around—always—but none could match Darla's wit and charm, and Susan quickly tired of them. Darla's experience was much the same. "Why is it," she said one night after returning home, flopping on Susan's bed and lighting a joint, "that whenever I go out, I can't wait to get home?"

If there was something unusual about their intense friendship, neither seemed to notice or care, at least not yet. After graduation Darla got an acting job in a small repertoire theater in New York. "I found a very expensive dump for us," she said to Susan, who was temporarily living at home while trying to sort out her plans for the future. "You'll love it," she said, adding, "Besides, I miss you like crazy." Grabbing at the bait, Susan packed her valise and settled into the roach-infested flat. Two months later she found a job as a lab assistant.

For the next year, life continued almost as it had in college. Both dated regularly, but neither seemed to find a man she wanted to get involved with. Susan dated a psychiatrist on the faculty of a prestigious hospital, who drove her crazy analyzing her lack of passion for him as a vestige of her repressive upbringing. ("The truth was, he just didn't turn me on.") Darla, with her good looks and vivacity, also had the pick of the town, yet she rarely went out with a man for longer than a two-month stretch.

"I think the problem was that we always seemed to end up having more fun with each other," said Susan recollecting, "so neither of us had any dire need to find someone permanent. It was easy enough to have your sexual needs taken care of without having to move in with the guy."

Meanwhile, Susan's mother was becoming concerned. "A city like New York, with millions of available men, and you mean to tell me you can't find one you like?" she continuously implored. "I think that roommate of yours is having a bad effect on you." Secretly, Susan suspected her mother thought she was a lesbian.

Susan was only twenty-three when her relationship with Darla was becoming suspect, subject to scrutiny; and as much as she wanted to shrug off the implications, they were beginning to get to her. She knew she loved Darla, but there had never been any physical relationship between the two women, aside from what most would consider acceptable affections. The fantasy of making love with Darla had once emerged in a dream, but the idea of translating the fantasy into reality was abhorrent to her. Still, Susan was beginning to wonder if she was normal, or if there was something wrong with her. She entered therapy.

Her timing was more auspicious than she had suspected. A month later Darla was offered a small part in a soap opera, which required that she move to Los Angeles. Susan was devastated. She tried making a go of it alone, but their small apartment began looking more tenamentlike than funky without Darla's effervescence to liven it up. When a woman who had been a mutual friend suggested Susan become the fourth in their communal living arrangement, she grabbed the chance.

Once again surrounded by women, she felt herself less lonely and desperate. While she got along with all three, Bobbi, a plump, matronly person, most touched her heart. When Susan was sick, Bobbi would prepare a batch of chicken soup and was more than happy to nurse Susan back to health. She also had a stupendous sense of humor. "I just loved being with her. We always had a wonderful time together. A few of my other friends outside of the apartment would, from time to time, comment on how matronly she seemed, and how strange it was that we were such good friends. They didn't understand that she was just the kind of friend I needed—someone to love me and care for me in a way my mother never had. It was a very gay time in my life."

Meanwhile, back at her shrink's, Susan's psychiatrist (a man) was looking for some dark, deep-seated reason to explain her attraction to women. The implication was that her love of women was a sort of regression—perhaps, he suggested, she was stuck in the genital phase, as she could not have orgasms without clitoral stimulation. Bobbi heard this and exploded, then gave her a copy of Masters and Johnson. "Don't listen to that man," she admonished. "His ego's just bruised because you haven't developed a swooning transference." Susan read the Masters and Johnson book. A week later she quit therapy.

The next three years passed without incident. Susan convinced herself that there was nothing wrong with her, other than the fact that she had not married on schedule. Having everything she felt she needed—a good job, a comfortable home, good friends, she still felt no propelling need to find a man to fill her life.

"The feeling was that I really didn't need a man. I was just as happy being with women. There was Bobbi, and Darla, whom I wrote and phoned regularly. I had lots of boyfriends who wined and dined me and took me on trips. Sex was adequate—nothing earth-shattering. I didn't feel I was going to go out of my mind if I didn't have intercourse every minute."

As time passed, however, the old fears began creeping up. Darla had written Susan announcing her engagement. Bobbi, who never seemed concerned about marriage, suddenly became obsessed with finding a man, threatening to do herself in if she was not married by the ripe old age of twenty-eight. Susan felt confused and became increasingly anxious. "Before, I could rationalize the whole thing by saying that women were getting married later and later because they wanted to establish their careers first. But suddenly there was Darla getting married, and Bobbi who kept saying she'd die if she wasn't married by the time she was twenty-nine. It seemed I was the only one who wasn't obsessed about the marriage thing."

Once again Susan entered therapy.

Then came the rude awakening. Returning home from a two-week visit to her parents, Susan found Bobbi's room empty. "What the hell's going on here," Susan shrieked.

"Bobbi's gone off and gotten herself married to that French pianist," one of her roommates told her.

Susan was thunderstruck. "She did what?" she cried in disbelief, finding it hard to fathom that her friend was now living in conjugal bliss with a man she had met only three weeks before.

"I fell apart. A dam broke. I cried hysterically for days. I was absolutely heartbroken. I mean, how could she do this to me? I felt so let down, so betrayed, I didn't think I'd get over it."

She did get over it, but not before she was faced with the ultimate realization: that she loved the company of women, that she felt perfectly content without a full-time man in her life, and that she was not a lesbian. Sure, she'll admit, there was sometimes a fleeting erotic element in her friendships. In fact, one out of five women have homosexual encounters which arise out of close friendships and then go on to become heterosexual women.[29] But when it came to acting on her impulses, she realized she had no desire to.

It was in the midst of all these realizations that she met Dick. He was different from the other men she'd been involved with—softer, more gentle, more nurturant. He was, in Susan's words, very "mothering." They began seeing each other regularly. A year later Susan crossed the threshold.

Today she is happily married, has two children, and wouldn't change her life for anything. And yet, she has to admit, she wonders from time to time whether she could have enjoyed her life equally well if her single friends hadn't gotten married, if they had continued to live as they had before.

"I have this impression that if Bobbi hadn't gotten married, if Darla hadn't gotten married, I could still be out there, for God's sake. I could be living very happily with my career and my women friends in this sort of nowheresland. I loved sharing a house with women. It was just fun. I could have done that, I think, for the rest of my life. If not for the feeling that I was abnormal, that is."

Is Susan's fear well founded? Probably not, although when I asked Jane Flax whether there was any one psychological dynamic that could be correlated with lesbianism, she said, "A cold, indifferent mother."† More likely in Susan's case was that having close relationships with

---

†NOTE: Dr. Flax does not, however, view lesbianism as pathological. In addition, while having a nonnurturing mother can be correlated with female homosexuality, it is not, in and of itself, a causal agent.

other women over the years was a way of making up for the love she never got from her mother, a kind of compensatory device that gave her the foundation she needed to switch to men.

But what about Bobbi and Darla? Did they have less than terrific mothers, too? When I asked Susan that question, she chuckled. "God, no—as a matter of fact, when any of us really needed mothering, we'd go to one or the other's house, where we'd find more chicken soup than we could eat."

What, then, might account for their strong ties to women, so strong for Bobbi, in fact, that she had to break her connection to Susan completely for a while? One possible explanation is that women who are uncertain about their own autonomy might find they have an easier time hanging on to their independence around women than around men. In a recent study of lesbians, for example, the researchers found that there were certain characteristics among gay women that did not exist between opposite-sex couples—in particular, that power in gay female relationships was not determined by how much either partner earned.[30] It is also significant that while homosexual men tend to have homosexual encounters before heterosexual ones, many women turn to lesbianism after having a long-term heterosexual relationship. In fact, there is a significantly high percentage of lesbian women who were once married.[31]

Another more threatening possibility is that women can get along better without men than they think they can. When all the studies are put in the hopper, the finding that comes out again and again is that women who never marry do far better than their never-married male counterparts. They are mentally more stable and suffer less from neuroses.[32] They are happier, with one study claiming that the happiest of all were women who had female roommates.[33]

In fact, the real question that should be asked, Dr. Flax told me, is not why some women are lesbians, but why more are not. "When relationships between women friends are strong, there is a basic connection, a sense of being able to flow in and out of one another's experience more easily than with a man. Even in the best relationships with men, you're often translating your experience into another language. Women are generally more nurturing and understanding than men; they have a greater sensitivity to each other than men do. If you put taboo aside for a moment and really think about it, it's amazing that there are as few lesbians as there are."

What is it, then, that keeps most women "in line"? In part, Dr. Flax says, it has to do with society's fear of homosexuality. Also, women's ego boundaries are so permeable that a physical relationship with another woman could prove psychologically damaging. "Making love with another woman can dredge up unconscious memories of the early sense of merging with one's mother. Sexual relations with men are much safer—they're more bounded, much more differentiated. They allow a woman to keep a sense of separation that she might not have with another woman."

The possibility that many of us, deep down, may be warding off our desire for greater intimacy with other women should give every woman food for thought. It's too easy to say that women who don't sing the praises of men, who don't have a better time with men than with their women friends, have some underlying psychological disturbance. It's a lot more difficult to consider that, sex aside, women may not need men as much as we've been led to believe we do.

Chapter 5

MARITAL BLISS OR
THE LONELY CROWD?

AND so they are wed, she in her grandmother's wedding gown; he, handsome in his black tux. It is a ceremony fulfilling the fantasy of a lifetime, her greatest achievement really, and the sigh of relief is almost audible.[1] Wrapped in her husband's arms and fingering that little band of gold, she feels she needs nothing, and no one, else.

That's the illusion of romantic love that most of us were reared on, and during the honeymoon stage of marriage it feels like a dream come true—which is why most women are prone to putting their relationships with other women on the back burner after marriage.[2] But what happens to her friendships once the romance cools, when the burning passion is less frequent than the burnt toast? Women will be welcomed back into her life. Even if she considers her husband her best friend, she'll probably ignore the idea that marriage is a private affair and confide even more in her women friends than she did when she was single.[3] She's also likely to say that she needs her friends more than ever before.[4]

If marriage is the be-all and end-all of a woman's emotional life, how do we explain all the women who say they couldn't make it without their friends, to the point that some feel no friends would be worse than no marriage?[5]

The most obvious answer is that no matter how terrific the man, no one person can fulfill all your needs. The problem is that many young women have been led to believe in the power of the All-Encompassing One. And so when their husbands turn out to be human, they feel let down. Or they begin to question the value of their marriages.

MY ONE AND ONLY

Writing about what married women's friendships were like a century ago, sociologist Jessie Bernard says: "Here was a world to which men had little access and of which they had little understanding." She goes on to tell us that men were considered "aliens," necessary as protectors and to keep the population growing, but certainly not the ones women thought to turn to about matters of the "heart." In fact, she says, if women had depended on their spouses only for emotional nourishment, most of them would have probably starved to death.[6]

Unfortunately, the coming of Freud and the stigma attached to anything "homo" put a damper on women's intense relationships, and the tight bonds women had with each other fell under scrutiny. The whole domestic world of women, in fact, became denigrated—over time, even women themselves wanted no part of it. The entire field of psychiatry suggested that only your shrink should know about your personal problems, and that didn't help much either.[7] The accumulating effect of all these messages led to the development of another assumption: Find a husband, and you've found emotional bliss.

Catherine Hansen is one woman who married with that idea in mind. "I had this fantasy that it would be just the two of us, and that was it," she recalls. And for a while it was, with her husband, Tom, as engrossed in the marriage as she. At night after work they'd sit and talk for hours over a leisurely dinner, and on the weekends they'd spend every spare second together. Marriage promised emotional security, and she'd gotten just what she had bargained for.

Two years later, however, Tom began expanding his career horizons.

He began coming home later and later, and Cathy felt hurt and resentful. "You're not there for me anymore," she'd wail.

"That's ridiculous," he'd reply. "You just expect too much from me."

That's not how it appeared to Cathy. She began monitoring herself, making sure she wasn't becoming too much of a nag. And she started making mental notes of all the times he had disappointed her. "All the hurts, they just stayed right here," she said, pointing to her stomach. "It was like being on an emotional seesaw. When Tom was ready to listen, I'd be happy. When he wasn't available, I'd feel miserable and resentful."

She was not the only one feeling resentful. "Cathy was beginning to feel like a burden," Tom told me. "I felt like she wanted me twenty-four hours a day. I was beginning to feel really trapped."

His response was to stay away later and later, which, of course, only raised Cathy's hackles. Then the explosion. "Why don't you dump some of your problems on your girlfriends," he yelled.

Cathy was shocked. Girlfriends were for fun, but husbands were for things like problems and worries. After all, if you couldn't turn to your spouse for those kinds of things, what use was it being married? What she didn't realize was that imbuing one person with sole power of attorney over one's emotions puts too much strain on a marriage,[8] that togetherness is terrific, but only up to a point.

At Tom's suggestion they sought the help of a marriage counselor. No doubt about it, said the therapist, Cathy's needs were at the heart of the problem. Not that she needed too much, mind you, but that she expected Tom to satisfy all of her needs. Tom was also right, said the therapist, about suggesting Cathy use her friends to fill some of the void that Tom could not.

"But I don't feel I should have to need anybody else," she answered.

"Mrs. Hansen," the therapist replied, "I've been married for twenty years, and if I had counted on my husband every time I needed some nurturing, I would have hated him by now."

Reluctantly at first, Cathy tried the therapist's suggestion. Instead of going directly to Tom, she'd pick up the phone if she was upset. If she was feeling lonely, she'd arrange a dinner date, maybe even treat herself to the theater. And while initially she felt begrudging, it didn't take long for her to take real pleasure in the women she knew. "I began to feel I needed Tom less," she says, "which, of course, wasn't really true. What was true was that now there were other people, my friends, that I was looking to for some of what I had expected from him. And do you know what happened? I found that most of the time when I turned to Tom, he was really there for me. I guess I just needed permission to have some of my needs met somewhere else."

That's because when you've been told all along that marriage is sacrosanct and the provider of all emotional nourishment, it's difficult not to question the legitimacy of the marriage when things don't turn out that way. Which, given the shortcomings of husbands—or wives, for that matter—as people, it almost never does.

THE COMMON BONDS OF WOMANHOOD

While needing women friends because no one person can fulfill all of your emotional needs is the most basic reason women still need their friends after marriage, many other women give another reason: There are certain things about being a woman that only another woman can understand. Particularly when it comes to experiences that men have no familiarity with, such as labor or menstrual pains, or the "biological pull," talking to a man may feel as satisfying as talking to a Martian.

At cross-purposes: That's how it felt to Wendy when she and her husband spoke about having a child. A highly successful career woman who headed a major woman's publication by the time she was twenty-eight, having a child hadn't been on either of their priority lists. But hitting thirty, Wendy was having second thoughts about it; by thirty-three, having a child had become an all-out obsession.

Her husband couldn't understand it at all. "It's not rational," he'd tell her. "You know you don't want to stay home with a baby, to sacrifice your career, and if you can't stay home, then why have a child?"

"He's right," she'd tell herself, "it really doesn't make any sense." Still, she could not shake the feeling.

She confided in her friend, also a career woman, who'd had her first child a year earlier. "I know I'm not being rational," she said with an air of self-disparagement in her voice, "but I have this urge to have a baby."

Her friend's answer was swift and to the point. "So who says having a baby is supposed to be a *rational* decision?"

Wendy eventually decided to have her child, over her husband's objections, and while he loves his little girl, he still admits he could have lived his life just fine without ever having had a child. "He couldn't understand how I felt, and I finally gave up trying to explain it to him. There are some things he'll just never understand, and that's one of them."

Nor does she really need him to. When studies are conducted on women's feelings about pregnancy, it's the way her friends feel and how much support she gets from them that is the big determinator of how content she'll feel—not the way her husband feels.[9] That's because, like Wendy, most of us discover that there are certain female experiences which only another woman can validate, which only another woman can fully appreciate. It doesn't have to be children, of course, but almost anything men don't relate to: clothes, a detailed psychoanalysis of last night's dream, the simple need to relate every detail—all the intricacies of life that women thrive on, and most men detest. Nor does the "cross-communication," as Wendy put it, necessarily create tension in the marriage. "I'm not interested in the World Series and he's not interested in astrology," one wife told me. "So he talks to his friends about baseball, and I talk to mine about metaphysical things. It works out fine for both of us."

FEMALE COLLUSION

Another, less obvious reason that bonds married women together is their collusion against men. Behind every defiant wife there's usually more than a little help from her friends.

One woman found herself in a head-on collision with her husband when she brought up the idea of going back to work. "I had reached a point where I was done staying home, done doing the cooking, done being everyone's mother," she explained. "My husband hated the idea —he actually said he forbade it." She whimpered and complained and nagged, all to no avail.

"You're going about it the wrong way," her friend told her. "You've got to say to him, 'Look here.'"

She tried it. "He was so shocked that he had to listen," she grinned. "And it suddenly dawned on him that he couldn't forbid me to do anything." Her husband, of course, took a while to adjust. "He called my friend a 'bad influence on me.'" Her friend gave her the right answer to that one, too. "Tell him that if someone who influences you to become an individual is a bad influence, you'll take all the influencing you can get."

"He hasn't said a nasty word about her since," she told me.

Then, of course, there's the whole issue of affairs. Men may have traditionally been the ones going out on the sly, but there is evidence that women are quickly catching up in the nonmonogamy department (although women do have fewer outside partners than their husbands).[10] And women, like men, are bound to feel guilty, to say nothing of enjoying that little boost of approval from their friends. If a woman says to her friend, "I met this fabulous man and I've been fantasizing about him ever since," and her friend says, "By all means, do it," she is, in effect, getting the permission and validation she may need to take the plunge. On the other side, her friend becomes privy to the vicarious pleasure of it all, or perhaps works up the gumption to go try it herself.

"I was frankly shocked at how supportive my friends were when I started having a series of affairs," one woman confessed. "Not one of them suggested that what might really be happening was that I was miserable in my marriage. At first, I thought they were getting pleasure out of listening to my escapades, but later I realized they were all unhappy in their marriages, too. I was the one really to get the ball rolling." Within months all the women had taken on lovers. In a year almost all of them had asked for a divorce.

Of course, extramarital affairs aren't necessarily an augury of divorce. Occasional infidelity need not even signify that a marriage is in grave danger.[11] Either way, having an affair is still so emotionally loaded for women that they often feel the need for an outside supporter to rally to their cause.

And if friends aren't supportive? If a woman declares her extramarital proclivities only to find her friends overwhelmingly disapprove? The experience can be shattering, and possibly lead to an end to the friendship. A woman who opts for nonmonogamy is a woman who is often experiencing a temporary feeling of alienation from her husband. Now she feels isolated from her friends. "I always counted on my friends to support me in the way my husband couldn't," a housewife told me. "So when they were judgmental about my affair, I felt very distant from them. I didn't want a divorce, but I had never slept with anyone other than my husband and at thirty-five felt a need to try it. My friends thought this was disgusting." How did she deal with disapproval? Not by ending her involvement. "I just looked for some new friends."

Friends may object to affairs for moral reasons and because a friend's affair, like divorce, often triggers a woman's own forbidden feelings. Sometimes, too, extramarital involvements raise issues about the friendship itself. One woman admitted that she ended a friendship when a woman she knew began sleeping with a man at work because it made her feel her friend was generally untrustworthy. Her sentiments went something like this: If she can cheat on her husband, who's supposed to be number one in her life, how can I be sure of what kind of betrayal she might lay on me?

There is only one way, of course, to know how friends feel about affairs, which is to give them the facts and wait for them to respond. Unfortunately, it's often too late, although close friends will generally argue out their differences or agree to disagree on the ethics of it all. Either way, the collusion to make a statement about individuality and the trust women instill in each other speak to the tightly knit bonds between women after they've crossed the threshold.

Which is why, not surprisingly, men so often feel threatened by them.

TO WHOM SHALL I BE TRUE?

"My husband is very jealous of my friends," one twenty-six-year-old wife confesses. "It comes out in all sorts of ways—when I've been on the phone, he'll ask me in almost a little-boy whimper, 'Who was that you were talking to?' And we used to fight all the time about my going out with my friends. The implication was, 'How could I really love him best if I wanted to spend time with other people?' He's gotten better, but he's still not comfortable with it."

This husband's sentiments are not only the flip side of the "my one and only" ethic, or a suspicion that his wife is using her friend as a confessional for her infidelities, but a reflection of men's deepest insecurity—the fear that they need women more than women need them. Margaret Mead once said, "Men have always been afraid that women could get along without them."[12] And for good reason—there's a primary bond that women share with one another, stemming from the bond they had with their mothers, a bond they do not share with men.

Men also haven't been encouraged to share emotion with their male friends, which leaves them precariously dependent on their wives.[13] Little wonder a husband is jealous when his wife has other people to be intimate with, when he's left to his own devices.

There's also the question of what it means to be loyal. When women turn to their friends for marital advice, which all but the most conventional women do with great regularity,[14] the outcome is usually to improve the marriage. There's nothing like getting an objective view, and a true friend will try to hear the story from both sides. At the very least, a woman is likely to feel a lot calmer after talking it out—and certainly a lot richer than if she'd spent an hour on the couch.

At the same time, confiding that we're concerned that a husband drinks too much or is having impotency problems violates certain rules of privacy and can be dangerous, especially if husbands find out. "I once let it slip that I had told a friend about some difficulties we were having and all hell broke loose," said one wife. "We had a big blow up, and he made me promise that I'd never talk about personal things like that again." Did she keep her promise? Well, not exactly—she's just learned to be a little bit smarter. "I keep my mouth shut and figure what he doesn't know won't hurt him. The truth is, I think it would be worse for the marriage if I kept things all inside."

Which isn't to say that she doesn't understand her husband's feelings. "I wouldn't want him telling anyone about our sex life either," she admitted.

How do wives resolve the dilemma? Sometimes by keeping certain topics off-limits to friends—more often with a healthy dose of rationalization. As one woman put it, "My husband's my best friend. It's just that I define what that means differently than he does. He sees telling friends about marital problems as a betrayal; I see it as necessary for my mental health."

The comforting thing, or discomforting thing, depending on one's outlook, is that a number of women I spoke to say their husbands are following their lead and developing more intimate friendships of their own. And in the process, the wives tell me, they are getting a feel for what it's like on the other side—the pangs of jealousy, the flashes of anger when they suspect their husbands are "telling too much,"—and learning to become better friends to their spouses because of it.

THE OTHER HALF

But this is only part of the story. Although many women say their friends are an important addition to their relationships with their husbands, the icing on the cake, other women give another reason for needing close ties with women: Their husbands aren't very good friends. In fact, when wives are asked to make a list of their closest friends, half the time the husbands aren't even mentioned.

The absence of friendship in many marriages was most thoroughly documented by Dr. Joel Block, who surveyed over two thousand men and women. When he asked his respondents what made for a good marriage, both sexes responded almost unanimously, "Friendship." Yet when he questioned the same men and women about whether they considered their own spouses as friends, only 38 percent said their spouses had the qualities that made for a good friend.[15] Dr. Robert Bell found similar results. Only 50 percent of all wives and 60 percent of the husbands considered their spouses their friend.[16] Even more startling results emerged when Dr. Bell asked married women to name the three people they most enjoyed spending their time with—two thirds of the women had husbands on their lists, but 98 percent listed a woman friend.[17]

Could this be true? Half of all women said they don't think of their husbands as friends? More women would rather be with a woman friend than with their spouses? At first glance, these data appear incredible. But when we dig deeper, we learn that friendship between husbands and wives is rarer than most of us would like to believe. The question is, why?

THE HOUSE, THE KIDS, AND OTHER SLIGHTS TO COMPANIONATE MARRIAGE

Part of the problem, according to Dr. Block, is that the newness and excitement of early marriage simply gets lost with time. "Most people think that marriage is at first made up of discovery, of having novel emotions and impressions, of conflict, and of finding new ways of sharing, all of which slowly evolves into a more stable, but ever more complete and satisfying friendship," writes Dr. Joel Block. What really happens, however, is another story. "When the fire of romance is banked, and as passion cools, the marriage frequently becomes boring and stale . . . words like monotony, humdrum and fed-up describe the state of many marriages."

Nor does the endless list of day-to-day burdens and responsibilities—paying the bills, buying the house, cleaning the toilet bowl—do much for romance, to say nothing of what happens once the kids start coming. Kids of any age, revealed a Cornell University study, decrease the amount of time couples spend together by 50 percent. Having a preschooler at home cuts into intimate husband-wife time even more; couples with little ones are three times less likely to consider their spouses as friends than couples whose kids have left the nest or who never were parents to begin with.

"It's not just the quantity of time, but the quality," you say? The researchers found that all too often quality suffered, too. "Conversations once spiced with exchanges about books, ideas, and personal relationships," they tell us, "were almost entirely concerned with routine affairs—'What did you do today, dear?' . . . 'Oh, nothing much . . . What did you do?' . . . 'Was there anything in the mail?' . . . 'The plumber came to fix the sink.' "[18]

But there's more to worry about than the fact that running a household and raising children temporarily steals some of the intimacy between mates. Children grow up. The ebb and flow of daily responsibilities change over time. Even then, says Dr. Block, friendship between husband and wife is often not revived.

That's because there's a deeper psychological dilemma many husbands and wives must face. Freud once said that what a woman looked for in a husband is her mother. And men may be terrific at a lot of things, but mothering is not often one of them.

EMOTIONALLY DIFFERENT SPECIES

In an article on friendship between the sexes, author Letty Cottin Pogrebin wrote: "We may be oriented toward the opposite sex for sex, but for other kinds of intimacy we tend to be gender loyal. This is no accident. True friendship is rare between women and men and because sex separatism is so rigorously ingrained during childhood. Most parents rear male and female children as though preparing them to live in two different worlds."[19]

The discrepancy in the male-female experience is both social and psychological. From the beginning, mothers see their sons as more separate than their daughters, encouraging boys from a very young age to master their environment. Girls, who are rewarded for staying attached and dependent, get the opposite conditioning. Not surprisingly, boys come to view themselves as separate from the world, and girls as attached to it, creating a kind of communications gap between the genders. "Talk to me!" we plead. "What's there to talk about?" they answer. It's not that they're being callous or that we're nags, but men and women simply don't see eye to eye when it comes to certain forms of communication.

Added to these differences is the demand that boys renounce their mothers in order to develop a masculine identification. A boy learns that in order not to be a sissy, he has to cauterize many of his feelings: After all, big boys don't cry. Not only does this widen the gap between boys and girls, but establishes a situation in which boys, and later men, come to develop a kind of contempt for women. "If being like Mom, or any girl for that matter, is 'unmasculine,'" registers the unconscious message, "then 'girly' things like nurturance, and girls themselves, must be inferior."

Although shutting off his softer side serves well to prevent problems with gender identity during the developmental stages, the strong, silent type doesn't do much for providing loving support within a marriage.

The conflict is strikingly revealed in a host of studies conducted on the emotional aspects of marriage. Judging from what researchers have learned, women contribute about twice as much emotional support in their marriages as they get.[20] It also isn't uncommon for men to respond to their wives' problems "by criticism, by rejection, by dismissal of them as unimportant, or by merely passive listening," concludes a study of over seven hundred families.[21] Complain about it? That only makes matters worse; the more emotional a wife gets, the more rational her husband is likely to become.[22]

The result is that many women are left emotionally disadvantaged in their marriages—they need more, but they get less. "Men satisfy their needs for intimacy largely within the marriage," concluded one researcher, "but women must seek gratification for such needs with their own sex."[23]

And among no marriages is this more true than in those where man and wife are living their lives in separate realities to begin with.

EMOTIONAL DEPRIVATION AND THE FULL-TIME HOMEMAKER

Joel Block's friendship survey uncovered an interesting finding about why some couples were friends and others weren't. Wives who worked or who were preparing for a career were most likely to consider their husbands as friends. Less fortunate were women involved in more traditional marriages, where the woman takes care of the house, the children, and the cooking, and the husband is assigned the role of breadwinner. These couples, found Dr. Block, were not only less likely to have a basis for marital friendship to begin with, but had the makings for a growing wedge between spouses that deepened over time.[24]

What happens to a housewife when she wakes up and realizes that just because her husband buys her a house, two cars, and a Caribbean vacation, it doesn't mean he can provide the kind of emotional nourishment she needs? According to sociologists, she'll feel emotionally starved and become depressed.[25] That is, unless she's lucky and resourceful enough to have women friends to fill the void.

I met a group of women like these in the posh suburbs of Philadelphia. They were well-to-do, attractive women in their late twenties. Their husbands were either corporate golden boys or professional men —an attorney, a dentist, a corporate VP—and had done well in providing their wives with the amenities of life. The women said they were happy in their marriages, and yet they spoke about a certain feeling of distance from the supposed primary person in their lives. One of the women, whom I'll call Jan, expressed frustration because her husband refused to celebrate birthdays—"He thinks they're silly," she said. Meanwhile, year after year she looked in the glove compartment, under the bed, in the cupboard for the present that never came. Another, Ina, felt totally detached from her husband's work, and secretly wished she could turn invisible for a day so she could go with him to the office and learn about what he did all day. Betsy, whose husband traveled regularly, admitted she became furious when her husband wouldn't take the time to call her to let her know that his plane would be late. Her husband, she said, was simply too embarrassed to leave a big business meeting "to call little ole me."

If husbands turned their backs, however, their women friends were there with open arms. "I call my friends a million times for everything," said Jan.

"Why don't you call your husband?" I asked.

"He'd hang up on me."

The others laughed. Economically, their lives were cushy. What they hadn't considered was what it would be like being at home alone with children from as early as seven in the morning to as late as eight o'clock at night. Nor had they done much thinking about what the traditional division of labor does to the friendship element of marriage.

"I'm much more involved with my friends than with my husband," admitted Ina wryly. "My husband gets bored after ten minutes of hearing the kids did this today or did that. It's really my friends that I count on to listen. I can tell them the nitty-gritty, whatever I want. Steve isn't at all interested."

"Women give you a lot that men don't," said Betsy. "Like patience. A lot of things my husband considers nonsense, my friends think are very important. And there are some things that we can tell each other that we can't tell our husbands. For instance, a few years ago I was having a sexual problem with John. He wanted to have sex anytime, all the time, every night of the week. A lot of the thrill has left for me, and I was exhausted with the kids, but I couldn't tell him that I just wasn't interested. But I could tell my friends." Shaking the bangs out of her eyes, she glanced over to her two friends, who had broken out into broad grins. "And it was sure nice to know I wasn't the only one who felt that way," she added.

Given the amount of time they spent with each other, dropping in for coffee or going shopping or on the phone, I wondered if they ever felt more intimate with each other than with their mates. There was no doubt in their minds. Self-consciously they spoke about how surprised they were that the women in their lives were so important, how "they'd die" without one another.

What they couldn't see was that the root of the problem with their husbands was the life they had chosen for themselves. "Men just aren't as understanding as women," blurted Ina, who complained that her husband sometimes treated her like one of the forty-some odd staff members he had working for him at the office. "We just relate to the world differently."

"Did she ever consider that might be because she and her husband were operating in contexts that *were* totally different? Well, no. You see, she and her husband had agreed that it was best for a wife to stay home full-time. Besides, she said, she knew lots of working women who spent so much time at their jobs that they really didn't have much in common with their husbands either.

A convenient rationalization, but not one that holds much water. Even when a husband and a wife agree that having her at home with the babies while he traipses off to work each day adds up to a fair trade, the psychic equation is this: The more traditional the marriage, the greater the emotional distance between the spouses. Said another way, the less a man participates in the domestic chores, the greater the relational void.[26]

Only Jan was able to make the link between her relationship with her husband and the traditional marriage in which she was living. "There's no doubt that since I've been home full-time, Bob and I have become more distant. He does his thing all day and I do mine. And when he gets home, he doesn't want to hear about my day or talk about his. I also feel he's lost respect for me, because sometimes when I ask him to explain a particular law case, he says I wouldn't understand. It was never like that when we first met in college. He considered me his equal. But since I've had kids, it's as if I lost my brain, from his point of view. He just doesn't see what I do as being as important as what he does."

She's right; he probably doesn't. When studies are conducted on husbands whose spouses are full-time wives, the men almost unanimously
hail the virtues of their wives as homemakers. The problem is, these
same husbands say they have little respect for their wives as people.[27] If
men have to develop a certain degree of contempt for women in general
in order to establish their masculinity, it shouldn't surprise us that they
would have the most disdain for women who most resembled their own
mothers.

That's not to say that Jan, Ina, and Beth feel that in the balance of
things their marriages aren't satisfactory. A lot of women marry for
reasons other than friendship, with economic well-being at the top of
the list. At the same time, the cost of that arrangement is often less
intimacy in the marriage. And if they are able to feel reasonably content
with their lots in life, it is because they have each other to fill in the
patchwork their husbands do not.[28]

And what happens to women like these when they don't have close
friends? Often the marriage ends in divorce. "I've seen many women
who report that their marriages are less than satisfying on an emotional
level, but the support they muster from their women friends allows
them to remain in the marriage," says Angela Fox. "What is so telling is
that when a woman loses that support, when her friends move or the
friendships break up for other reasons, she is far more apt to terminate
her marriage. One patient, for instance, was uprooted from her community when her husband was relocated, and when she moved with him,
she was forced to leave her friends behind. Nine months later she initiated divorce proceedings. Without her friends to shield her against her
feelings of loneliness in her marriage, she was left defenseless against
her feelings of disillusionment."

For others, finding the way out is not as easy. The number of women
who can support their families on their own is still relatively small.
Which is why many women collude to keep the image of a satisfying
marriage afloat.

"I have no problems dealing with whatever gaps there are in my
marriage," said Ina defensively, near the close of our interview. "I've
just changed my expectations. If you don't expect your husband to
understand you a lot of the time, you're not so disappointed."

THE WELL-INTENTIONED "LIBERATED" HUSBAND

Of course, wives who work aren't necessarily guaranteed marital friendship either. Having a career may be good for a woman's ego, but the time demands of unrelated professions on the dual-career couple may make the spouses almost strangers to each other. A musician for a major symphony orchestra, for example, tells me it's been a long time since she's considered her husband a close friend. That's because they're on completely different schedules. "We're more like compatible roommates these days," she tells me. "He works from nine to five, I have concerts in the evenings, including weekends. The truth is, we hardly get to see each other."[29]

A more common scenario for the working wife is to find herself up against a husband who does not fully support her working. While most husbands love the extra money women earn, many men feel cheated when their wives are no longer there at their beck and call—after all, many men are looking for mothers in their wives, too. Even if he says that he's fully behind her, he may feel threatened by her growing independence. Many husbands enjoy the "superior" position that being the primary or sole breadwinner affords him; they like the idea of having their wives financially dependent on them. And for good reason—the more money a woman earns, the better the chance that she'll up and leave the marriage if she's dissatisfied with it.[30] Even if a wife has no intention of walking out, her success may feel like a slap in the face to a man whose identity is almost entirely wrapped up in his achievements. "I was raised to believe that a man could take pride in being the provider," one forty-year-old man confesses. "Today my wife earns about the same income I do. Sure, I'm proud of her. But I can't help but feel that something's been taken away from me."

He is not alone. Dr. Block reports that marriages are more likely to evolve into true friendships when husbands believe in women's liberation.[31] But a study done at Virginia Commonwealth University suggested that, while men often say they're in favor of female equality, deep down they don't really feel that way about it. Based on a written attitudinal test, men were classified as sexists and nonsexists. They were then shown a profeminist movie. After the film they were given another written test to see if and how their attitudes had changed. The men who were originally classified as sexists showed a dramatic increase in hostility toward the women's movement. What was surprising was that the nonsexists showed an even greater increase. In fact, when all of the scores were tallied up, sexists and supposedly nonsexist men were equally hostile toward the movement. Simply put: Saying you're a liberated man is one thing; meaning it, another.[32]

What happens when a working woman turns to her husband for support if he's one of these well-intenders? Oftentimes she's frustrated and disappointed. According to psychiatrist Ruth Moulton, a working woman, and a career woman in particular, needs more than a small dose of encouragement from her spouse. And given the fact that she's probably had an encouraging father or other male mentor who launched her ambitions to begin with, she'll come to expect the same kind of backing from her spouse. Unfortunately, says Dr. Moulton, while many men start out with encouraging words, they often end up feeling used and resentful.[33] Which is why meaningful support from her women friends is that much more critical. Even among the corporate elite, these feelings prevail. A recent study reported in the *Wall Street Journal* claimed that 50 percent of wives who held corporate positions had husbands who could be classified as "subtle-obstructionists."[34]

"You should become a doctor." Those were Donald's first words to Patricia when he observed her greater than average nursing talent in the emergency room, thus planting a new bug in her head. Patricia was flattered and tickled to find a man who respected her abilities and was seemingly unthreatened by them. She could not have guessed that that would all change once they married a year later.

The two planned a life strategy. She would go back to school for a year to take the premed courses necessary for application to a medical school. They would then have one child, followed by her entering medical school, during which time she and her husband would share in the rearing of their newborn.

The next few years of her life were as well timed as clockwork. She took her premed courses and her boards. She was accepted to a medical school in the same city where Donald was completing his residency. She had Julia. Nine months later she entered medical school.

The workload, as hard as it was, was pretty much what she had anticipated. What she had not counted on was Donald's withdrawing his support. "Even though we had this agreement that we would share the child care equally, that's not how it turned out. Sure, he'd change a diaper once in a while, or watch the baby when I was in class and he was off, but I was the one who ended up doing most of the work—bathing her, diapering her, dropping her off to the baby-sitter."

Donald's attitudes toward her career also seemed to do an about-face. "It was as if he had walked with me to the lion's den, and then let me loose, shutting the gate behind him," she says. "And he was always complaining that I wasn't spending enough time with the baby. He was beginning to sound like a man who deep down wanted a hausfrau for a wife."

Unlikely. If he were one of those men who cannot tolerate the idea of an equal partner even on the intellectual level, he never would have married a woman like Patricia. At the same time, men who support their wives before they have children may pull back some of that support because once she has had a child, he no longer perceives himself as an equal. Every man knows that having babies is something he can't do, which is all fine and good as long as he can find something that he can do that his wife can't. But if a woman can do everything a man can do *and* have babies, what use is a man? What does he have that she doesn't? When he's married to a woman as competent as Patricia, the answer is, not much. Which is why men like Donald may begin clutching on to the idea of achievement as if it were his terrain alone.[35]

Whatever was behind it, making the grade that first semester was like fighting an uphill battle, and Patricia barely squeaked by. She passed two courses by the skin of her teeth and failed a third. Donald, rather than seeing her stress as a result of having to take primary responsibility for their child, as well as studying for exams, began to question her ability to get through. "If you can't stand the heat," he had said to her after she received her failing grade, "then maybe you should get out of the kitchen."

Up to that point Patricia had avoided becoming friendly with the other medical students; she had enough on her hands without the worry of yet another commitment. She also had trouble reconciling herself to the fact that her husband fell far short of meeting her needs: Like many other women, her feeling was that marriage was a private affair, something not to be shared with "outsiders." Yet she was feeling so pressured that when a first-year resident invited her to lunch, she gladly accepted. She spent the rest of the afternoon spilling her heart out. "How do you do it?" Patricia wailed, observing that the resident had a young child of her own. "Maybe my husband's right—I shouldn't be here."

The resident's ideas about what was happening in Patricia's life couldn't have been clearer. "He's threatened by you. Maybe he says he wants you to succeed, but way down deep, he's afraid you'll be as good as he is, maybe better." These problems, said the resident, were so common that some of the women had formed a support group to deal with them. Would Patricia like to join?

"The group changed my life," Patricia confessed. "For a while I was beginning to wonder if maybe I really couldn't hack it. But other women seemed to have almost the identical problems that I had. It was good to know that I wasn't the only one. It was also good to have someone standing beside me saying, 'Come on, Patty, you can do it.' "

She did, although it took her a year longer to get through. Meanwhile, Donald, not surprisingly, resented the support system his wife had found for herself, a group from which he was excluded. "You're so pressed for time, I can't see why you waste it with those women," he'd say.

"Maybe if I got a little more help from you, I wouldn't need to look for it elsewhere," was her reply.

The tension between the two continued to build. Patricia felt sabotaged by Donald's lack of cooperation. The more Donald pulled away from what he considered "women's work," the more resistant Patricia became about doing anything that was linked to the traditional female role. "Except for taking care of the baby, I went on strike," she admits. "I didn't clean, I didn't cook, the laundry piled up. It was as if the more he fought my independence, the less feminine I allowed myself to be."

Donald, on the other hand, felt threatened by his wife's impending independence and success. "It wasn't that I really didn't want her to be successful," he says in retrospect, "but I couldn't help but feel that the possibility of her making as much money as I, more maybe, was a slight to my masculinity. I guess I wanted it both ways—to have a partner, but to be the head of the household."

He's not alone. In fact, there's a lot of evidence that says the best way to upset the applecart in a marriage is to have a wife who does better than her husband. The patterns are so pervasive that many professional women themselves say they're more comfortable if their husbands earn more than they.[36]

The dilemma is that what men need in order not to feel threatened by their wives' success is often the same thing that keeps women in their place. According to psychiatrist Richard Robertiello, "A man needs a woman who will affirm his masculine power, enjoy it, enhance it and gain something from it, rather than envy it and try to destroy it."[37] Easy enough if translated to mean that women should be more accepting of their husband's need to be one of the boys, or to prove his masculinity through sports and physical prowess. The problem is that all too often, helping a man affirm his masculinity means making ourselves less competent for the sake of his ego.

The question is: Why do men feel so threatened? On the obvious level there's the fact that men traditionally have had more power than women, and people in power don't like to give that up. Psychologically, the resonance goes deeper. Most men, like most women, begin life with a powerful emotional attachment to their mothers. In order to "become a man," he has to sever that attachment and find a way of offsetting his emotional dependence on his mother and on women in general. Being the primary breadwinner does just that—at least under those circumstances his wife will be reasonably dependent on him. But a wife who threatens to outdo her husband financially puts her spouse in a precarious position. If she becomes financially independent, he wonders, then what? What will she need him for? This is why so many men covertly sabotage their wives' careers.

But sabotage wasn't something Patricia was willing to live with, and her marriage would have continued to deteriorate if the chief surgeon, under whom Donald was doing his residency, hadn't intervened.

"You seem to be under a lot of stress," said Donald's old college mentor after a session in surgery. "You're a brilliant surgeon, but your work just hasn't been up to par. Anything bothering you?"

Donald had never considered sharing his problems with any man, let alone his mentor; like many men, he viewed that kind of intimacy as a detriment, a vulnerability that men weren't supposed to have. Then again, he knew that his problem with Patricia was causing his work to slip.

"Oh," he said, trying to sound matter of fact. "It's Patricia. Dr. Strauss says she has a golden future, and while I'm happy to hear it, I sometimes feel that I'd rather have a 'wife,' not a professional dynamo. You know, someone who needed me a little more, who I could take care of."

The senior physician nodded his head. "I know exactly what you mean," he admitted, scrubbing his hands, and then proceeded to tell Donald about his own marriage which had ended in divorce eight years earlier. His wife, he said, had been a corporate wizard—tops in her field. He had wanted to be behind her all the way. But emotionally, he just couldn't do it. "It was my own damn ego," he explained. "I didn't mind that she was bright, but, as a man, I wanted to be the big star. So I started getting on her back, complaining about the traveling she had to do, accusing her of being more like a man than a woman. The fact was, she was a free woman and I just couldn't handle it," he confessed. "Finally, she just walked out."

Seeing his own mirror image in his mentor's words shook Donald up. "That conversation was a real turning point for me," admits Donald. "I mean, to hear it from your wife is one thing, but to hear it from another man is something else." Donald looked inward, and for the first time confronted many of his insecurities about his own masculinity. It was, he admits, a painful and often difficult process. And as his attitude began to change, Patricia became less rigid, too.

"All of a sudden, it didn't seem to matter so much if I did more of the cooking and he took care of the bills. Once I felt that he really saw me as an equal, it was okay to be a woman, too."

Now, five years later, Patricia and Donald have a joint practice. And they don't need to worry about most of the household responsibilities because they're fortunate enough to be able to hire live-in help. The biggest change of all, both confide, however, is the evolution of a friendship between them.

"There's love and there's romance, and then there's friendship," said Patricia. "And just because you have the first two doesn't mean you have the latter. We've worked on making sure that we do, and the payoff has been stupendous."

Which isn't to say that Patricia doesn't need women friends anymore. "There are some things that men will just never understand the way a woman does," she admits. "We're living in a time when there's a lot of change taking place, and as much as men try to understand women's struggles, they just can't on a personal level."

Then again, Donald adds, neither can a wife understand his trials and tribulations as well as a male friend. "It works two ways," he told me, "and having a few good male friends to confide in has opened my horizons."

Patricia smiled. "It's also taken the emotional burden off of me."

THE RECIPE FOR FRIENDSHIP IN MARRIAGE

Patricia and Donald learned two important lessons. The first is that friendship is the emotional glue of a marriage, that without it, there's nothing more than a roommate type of situation, two people crossing in the hall on the way to the bathroom.[38] More important, Patricia and Donald discovered that if there's anything critical to marital friendship, it's equality and mutuality. "Gender hierarchies are not conducive to friendship," says Letty Cottin Pogrebin. "Sex can flourish between unequals and love can thrive between them, but friendship requires equality. Unlike love, it cannot be unilateral or unrequited. Unlike sex, it cannot be imposed. Friendship must be mutual."[39]

But what exactly does it mean to be equal, to have a relationship based on mutuality?

In part, it's a matter of psychological attitude, a sense of another person's rights and talents as an individual and a commitment to allowing that individual to grow. And because men tend to feel threatened by their wives' success, they will have to find a way to give up the idea of a one-ring circus in which they are the ringmasters. And in fact, there is some hope that some men, at least, are willing to do so. A recent large-scale survey of couples discovered that men were happy if their wives were successful, taking great pride in their partner's achievements—a dramatic change from a decade ago. But the researchers also noted the pleasure quickly soured if it appeared their wives might do better than they did.[40]

In order for husbands and wives to be better friends to each other, there will also have to be a closer emotional connection between the two. *Vive la différence* may make marriage more interesting, but if a wife has to beg her husband to talk to her or if a husband views his wife's emotionality as some kind of psychological defect, there's bound to be trouble. Here, too, some signs of hope are on the horizon. Only twelve years ago it was political suicide for Edmund Muskie when he cried in front of millions of television viewers because someone had insulted his wife. Today Olympic gold medalists shed the tears freely— even Ronald Reagan has been known to become teary-eyed. Walk through the street of any metropolis and you'll see men, for the first time ever, pushing strollers through the park together, as if that were the most natural thing in the world. And yet, for all the changes some men are making, the emotional rift between husbands and wives remains strong. While both men and women agree that friendship is critical to the happiness of a marriage, they fall into disagreement with how that should be accomplished. "Communicate more," say the women almost unanimously. "I don't think talking more necessarily solves anything," say the husbands. As for what would make a difference, well, admit the men, they're not exactly sure.[41] Kate Millett once said, "Men repress, women express." For many couples that still seems to be true.

Until some of these differences are resolved, having women friends will continue to be critical to the emotional well-being of married women, as well as to the stability of the institution of marriage. Which isn't necessarily detrimental to the marriage. While there are some women—disgruntled women—who talk each other out of remaining in what they see as a stifling, unequal relationship, there are many others who are collectively trying to find solutions to the age old male-female intimacy gap. What kind of strategies can you use to deal with a less than cooperative husband? What can you do to get your way without threatening him at the same time? Most of all, how does a woman who believes that marriage should be a fifty-fifty deal cope with the reality that it most often isn't without heading for the divorce courts?

Feminist and sociologist Barbara Forisha, for example, writes that she'd rather try to find an overall sense of balance in her marriage than spend her life arguing about who's going to slice the celery. She realized that she'd rather cook and do the laundry than bring in the car to the garage or wait in the rain to buy theater tickets. "I am not advocating a return to traditional norms, in which men and women became very separate from each other and seldom shared the high point of communion which happens periodically in the best of relationships," she says. "However, I am also not advocating the pursuit of equality all the time. I am suggesting that we strive for a delicate balance in which each part of ourselves, the old and the new, gets its due, and the symbolic ritual of traditional sex-role behavior paves the way for a fuller acceptance of human beings in both work and love."[42]

Whether you buy Dr. Forisha's ideas about balance or not, just being able to brainstorm about the possibilities not only draws women closer, but gives us ideas to ease the tension, to help our own marriages over the rough spots. And if we are honest with ourselves, we're likely to find that it isn't just husbands who hold traditional ideas about the way things should be, but that we ourselves play a part in keeping women in their place. "When my friends and I complain about our husbands, two things come out," one woman admitted. "The first is that on some level, all men want mothers who will tend to them the way their mothers tended to them. The second is that on some level we wouldn't mind having someone take care of us financially either."

And what if men and women do begin to resolve their differences? If companionate marriage becomes the norm, would women friends become less important? I don't think so. There will always be needs that women have for other women, no matter how terrific the marriage. And without the legacy of gender differences, we'd all probably have a lot more men, including our husbands, in our circle of friends.

Chapter 6

FULL-TIME MOTHERS, FULL-TIME FRIENDS: A LIFESTYLE AT RISK

T HE woman who greeted me at the door was blond, petite and looked cheerfully harried.

"You must be Eva," she said, trying to juggle a baby, a bottle, and a stuffed Miss Piggy so that she could extend her hand, at which point her son conveniently decided to have an "accident."

"Welcome to Kiddieland," she chuckled, holding her nose as she led me through the small but homey dining room that was strewn with toys, through a hallway, and into an even more cluttered living room—despite the fact that the only furniture was an old plaid couch and two folding chairs. "You're just in time—everyone arrived a few minutes ago."

THE MOTHERS

The women, whose names were Diane, Val, Ricki, and Merri, were all pleasant-looking and in their mid to late twenties. All four had high school diplomas and Val and Diane had gone on to secretarial school, while Merri and Ricki had worked in clerical jobs before they were married. All had given up any outside commitments when they became pregnant. Their husbands were salesmen and laborers, and while not earning abundant livings, all earned enough money for their wives to stay at home. Ricki and Diane each had two children, ranging in age from six months to three years; Val and Merri both had one-year-olds but were already planning for their next. And all agreed that when kids were young, their place was at home.

The women and the details of their lives, however, weren't nearly as interesting as the scene in Diane's living room. There seemed to be children everywhere—on laps, in arms, in the playpen, pulling at a pants leg. Merri breast-fed, while Val, who had developed mastitis, fed from a bottle. Diapers, which the women carried with them as automatically as a business woman carries her attaché case, were everywhere, with a communal changing table ready for use near the bathroom. The women were dressed neatly but simply—as Val later put it, "Why worry about clothes when you're just going to get spat up on?"

"It looks as if it took quite a bit of organizing to get you all together," I said.

"Oh no," said Diane. "We get together like this at least three times a week."

The group had been formed bit by bit. "I went to school with Ricki, have known her all my life," said Val, "and so when she moved down the block, it was almost natural for us to become close."

"And my cousin knew Ricki, so when I moved here, she gave me her phone number and I called her up, and well, that was that," added Diane.

"I guess I was the newcomer," Merri told me, sweeping her bangs out of her eyes. "Val was having a garage sale and we had just bought our house. Anyway, we got to talking and found out we only lived a few blocks away. It was through her that I got to know the others."

In any suburban clique, there's always the possibility of attracting women who don't fit in with the group—there's no telling, not at first anyway, who might be a back stabber or a social snob, or who might be convinced that her own mothering is beyond reproach. But Val, Ricki, Diane, and Merri were lucky.

"I guess you could say we just clicked almost immediately," Merri offered.

Their relationship, which started by having coffee at one woman's house or the other, developed into a staunch alliance and support system. They talked about the newness of being a mother, and acted as baby-sitters if one or the other had to go to the dentist or doctor or simply needed some breathing space. They spoke of the long hours alone when their husbands were at work, and the sense of competency they felt around one another, which they often did not feel around their husbands. Like the women's sphere of past centuries, they had formed their own little world in which they were the queens of the castle. It was a place where the values of nurturing and mothering were supreme, outranking any possible achievement in the outside world, and which made the women feel loved, cherished, and safe. While the rest of us imagine that such a world is defunct, the relationship between the four women was a testament to the fact that it is alive and thriving.

Mostly, their conversation focused on children and mothering and the critical need for friendship. There were the ordinary trials and tribulations of motherhood, of course: What do you do when the baby teethes? and 101 methods for dealing with a colicky child. But even feelings that one might suspect would arouse disdain, or at the least raise a few eyebrows, were discussed openly.

"There are things I can say here that I'd be embarrassed to tell anyone else," said Merri. "For instance, when Jeremy was first born, he was a crier. I wasn't prepared for it; I didn't get more than four hours of straight sleep for six months, and there were times that I had fantasies about throwing him out the window." Not an eyelash flickered. Apparently, they had heard it before.

But their discussions ranged far beyond the physical aspects of caretaking.

"Diane's our resident shrink," said Ricki, who had just coaxed her three-year-old into playing with some blocks. "She's always questioning, asking about how we think girls should be raised as opposed to boys, or whether they should be treated differently at all, or how it would feel to have a daughter who liked playing with guns or a son who liked helping out with the dusting."

"Or how every little thing you do is supposed to make this big dent in your kid's personality, and how that's such a heavy responsibility," added Merri, when a shriek filled the room.

"Damn it," mumbled Diane, picking up her little one from the carpeted floor. "Here he goes again." She stuffed a plastic nipple into her baby's mouth, only to have the little mouth angrily reject it. She tried it again.

"He's not hungry," said Merri with a mixture of sympathy and annoyance in her voice. "Don't feed him; walk him."

Diane started pacing, grumbling under her breath how she'd had it, while the rest of the conversation resumed. I looked at Merri, who had reflected the first sign of dissension in the group.

"Diane's always stuffing in the nipple and it bugs me because it doesn't do any good," she said defensively.

"Come on," said Val, sounding exasperated, "you should know what it feels like to have a child that cries on end."

"Yeah, but the answer isn't to feed, feed, feed."

Ricki, whose daughter was sitting on her lap tying her mother's hair in little knots, sat back for a moment as if to take an objective view. "If there's anything we fight about, it's what's wrong and what's right in terms of raising your kids. For a while a lot of what we said was behind the back—not really catty, but also not out in the open. But after you spend so much time together with the kids, it's hard to keep things behind closed doors. So we've had our moments, like when everyone thought I was breast-feeding for too long, claiming I was hanging on to my child too tight. Or when last year Diane complained that Deena was a clingy child but anyone could see that she was the one who was clinging to Deena. And sometimes it gets a little heavy because the implication is that you're not being a good mother."

"But it always works out," said Diane, returning with child sound asleep in her arms, "because we all know that none of us is perfect, that we're all vulnerable. So it usually ends up being productive, particularly if what the women are saying is right."

"Aha, you admit it," said Merri with delighted amusement.

Of course, not all young mothers are this fortunate. Theorists have known for a long time that a lot of issues that a woman never resolved with her own mother get addressed when she has a child, including her wish for a perfect mother. That's why there's often a lot of underground competition in certain friendship circles about whose kid broke the first tooth, whose child is smarter or prettier or more outgoing—and why women are more critical about other women's mothering than about anything else.[1]

"Some women try to become the perfect mothers to their children that their mothers weren't to them," Jane Flax told me. "So they set these incredibly high standards for themselves and need to see themselves as better mothers than the women they know. It may look like competition, but it isn't. In fact, it's usually the woman who's the most judgmental of other women who's the one that's the most critical of herself."

Why, I wondered then, didn't Diane, Val, Merri, and Ricki experience these problems?

"Because once women work out the fantasy of being the perfect mother, once they accept their own human limitations and imperfections as mothers, they are also willing to accept those limitations in others." It appeared that the four women had.

When I asked about any other conflicts, only one came to mind. There was, they had to admit, some jealousy in the group concerning who was closer to whom. Merri had called Diane instead of Ricki when her baby had to be rushed to the hospital with a violent stomach flu; Ricki had been insulted. And yes, they admitted, there were times they felt more comfortable with one friend than with another. But after all, wasn't that human nature?

I agreed that it was, and that night when I thought about my decision to work when my own children were small, I couldn't help but wonder what I had missed out on.

MID-LIFE CRUNCH AND THE I'M-JUST-A-HOUSEWIFE SYNDROME

Unfortunately, early motherhood and the nurturing friendships that develop around it do not last forever.

Traditionally, getting married and having children were considered the pivotal events in a woman's life. But recently, behavioral scientists have become aware of a far more tumultuous period in a woman's development: sending her last child off to school.

Whether a mother sighs in ecstatic relief the day she puts her "baby" on the school bus or weeps at the loss of the most gratifying period in her life, she's nevertheless aware that she is entering a new stage. Of course, no mother is immune to the pangs that come the first time her child says, "But I don't want to have milk and cookies with you, I want to play with my friends," or to the unpleasant reminder that her youth is slipping away when her child describes her teacher as "old," only for the mother to discover that this woman who's supposedly on the verge of decrepitation is almost exactly her age. But for the woman who's devoted all those years solely to her children, the message has an added sting. Not only is she getting older, but the whole of her identity is being pulled out from underneath her.[2] Earlier she probably wondered, "Is there enough time in the day to do it all?" Now another question seizes her attention: "What am I going to do for the rest of my life?"

The galling thing is that it's a question she often isn't prepared for. Her own mother, after all, probably just kept on doing what she had done before—raising the kids through adulthood as she patiently awaited the grandchildren who she could then help raise, too. But as our society has become more mobile, adult children are less and less likely to live close to Mom. The result is that the function of the grandmother is slowly becoming extinct.

But there's more to the homemaker's present-day dilemma than this. When her mother was a mother, almost all women stayed at home, (with the exception of wartime when women flooded the labor force). In fact, the woman who had to work was generally considered a pitiable creature who hadn't netted a good catch. Staying at home was considered a luxury, a privilege. She didn't have to defend herself or bolster her position—everyone else did that for her.

If anyone bore the brunt of criticism, it was the career woman. From the homemakers' point of view, they really weren't "women" at all. And there was a spate of psychological research to support that view, condemning women with such "deviant" ambitions as not quite normal, at best, and at worst, poor victims of childhood trauma. As one social scientist described it:

. . . the girl who aims for a career is likely to be frustrated and dissatisfied with herself as a person. . . . She is less well adjusted than those who are content to become housewives. Not only is (she) likely to have a poor self-concept, but she also probably lacks a close relationship with her family.[3]

The sixties began seeing a changing tide. The idea that a woman might expect to have a family *and* interesting work gained increasing acceptance, that is, so long as she continued to put her family first.

Which naturally meant that she would graciously accept the inequality in the work world that went along with motherhood.

By the seventies even this attitude had begun to change. In fact, the tables had almost completely turned from the fifties. Now the career woman was the one receiving all the accolades, and it was the full-time homemaker who was seen as the deviant. The notion that working mothers had low self-esteem was also overturned: it was now being reported that the woman who stayed at home was the one with the problems.[4]

Once heralded as women's God-given duty, the status of "occupation: housewife" has taken a nosedive. When one researcher added up the values assigned to all the functions of being a mother and wife in the *Dictionary of Occupations,* she found that not only housework but child care were at the bottom of the heap.[5] The result of all this imprinting on many homemaker's feelings about themselves has been dramatic. Once proud of who she was, the homemaker of today has come to dread the question "And what do you do?"

After all, she's "just" a housewife.

FILLING THE VOID

The woman whose children have left the hearth, then, finds herself bombarded on two fronts. She has a lifetime ahead of her to fill. But if homemaking isn't an option, then what?

Some women postpone the conflict by becoming pregnant again. As long as there's a young child at home, there isn't any conflict. Not surprisingly, the more children a woman has, the less likely she's going to leave the home—ever.[6]

Still others fill the gap by becoming increasingly involved in developing creative homemaking skills or by joining volunteer organizations. And for many women the desire to help, which has at its root a continuation of the maternal role, provides tremendous gratification that can give women the same kind of fulfillment that the woman in the labor force receives from a job or career.[7]

But for many women these options aren't enough. They don't want more children, and they don't see volunteer work as doing anything for their self-esteem, let alone their pocketbooks. After all, if it isn't paid, how important can it be?

The ultimate answer for these women is to enter the labor force, and some women make the transition with relative ease. Women who, for example, were teachers or nurses before they married find that their skills are still in demand.

Unfortunately, many other women face gloomier prospects; the "simple" act of finding a job, they quickly discover, isn't so simple at all. Expecting to be wives and mothers forever, many women never bothered to cultivate any marketable skills before they married. Others have been out of the labor force for so long that the skills they once had are almost antiquated. "Women, particularly women who never stopped working, can be very insensitive to these issues," Angela Fox told me. "Their attitude often comes across as 'Just get off your butt and find a job.' But for a woman who's been home so many years, even if she has marketable skills, it can be very threatening to go back to work. It's a whole other world out there that she has very little familiarity with. To add to the problem, many women who choose to stay at home full-time are dependent to begin with."

Many women also face a lot of resistance from their husbands, who have gotten used to a spic-and-span house and dinner on the table every night, and who enjoy being "spoiled."[8] "The biggest problem I'm having with my husband now is that while I want to go back to work, he wants me to be a housewife," confessed a talented thirty-two-year-old cartoonist. "It wasn't always like that—I had worked for almost ten years before I had my first child and decided to stay home for a while. But over the years he's become accustomed to having the house neat, his socks picked up, his dinner ready and waiting, and my taking almost sole responsibility for the kids. I'm afraid that if I went back to work now, my marriage would be ruined."

The most difficult hurdle of all, however, is not practical but psychological: Women who have stayed at home for many years often become hooked on being caretakers. And a lot of that addiction comes from having caring, reliable friends who are constantly available to provide emotional nourishment. Given women's pull toward nurturance, it's hardly surprising that leaving an environment in which love is in constant supply is so difficult.

And why the woman who makes the smoothest transition back to work usually has a little help from her friends.

For three years, at least three times a week, Jodie Matthews' day was absolutely predictable. She would return home from dropping her children off at school, read for an hour, and slip into a long, luxurious bath. A dead look-alike for Cheryl Tiegs, she would then put on one of her Ralph Lauren polos and Geoffrey Beene slacks. After blow-drying her hair and putting on her makeup, she would either pick up the phone to call her friend Risa or would wait for Risa to call her.

"Well, what's up for today," one would say to the other. Sometimes they agreed it was best to catch up on the housework and would spend their days alone, calling each other regularly at two-hour intervals. But most of the time they would make plans to spend the school-day hours together—shopping, going to a movie, taking a swim at the local spa, or just talking, which being "like sisters," they did openly and with great frequency—about husbands, their kids, life and death. It was a ritual Jodie loved and once thought could last forever.

In fact, if anyone would have suggested to Jodie ten years ago that she'd be enrolling in courses so that she could find interesting work, she would have snickered. Raised in a household where it was considered a privilege to be the pivot around which the family was spun, becoming a mother and wife had been her only aspirations. She'd also be the first one to admit that a primary criterion in choosing a husband was finding someone who would take care of her—finding "a father figure," actually, which was why when she met Peter she was convinced that her life would be as homey as kitten's fur. "He was sixteen years older than I, and I looked up to him with a kind of reverence," she says. "I loved being taken care of and he loved taking care of me. We were perfect for each other."

For the next ten years Jodie's life couldn't have been more perfect. She had two sons with hair as blond as golden spun thread, and adored being a Mommy. Her small house had a fresh scrubbed look like Jodie herself and was often filled with the aroma of freshly baked carrot bread. Did she feel bored? Ungratified? Not on your life. She had her husband, her children, her friends, her home. "Peter would sometimes say affectionately that I reminded him of Donna Reed, and in a way he was right. Being a homemaker was the most natural thing in the world to me and I loved it."

Then at thirty-two her life, which had fallen into place as neatly as a child's jigsaw puzzle, started coming undone. She had just sent her youngest boy to first grade, and all at once Jodie began feeling as if the rug had been pulled out from underneath her. "I felt like I was slowly being phased out of a job, like a secretary whose functions are being taken over by a computer. All of a sudden, I had this six-hour-a-day void to fill. And I knew it was going to get worse—as it was, when my nine-year-old came home from school, he was more interested in playing with his friends than in being with me."

That same year she and Peter moved to another state, and Jodie was forced to leave behind the group of friends she had painstakingly developed over the years. And as studded as her old neighborhood had been with mothers, her new community was equally replete with young avant-garde professional women, many of whom were postponing having children or who said they wanted no children at all.

After six months of being more or less isolated, Jodie became depressed, then panicked. She began dreading the hours her children were out of the house, grabbing on to any excuse—a sniffle, a feigned stomachache—to have one or the other home with her. "You've got to find something to do with yourself," Peter told her one evening when she burst into tears because her oldest son wanted to spend the weekend at his friend's house.

She knew Peter was right. But then again, what exactly was she supposed to do? Run out and get a job as a cashier at the A & P? That was about all her skills afforded her, and that didn't sound like liberation at all. Instead of grappling with her own wavering identity, she made Peter the villain. "You've encouraged me to lean on you for everything all these years," she'd scream as if he had tied her to a ball and chain. "Besides," she would add, "maybe if you didn't need a mother as much as the kids, if you picked up after yourself or cooked from time to time, I wouldn't be in this position."

Later Jodie would admit, "The truth was that even though I didn't know what to do with myself, I wasn't ready to go to work. I had built a life for myself as a mother and wife, and that was all I knew."

Jodie decided to become active in a local charity, where she met Risa, a woman whose position duplicated Jodie's exactly. She, too, had recently sent her little one to school and found her identity as a mother tottering. The women connected almost instantaneously. Jodie admired Risa's sense of humor, and she would double over laughing as Risa sorted out old clothes from rags that weren't fit for a pauper singing "Tiptoe Through the Muumuus." And when Risa stormed out the door because she had been scolded for putting too many ripped up dresses in the "unsalvageable" pile, Jodie followed. "We can find something better to do than sifting through someone else's do-rags," Risa told her.

Over the course of the next few months, Jodie and Risa began seeing more and more of each other—shopping, traveling into town, taking in a movie. And what started as an acquaintanceship quickly grew into what Jodie describes as the most rewarding friendship of her life. "I was very much infatuated with Risa," Jodie recalled. "She was witty and open and I trusted her completely. She was the type of person you could share anything with and she wouldn't reject you." There was so much warmth there that they occasionally called each other "Mom."

With Risa close by, Jodie's feelings of boredom and disquietude went away. No longer did the days seem long and unproductive—with Risa in her life there was always fun to be had. Even Peter noticed the change. "Thank God for small miracles," he'd say when he came home to a chipper, seemingly contented wife.

"I couldn't have been happier," Jodie told me. "It was as if I had found my best friend for life."

Without knowing it, she had also found a way of postponing her impending identity crisis. It's not uncommon among women who are trying to hold on to their identities as nurturers to strike up new friend-ships or strengthen old acquaintanceships as a way of allaying their anxieties about making a change in their lifestyle. If women feel a void in their lives as nurturers, what better way could there be to fill it than by finding someone else to nurture, and be nurtured by?

Jodie's contented state of mind, which indeed sounded enviable, lasted three years. And, Jodie suspects, it may have lasted much longer if she had not been shocked out of it.

It was supposed to have been a routine doctor's visit. Then the som-ber announcement at dinner. "I've got high blood pressure," Peter said.

Shock. Then the snap. "I don't know how to explain it," Jodie said, "but my whole view of things changed after that." Her morbid fears about Peter collapsing at the dinner table gave way to an obsession with low-salt/low-cholesterol cooking, then to a stunning realization. "It oc-curred to me that there might come a day when I would be living alone, when I'd have to make a life of my own." A life of her own? She couldn't even imagine what that would be like. "My husband, my kids —they *were* my life."

Of course, Peter wasn't exactly ready to be written off—he was only forty-seven and the doctor saw no real problem if he watched his diet. But a few years later Jodie can speculate on what she thinks was at the real heart of the problem. "I suspect that latching on to Peter's health problems was my way of trying to face up to the fact that my children were getting bigger by the day, that each year they needed me around less and less, that someday they wouldn't need me at all. And then what would I do?"

Some mothers, unable to make any changes in their lives, become overly involved in the lives of their children, living vicariously through them.[9] But deep down Jodie knew that latching on to one's children that way is not only destructive to a child's independence, but to the mother-child relationship.

She confided her fears to Risa. "I've really loved these years with you, but I feel as if I have to make plans for the future."

Sadly, Risa agreed. "Yeah, it's been great," she sighed, "but I suppose it can't last forever, can it?"

What may sound like a simple admission was a critical step for both women. Not only were they willing to question what had been a life's strategy they had planned for as long as they could remember, but they were in many ways putting their friendship on the line. As close as working mothers often are, they do not have the luxury of leisure time to build their relationships. They cannot call each other up every day— to talk, to vent, to exchange ideas—and expect there to be someone ready to lend them a sympathetic ear. They cannot be the kind of all-available, ever present "mothers" to one another that women at home can be, that Jodie and Risa had become to each other. And to any woman who's experienced that kind of relationship, it is not something that is easily given up.

The next few months began with great plans for their future forays into the working world. There were résumés to be written, contacts to be made, job hunting to be done. Yet at the end of three months they had gotten no further than determining which heading looked best on their almost nonexistent curricula vitae. The time they had set aside to get their plans together almost invariably boiled down to a discussion about the kids, or a leisurely drive to the beach.

Aware of the stall, their first inclination was to blame their inexperience—after all, could you really consider being on the PTA bake sale committee "Fund-Raising Experience"? Their husbands were also convenient scapegoats—how would they react when their well-planned meals were sometimes replaced by a Swanson tray? But there was something else at work which neither woman could put her finger on—the presence and availability of the other. And on some level it was beginning to register that going to work came with a steep price tag that neither had really counted on—the day-to-day intimacy with each other.

The dilemma came to light one afternoon as they were riding down the elevator in Risa's apartment building. Two weeks before, the women had treated themselves to lunch at a posh restaurant, and as they walked out the door, the waiter ran after them.

"Excuse me, Madame," he said, waving a fabulous Pucci scarf and looking directly at Risa. "I believe you've forgotten something."

Risa had never seen the scarf before. "Oh yes—how careless of me, and my favorite scarf, too," she said without flickering an eyelash.

Jodie broke up. "I don't believe you actually did that," she said as they giggled half the way home.

Now, riding in Risa's elevator, both women's eyes rested simultaneously on the handrail, where another forgotten scarf rested. Risa's eyes twinkled.

"Uh-uh," Jodie said, reading her friend's mind. "That one's *mine.*"

It would have been no different than many of the other silly times they had spent together, teasing, joking, had Risa not said when the hysterical laughter subsided, "God, I'm going to miss these times."

The unspeakable now spoken, and with all the cards out on the table, the two women broke down in tears. They spent the rest of the afternoon hugging each other and having a good cry. "It was as if we were mourning a lot of things at once—our roles as homemakers, our past lives, our relationship with each other. And we both knew that we were saying goodbye to something and hello to something else at the same time."

Indeed they had.

When I interviewed Jodie six months later, she was in secretarial school taking some courses she felt would be necessary to get the kind of job she could enjoy. And Risa, she told me, had found a job as a manager for a local dress shop. It's painful, Jodie admitted, not having her companion always there by her side. But in another way their relationship has become even stronger. "Not only is the time that we have together more precious, but in a funny way I feel more respect for Risa as a person. And," she added with a smile, "for myself, too." Her experience is the echo of many women. One study found that one of the first changes women noticed when they went back to work or to school for retooling was that they had greater liking and respect for other women.[10] And, one might suspect, for themselves.

Which isn't to say that the transition is easy. The desire to work may be contagious, with contacts with working women triggering the push to expand one's life in even the staunchest of housewives,[11] but it certainly helps when there is someone else with whom to make the plunge.

"If it hadn't been for my husband's health and for Risa, I could still be procrastinating about making a new start," Jodie told me. Suddenly, her nose crinkled with what was a new revelation to her. "Then again, if I hadn't found Risa, if I didn't have that kind of close friendship to buffer me against the changes that were occurring in my life, I might have gone to work a long time ago."

KEEPING THE ENEMY OUT

Unfortunately, not all stories have such a happy ending. When friends are at similar developmental crossroads like Jodie and Risa, support is the common pattern. But not all women want to make or are ready to make changes in their lives. What happens when one homemaker is open to grappling with the crises of middle motherhood and her friends are doing their damnedest to avoid them?

"I expected that my friendships would change when I went to work, that I'd have less time for the women I was close to, but I didn't expect that they'd all dump me," Katie Jaccoby told me.

Katie is now wiser and can see that in many ways she was a threat to Carol, Roberta, and Judy, the women with whom she had shared her first labor pains, the women around whom ten years of her life had been spun. But she had no such awareness when she became pregnant, gave up her job as a nurse, and moved to the community where she found her new circle of friends. She was twenty-three years old, married to an up-and-coming corporate attorney, and her life couldn't have been cushier. The idea that such a privileged woman could be envious of a working mother seemed preposterous.

"I had a nice house, a great husband, and wonderful friends who were very much like me. We had all worked a few years before we got married, and we all agreed that a mother's place is at home with her young children." When she quit her job, her husband was behind her all the way. So were her friends. "There were a number of working mothers in our town, and I guess you could say that we felt superior to them. We would watch the baby-sitter come, or see them take their two-year-olds to a day care center, and think, 'What did these women have children for?' It just didn't seem right to leave such young children with strangers."

Those sentiments lasted nine years during which Katie had a son named Scottie, a miscarriage, and then a hysterectomy. And during which Judy, Carol, and Roberta were central figures in her life.

"Our husbands were all very concerned with moving up professionally and weren't all that interested in the kids, so most of the time, we ended up relying on each other." Which, for the most part, was all right with Katie. "I loved those women, felt supported by them. We all took motherhood very seriously and felt we were doing something very important. I didn't feel at all torn about working—Scottie needed me at home, and I wanted to be at home with him. I can't imagine not having been there to watch him take his first step, or utter his first word."

But in what felt like almost a blink of an eye, little Scottie wasn't so little anymore, and when he entered third grade a feeling of panic set in. Was it that Scottie now preferred playing outside with his friends than being around Katie? Or the reflections in the mirror which bore testimony to the undeniable etchings in her skin which she knew would not vanish even after a good night's sleep? Or the fact that she and her husband seemed to have less and less to discuss these days? "I don't know what triggered it. I just began feeling bored—as if the excitement had gone out of my life. I just didn't feel I was doing anything very constructive."

Occasionally, a comment by Judy, Carol, or Roberta suggested they experienced similar rumblings. "I can see my epitaph," Carol had once said only half-jokingly. "It will read: 'To the memory of a martyr—Wife, Mother, and Treasurer of the PTA.' " But their complaints were always offset by what Katie later viewed as the great rationalization for staying at home: the welfare of their children. "They felt strongly that the best mothering was full-time mothering and anything less was, well, less."

Katie had bought that argument, too, when Scottie was little. But her son, who was now eight, had a number of friends whose mothers worked, and none of them seemed adversely affected by it. In fact, Katie would sometimes point out to her friends, they seemed happy and well adjusted. Take Johnny Richards, for instance, the boy who lived next door and was Scottie's closest buddy. He was the same age as Scottie, came home every day to a college-aged mother's helper who helped him with his homework, during which time his Mom would usually call and he'd tell her all about his day, and then go outside to play. "He was a real nice kid," Katie told me, "very well adjusted and mature for his age."

Judy, Carol, and Roberta, whose children ranged in age from five to ten, had different feelings about it. One day over coffee at Katie's house, for example, when Scottie and Johnny were playing soccer in the back-yard:

"I wonder what it's like for a mother never to see her child," said Carol with an air of loathing.

"Barbara spends time with him in the evening, and she calls him every day when he gets home from school," Katie countered.

"I wonder if she ever feels guilty about what she's doing to him," Roberta said in a tone that implied Barbara should have been charged with child neglect.

"Johnny seems very well adjusted to me," Katie once again asserted, only to be met by a chorus of "We'll see about that," as if the child were in a minefield and it was only a matter of moments before the explosion.

This type of response is not uncommon among women who are full-time mothers, discovered Jean Curtis, who conducted a study on working mothers. That's because the idea that a mother might be expendable threatens the full-time homemaker's whole rationale for remaining at home. The argument goes something like this: "If it's so easy to replace a child's mother, why stay at home in the first place? So continuing to stay at home becomes a justification for having stayed at home."[12] These mothers' defensiveness is also fueled by the fact that there's virtually no evidence that suggests that mothers of school-aged children who work are more likely to have children with emotional problems than mothers who stay at home. To the contrary, there is some evidence that despite the pressures of combining work with family life, women who work generally enjoy motherhood more than those who don't.[13] Which is why, one might suspect, women like Carol, Roberta, and Judy are so bent on proving this is not so.

A few months later Katie received a call from Barbara. "The school just called me saying that Johnny slipped and fell in the lunchroom. I talked to him and he's alright, but the nurse thinks he might have a broken toe and that he should have an X ray. I have a big meeting with an important client this afternoon, and if you can't pick him up and watch him until I can get away, I'll come home, but . . ."

"No problem," interrupted Katie, who didn't resent the favor but was struck by the fact that she had nothing more important to do that afternoon than buy some oyster sauce for a Chinese dish she was preparing for dinner.

Telling the story to her friends, however, unleashed a Pandora's box.

"What kind of mother would not drop whatever she was doing to be with her child in a crisis like this?" commented Roberta disapprovingly. "And to think of how she's using you."

"It wasn't a crisis," Katie argued, "and what's wrong with helping a neighbor out? Besides, the same thing could have happened to any of us if we were out for the day."

"Come off it," countered Carol. "There's a big difference between being away for a day and being unavailable to your child every day. And I can't understand why you're defending this woman."

Because, without knowing it, Katie was already taking preliminary steps to move away from her position as full-time homemaker. Unconsciously, she was looking for support from the women who were closest to her, support that did not come.

Of course, if Katie had to work for financial reasons, she probably wouldn't have met such resistance. It's the choice of wanting to work when she can afford not to that's disturbing to the full-time mother. "The prosperous housewife who wants to work . . ." notes sociologist Mirra Komarovsky, "must acknowledge that she wants to 'realize her potentialities' or 'be a person in her own right.' "[14] Which means saying that the traditional role does not suffice. The guilt of this acknowledgement, one study found, can be so unnerving that some women insist to their children that they have to work for the money, even though they are financially well off.[15]

Katie was not immune to these guilt feelings, and her friends' lack of support didn't help.[16] For the next year she tried warding off her discontent with staying at home by doing what she had been doing but more of it. "I became totally absorbed in Scottie's life—his schoolwork, his soccer team, his friends. I was becoming the epitome of the overly involved mother who hangs on to her child's every move."

Still, it wasn't enough. Even Katie's husband began noticing that she was more edgy and emotionally volatile than usual. "I don't think that staying at home is doing much for your disposition," he said one evening when she slammed a burned roast on the table.

"But I thought you liked having me home," Katie said with hurt and surprise.

"I liked having you home when you wanted to be here—I don't like being the whipping boy for someone who seems to be resenting every minute of it!"

Katie also couldn't help but notice that Scottie's favorite expression those days was "Get off my back, Mom."

"I began to realize that my staying at home had nothing to do with anyone else but me," she told me, embodying the findings of one study that found that husbands who supported the traditional role were less resistant to having their wives work than the wives themselves.[17]

It was in the midst of this psychological turmoil that Katie read *The Cinderella Complex* by Colette Dowling, a book whose underlying premise is that women are afraid of being independent. "It really had an impact on me. I read it in half a day. And all I kept thinking is, 'Yes, this is all true. She's talking about me, Carol, Roberta, and Judy.' And that's when I knew that I was going to have to get out of the rut I was in."

Feeling as if she had made an earth-shattering discovery, Katie brought up the book the next time the four women were all together. She explained, with heated enthusiasm, the book's main premise: that women run away from responsibility; that not working at this point was symptomatic of their dependency; that remaining dependent ultimately had devastating effects.

"Here we are, bored half the time," Katie told the group, "and yet not one of us has ever suggested that things could be different. We haven't even considered the possibility that our kids can probably get along just fine without us at home every day." The women were silent, eyeing one another surreptitiously as Katie continued her diatribe.

"Well," Katie finally said, realizing that she had been conducting a monologue, "What do you think?"

"I'm not much for all this psychological stuff," responded Roberta, admiring her manicure.

"I'd rather be bored under my own roof than working at a boring job under someone else's," added Carol.

Only Judy seemed sensitive to the real heart of the issue. "Look," she told Katie, pulling her friend aside, "if you want to go back to work, then do it. No one's stopping you. But obviously, we're not ready to do that. Maybe you're right; maybe we do like being taken care of, but you're not going to change that. All you're doing is rocking the boat."

Indeed she was: Katie was shaking the very foundation upon which her friendships had been built, a scaffolding that had been painstakingly built to support the traditional female role. And it's a basic tenet of group dynamics that the group tends to keep its members in line by virtue of its norms, that it has a way of reinforcing it's own values while keeping conflicting values, or the enemy, out. For Carol, Roberta, and Judy, the norm that was to be protected was that of the full-time, sheltered housewife; the enemy, independence.

By surrounding themselves with women like themselves, the women had kept the conflicts about being a housewife under wrap. Their lives were safe and their friendships were safe as long as they abided by traditional rules. What they needed were women who supported staying at home, who protected them from the fact that the role of full-time Mom was slipping away. What they didn't need were women like Katie, women who threatened the status quo, which was perhaps not very exciting, but was, at its most fundamental level, safe.

Which is why, one study on working mothers discovered, one of the first changes a woman notices when she leaves for the labor force is that her friends leave her.[18]

"When I finally did go back to work, my friendships with Judy, Carol, and Roberta took a nosedive," Katie told me. "It was anything but blatant at first, but suddenly I wasn't asked to be included anymore in the joint activities with the children. There were just these little exclusions, like not being told the ins and outs of everyone's daily lives. It got to the point that they just stopped calling me. The obvious explanation was that we were no longer in the same situation, that I didn't have as much spare time to spend with them. But I couldn't help but feel it went deeper than that, that they were both jealous and disapproving of me. Still, it hurt a lot—imagine, a decade of friendship out the window—just like that. I'm still not sure I understand what really happened."

What happened was that Katie's friends were struggling to preserve an endangered way of life. And if the defense has to be so strong, it's because the full-time homemaker's position has become increasingly weak. Statistics presented at a conference of the Coalition of Labor Union Women in 1984 showed that despite the hurdle of combining children and work, 60 percent of women with children under six are working outside of the home.[19] Women's attitudes toward the traditional mother-wife role have also undergone a turnabout. Fewer young women than older women agree that "having a loving husband who is able to take care of me is much more important to me than making it on my own"; that "my life is much easier than a man's since I don't have to worry about earning a steady income"; that "to be really active in politics women have to neglect their husbands and children," and "women should take care of running their homes and leave running the country up to men."[20]

What about the argument that women are working not because they want to but because they have to? Not so, says a New York *Times* poll. Given the choice, 58 percent of American working women said they would rather work than stay at home, and 31 percent of women at home said they'd rather be working.[21]

It's therefore not surprising that women who choose to stay at home have assumed a defensive posture. While not wanting to enter the labor force, they nevertheless feel denigrated by the emphasis on independence and achievements in the outside world. In fact, writes sociologist Jessie Bernard, "the constant assault on them . . . is the major fly in the ointment so far as they are concerned. The one thing that could make them happier would be the disappearance of all those successful and happy 'career mothers.' "[22]

Needing to justify their position, full-time mothers grab ahold of the longest straw they can find, which is the importance of motherhood, and lay the guilt on working mothers. Quite successfully, I might add. "It took me months to not attribute every problem that Scottie was having to my working," Katie confessed.

WOMEN WHO WORK AND WOMEN WHO DON'T

But the rejection of women like Katie is only half the story. A year after I interviewed her, Katie called to tell me that she had bumped into Judy.

"How's the old crowd?" she asked uncomfortably.

"Oh, I don't see them much anymore," Judy told her. "I started working a few months ago. I wanted to call you but I was too embarrassed."

Katie nodded her head in understanding. "So they gave you the brush off, too."

"To tell you the truth," Judy admitted, "it was really the other way around. Once I got a job, I found I didn't have much in common with them anymore."

If the defensiveness of the homemaker is easy to understand, the feeling that women like Judy have, that once they go to work they want little to do with their friends who are still at home, is less obvious. That's because the defensiveness of the working mother is a subject that's frequently ignored, as is the desire to be taken care of which looms among even the most successful women.

The fact is that inside of many working women, there is a woman who has not completely gotten rid of her need to be dependent. No matter how prestigious the job, there is still a part of her that would prefer to lie back and have her needs tended to. For some the need is right on the surface. The woman who is forced to work for financial reasons, particularly when her children are young, undoubtedly will feel jealous of her more privileged counterpart, often accusing her of being a slouch or a parasite. "The women in my community who have to work think that I'm lazy," one woman who decided to take ten years off from work to raise her children told me. "I'm not lazy at all—I have my hands filled with the kids and am very involved in raising them. But they're envious of my position, so they're very down on me."

But what about women for whom working is a choice, women who are gung ho on the career track? Even here, says Angela Fox, there's likely to be a conflict, an underlying fear that they can't really take care of themselves. "I see it in my patients all the time. These are women who have wonderful jobs, who make a lot of money, and yet they still think of themselves as not being able to take care of themselves. They worry about risk taking. They look at the man for a sense of security. One woman I'm seeing is going through that right now. She's thirty-five and has been taking care of herself financially since she's been eighteen years old. She's in the process of divorcing and what looms large in her mind is her ability to fend for herself. Meanwhile, through her nine-year marriage she was supporting her husband half the time. She didn't integrate that. She still looks to the man for the whole package of security. It's the child in her—the child that still feels she has to be attached to someone stronger to survive."

Of course, for women to admit this dependency would be too threatening, which is why it often comes out as a kind of loathing directed at the woman who is being taken care of. Writes Simone de Beauvoir in *The Second Sex:*

> A comfortably married or supported friend is a temptation in the way of one who is intending to make her own success; she feels she is arbitrarily condemning herself to take the most difficult roads; at each obstacle she wonders whether it might not be better to take a different route.[23]

Freud once said that the more you want something that you can't admit to yourself, the more you're likely to despise it. From this we might guess that the women who are yelling the loudest, who criticize homemakers the most, are the ones who have their own demons of wanting to be dependent to ward off.

WHAT'S SO WRONG WITH LEISURE?

Which leaves one question unanswered: If the road to being a working mother is so tough, and working is no panacea (as most any woman will attest), why don't all women who can afford to stay at home do just that?

For some women it's simply not a choice. "A woman who's been programmed to achieve early on psychologically can't afford to stay home," Angela Fox told me. "Too much of her identity is wrapped up with becoming successful outside of the home."

But what about women like Katie's friends, who claim to be content, who are not driven to achieve? The answer is that while homemakers often present a cheerful veneer, they are frequently psychologically distressed. While describing their lives as fulfilling, one study found that on projective tests the women were experiencing "considerable psychic turmoil, a depressed sense of emotional well-being and low self-esteem." The women doubted their attractiveness to men and did not feel "competent at anything, even child care and the social graces, let alone work and intellectual functioning." They felt "somewhat lonely and isolated . . . uncertain and on the sidelines," and while their lives had worked out as expected, they felt "an inexplicable sense of failure and disappointment, of having been left behind."[24]

Women who don't earn money also tend to experience themselves as relatively powerless in the family. While in Japan a husband's salary is handed over to his wife, and she's the one who controls the purse strings to the point of giving him an allowance, in this culture power is determined by how much money a person earns. And the less money a woman makes, the less of a voice she's likely to have in the monetary decisions of the family.[25]

Not surprisingly, these feelings often have a way of siphoning down into women's friendships. In my interviews I have been struck by how many homemakers told me that there was often an underlying competition about money and kids in their relationships with women, as well as considerable behind-the-back gossip, which, while feeling badly about it, they somehow could not control. My own guess is that it is not viciousness that is being expressed here, but frustration. Or as author Louise Bernikow put it:

No one speaks of the deprivation out of which this kind of conflict are made; no one notices the narrowing of the female sphere so that all that is left to a woman are her clothes, her looks, her husband. No one sees that energy misdirected misfires in the direction of the nearest victim, another woman.[26]

If working is no miracle drug, it does cure many of these ills. Even women who work initially out of need, who do not have glamorous or exciting jobs, are beginning to admit that there are many unanticipated rewards: "the enjoyment of social life on the job, the pleasures of workmanship, the bracing effect of having to get dressed up in the morning, some relief from constant association with young children and 'having something interesting to tell my husband about.' "[27] No matter how unimportant the job, mothers who go back to work also have a restored sense of self-esteem. In an experiment sponsored by the National Institute of Health, it was found that in the process of working or going back to school, "the women discovered they could exist as separate individuals in their own right; they no longer need to live only for their husbands and children."[28]

Many women are beginning to recognize this. Even women between the ages of forty-five and fifty-four are finding ways to overcome their dependency and are flooding the universities and the marketplace: By 1990 it is anticipated that almost 60 percent of women in this age group will be in the labor force.[29] And what about women like Carol and Roberta who cannot break free, even when the children grow up and move away? It's these women who are most likely to become hooked on tranquilizers.[30] Overinvolvement is another potential side effect of leisure living. A study of nonworking women in energy boom towns concluded that when well-to-do women are unemployed and don't join organizations, they become bored, depressed, and "obsessed with their families to the point of losing their self-worth and identity."[31] And the more cushy their lives are financially, the gloomier the prospects become—the highest suicide rate in the country, one study reported, is among women who are homemakers and who live in the most affluent areas of the country: northwest Washington, and Chevy Chase, Maryland.[32]

Despite the drawbacks of staying at home, there is still a sizable minority of women who do not want to work—either because they're truly dependent, or because the rewards of working just don't appear to be worth the costs. Then there are others who have become disenchanted with working or have difficulty handling the strains of the roles of mother and breadwinner. And as female participation in the job market increases, there's also bound to be a ceiling on jobs. What, then, are these women, whose self-esteem is sagging but who can't seem to find the way out, supposed to do?

There are no easy solutions. But my own guess is that in terms of the mother with young children, it would help if working mothers didn't make them feel so defensive, if the chasm between working and non-working mothers wasn't so wide. Recently, at a barbecue, for example, I spent an hour talking to a fascinating woman who was incredibly well read. Having heard through the grapevine that I was a writer, she said at the end of our conversation, "You know, I've been dreading this whole hour that you were going to ask me what I did, because, you see, I don't do anything."

"But I thought they were yours," I said, pointing to the two munchkins, one crawling, one playing on the lawn.

She smiled in genuine appreciation. "You're the first working mother I've met that seems to understand that just because I don't work doesn't mean that I don't do anything."

I did not have the guts to tell her that if she had met me two years ago, before writing this book, before getting an inside look at the life of mothers who choose not to work, that when it came to asking the question "What do you do?" I probably would have been the first one in line.

Chapter 7

THE NEW WOMAN, THE NEW FRIENDSHIP

WHILE women at home are trying to figure out what to do about atrophy of the brain, working women are wondering how not to crack under the overload.

THE COST OF HAVING IT ALL

Only a few decades ago burnout was something that happened only to men. But for the women I've spoken to, some as young as their mid-twenties, the fizzle's already begun. "I'm sure the women's movement never meant things to turn out like this," said a twenty-eight-year-old personnel director who is pregnant with her first child, "My days just seem like a vicious circle. My husband and I get up, shower, dress, and guzzle down a cup of coffee, and we're off to work. For the next eight hours, sometimes longer, depending on the time of year, I'm busy answering phones, meeting people—everybody wants you to do something. By the time I get home, I'm so exhausted all I want to do is sleep or stare at the tube. Half the time we eat out—not great when you're pregnant, but who has time to cook? We talk for a while, maybe I'll call a friend, then it's back to the same old thing."

Later in the interview she tells me, "I interview women my age all the time—women who say that they want to have 'careers.' Sometimes I feel like telling them, 'Forget it. Stay at home and be thankful you don't have to work.' "

As the saying goes, "She ain't seen nothing yet." What's this same woman going to do, how is she going to feel, once the baby comes? As it is, most married women who work will tell you they haven't got much leisure time. Women with children are even harder pressed; working mothers are reported to have less than two thirds the free time enjoyed by their husbands.[1] Of course, the tendency of the young and prosperous is to think you can hire most of the drudgery out—hire a nanny, a housekeeper, a college girl to run errands, and things will run just fine. But the fact is, few women who work can afford such luxuries, and the average working wife ends up putting in each day over two hours more work than the nonemployed wife.[2] And even when a woman can afford household help, there is no way you can pay someone to love your child.

What about husbands? An increasing number of working mothers don't have one. And in those households where there is a husband, he usually does not contribute enough to the household work to make much difference. Household responsibilities are still far from a 50-50 deal.[3] Even when they *do* help, studies show that husbands' paid work time goes down when they accept these additional responsibilities.[4] One researcher goes so far as to conclude that "every time a wife takes a paying job, she will work harder and her husband will work less hard, on the average."[5] The situation is pretty much the same when it comes to child rearing. While more men are pushing strollers and changing diapers, the psychological responsibility as well as much of the day-to-day caretaking responsibility, still rests with the mother.[6]

What, then, does it really take for a woman to "have it all"? Some experts say she has to work as hard as a man. They're wrong. She has to work harder.

TIME WARPS

Where does this leave us in terms of our friendships? You wake up at 6 A.M., feed the kids breakfast at 7, get off to work at 8. After a grueling day, you shop for a nutritionally balanced dinner that everyone will eat, run home and spend the next half hour listening to the din of La Machine, and secretly wish you could crawl into a dark, quiet hole. But the kids need to be fed, given attention, bedded down. And of course, you want to spend some time with hubby, too. With only twenty-four hours in the day, how much time is there to spare?

The answer is, not as much as we'd like. As one woman quoted in *New York Magazine* recently put it, "I'm on the go all day, and at night I have to be home with my husband and baby. Something has to suffer. Too often it's friendship." The article goes on to draw two blunt conclusions: Working mothers experience the problem most severely, and— "what else is new?"—men have had these problems all along.[7]

How have men dealt with the dilemma? Judging by the voice of experience, we find a simple answer—most don't have close friends. And those that do generally center their time together around a shared activity, such as squash or going out drinking with the boys.[8]

Maybe that solution is fine for men, but it doesn't work for women. Time may be short, our stamina may be pushed to the edge, but our need for supportive relationships with women is greater than ever before. Women have always needed other women's support for becoming independent to undo mother's taboo about separation; a feeling of approval that allows us to say, "I am becoming my own person and that's *okay.*" And of course, we need the feeling of validation that only another woman can give. As Margaret Thatcher recently said, "I don't think any woman . . . really has a happy life unless she's got a large number of women friends . . . because you sometimes must go and sit down and let down your hair with somone you can trust totally."[9]

And yet, we, too, like men, must come to terms with the changing structure of our lives. We no longer have the time to "kaffeeklatsch" or spend the afternoon goofing around. As we struggle to restructure our lives, we are also struggling to restructure our friendships. We need to find a modus vivendi between the intensity of seeing each other all the time and the isolation of superficial acquaintanceships.

And we have.

THE MA BELL CONNECTION

On a night like many others, the phone rings. It is my closest friend and she announces herself simply, "It's me."

She is just starting her own business and I know this week has been packed with meetings.

"How *are* you?" I ask, which in women's shorthand means "How do you *feel?*"

"Eh." Pause. Her meetings, she says, went fine, but she's sitting in her house with clothes strewn everywhere. She doesn't know what the hell she should be doing or where she's going. Should she get a file cabinet or should she clean up her house? As it is, her husband's already bitching and moaning about the sty. Then again, she'd actually just rather stay in bed. Or go on a vacation. Like three years.

I reassure her. "I got more pleasure from petting my cat today than doing anything else."

We laugh and then get down to business. Together we figure out that she's not too terrific about setting priorities. We make mental lists and then devise a game plan: This week write the proposal for the new business; next week clean up the slop and get a file cabinet.

"Well," she says, "how about you?"

I tell her about the problems we're having closing on our new house, how I have a manuscript to finish, the Bas Mitzvah of my daughter to get together, and a move to make in the next three weeks. And of course, I absolutely must have the floors scraped and the place freshly painted before I move in.

"You're nuts," she tells me. "Screw the floor and the paint."

I cross off the calls to the painters and the floor scraper from my check list.

All that in twenty minutes.

The next half hour we talk about our mothers (with whom, of course, there's always some problem), my kids, (who, of course, are always having some problem with me). She tells me not to feel guilty; most kids have problems with their mothers, even if their mothers don't work. We go on about how we should have married rich, half kidding, half serious —about how nice it would be to work only when you felt like it—and only at things you felt like doing. Of course, neither of us is cut out of the homemaker mold—but we luxuriate in the dream anyway.

"I sure could use a night or a weekend with you."

"Me, too."

We look at our schedules—she with her meetings, me with my move —and realize it will probably be four weeks before we can get together. It's already been four weeks since the last time. It depresses us—this work, this schedule-a-friend, this unburdening of our souls via telephone wires. "It'll sure be nice when we don't have to live our lives this way anymore," she says.

I know exactly what she means. I also know that in forty-five minutes we have given to each other a year's worth of therapy. We all get our first glimpse of who we are from our mothers—and both our mothers think that working while raising children is for the birds. We have become to each other the mirrors our mothers once were, and what is reflected back is "I think you're terrific," and "You're not alone; I feel the same way, too."

LONGTIME FRIENDS

Another source of alleviation of the potential isolation that can set in because of the difficulties friends have in seeing each other is the knowledge that there's someone out there who loves us, who can be depended on. Even if we don't see her for years at a stretch.

"She's like a lifeline," said the sophisticated accounting executive. "I've known her since first grade. We've been through everything together. There is a continuity about having her for a friend; she's part of my life."

How often did she see her? I asked.

"Almost never. She lives in California, and if we're lucky, we get to see each other once a year. But that doesn't matter," she adds, "because we've known each other so long, I feel so sure of her friendship, that I know she's always there for me. I guess you could say because of her I really don't need that many other close women friends."

Old friends are like long-distance runners—they go on and on, way past the point they need any "real" fuel to run on. They have enough holding glue to survive physical and even emotional distance; they just pick up where they last left off, with the time and space that separated them seeming like a figment of our imagination. As far as a sense of security, these women really luck out. As the executive put it, "I can count on her to be there the same way I always wanted to be able to count on my mother."

SUPPORT NETWORKS

A new arrival in the lives of working women is the support system.

"Women must be extraordinarily talented, independent and motivated to achieve professional success without the support of an informal network," says sociologist Sandra Candy. "Women in all roles, particularly nontraditional, feminine roles, need supportive relations, especially those of other women."[10]

Women all over the country are hearkening to the need for that support as evidenced by the mushrooming of all kinds of formal and informal support groups. And what they are finding is that, while the group is originally centered around a certain problem, strong friendships are often the result.

When Madeline joined a group for divorced mothers, the idea was to exchange ideas and information about managing the responsibilities of work and motherhood without a spouse. For eight weeks they discussed strategies for keeping their lives together. But as they later learned, the interchange went far deeper than "how not to slug your kid when he says he likes Dad better."

"About a month after the group officially disbanded, my ex-husband had come into the house drunk and started abusing me. I called the woman in the group that I had felt closest to. An hour later almost the whole group was standing at my doorstep. I couldn't believe it! One took me and my daughter home with her. Another who was an attorney started filing papers. The rest took care of getting the locks changed and the windows bolted. I then realized I would have done the same for any of them. We had become friends."

FRIENDSHIPS WITH NONWORKING mothers in the neighborhood are another support link if women can get beyond the stereotype notion that working and nonworking mothers have nothing in common.

For years I watched Patti Tobias from my window—dropping her kids off to school, then retreating into her house or disappearing completely for the day. "What in God's name," I wondered, "does she do all day?"

A year after we had exchanged only cursory hellos I got stuck in a rush-hour railroad jam. As the stationmaster announced all trains were delayed for at least an hour, I panicked—my husband was out of town, my kids had no way to get into the house after their swimming class. I called Patti and shyly asked if she would look after them until I returned.

That got us talking. Not only did I learn that she was an interesting woman who read vociferously—but she had some remarkable ideas on child rearing. I began to appreciate how wonderful it was to have a house that smelled like fresh-baked oatmeal cookies. We began an exchange—she watching my kids when I wasn't home, I picking up a book or some exotic spice when I went into the city. She can tell me when parts of a manuscript are fuzzy and can calm me down when I feel blocked. I can help her with the many fund-raising proposals she works on for the charities in which she is involved. We have become friends in the truest sense of the word.

No relationships between working and nonworking women are entirely free of conflict, however. There is a part of me that would rather be baking oatmeal cookies and a part of her that feels she is not being as "constructive" as she could be. Sometimes I resent the fact that she does not have to worry about work deadlines, and sometimes she feels threatened by the fact that I do. But the bottom line of our friendship is this: We have learned to accept one another's differences.

FRIENDSHIP IN TRANSITION: LEARNING THE NEW RULES

That women are defying the clock and finding ways to give and to support in the same climate that men have not been successful is a kind of minor miracle.

Which isn't to say that we've solved all the problems.

If there's any critical element to the permission women are giving one another to grow as individuals, it is in overturning the old message that nurturance is at the expense of autonomy. And by doing so we're saying that we don't have to become like men in the process.

But there are more ingredients to friendship than support. Friends get depressed. They can be emotionally dependent. They can need you at the most inopportune moments.

It's here, many women tell me, that the waters get murky. For every woman that is waving the flag about how supportive women are of each other, there are others who are asking: What does it mean to be a *real* friend? How much, given the persistent tugs of husbands, children, bosses, can we expect friends to go out of their way for us? Behind the pointing fingers, there's usually a fair measure of self-doubt: How much are we willing to stretch our necks out for them?

"Oh, I have lots of friends that I can talk to, that I let off steam with, that help me talk through a problem," a woman named Denise told me. "But to tell you the truth, in a crisis I'm not sure that there's anyone I can count on besides my husband. And frankly, I hope that I never have to test it." Is it any wonder that therapists' practices are booming at an unprecedented rate?

One study shows, in fact, that women who think of themselves as nontraditional don't even look for qualities such as reliability and availability in their friends.[11] Some women might pounce on that finding as a testimonial to how "grown-up" we've become, how "reasonable" our expectations are of one another. But for many of the women I have spoken to, the reason women feel so iffy about asking their friends for favors has a simpler explanation: They are afraid they'll be rejected. Or the flip side—they don't want to be in a position of having to reciprocate.

Of course, defining what it means to be a true friend is as old as the concept of friendship itself, and is by no means exclusive to the "new" woman. But the fact is that coming through for a friend in need was a lot easier when our lives revolved around the home. Not always convenient, mind you, but at least we didn't have to worry about what the boss would say if we missed a deadline because we shopped for a sick friend. And there wasn't this nagging guilt that we weren't spending enough time with our husband or children. Or wondering how much we can commit to others when we don't have two minutes to ourselves.

Women aren't used to having to look at their friendships this way. We've been entering the work force so that we can develop some measure of independence—emotional and financial. Of course, we expect our friendships to change—how many working mothers have the luxury of spending a whole afternoon gallivanting around town? But most women have never talked about what the changes in our life scripts really mean in terms of what's reasonable to expect from one another. "Women who are in the process of redefining themselves are also going to have to redefine the nature of their friendships," Jane Flax told me in an interview. "Our husbands depend on us, our children depend on us, we're even responsible for putting food on the table—but everyone has limits." The question is, what exactly *are* those limits?

Some of the boundaries become obvious the minute we make our forays into the working world. You're in the mood to talk, but the other end of the telephone line doesn't cooperate. "I'm sorry that I'm not available to come to the phone right now," says the mechanized friend-voice, "but if you'll leave your name, phone number, and the time of your call . . ." Or you're dying to tell your friend about that hefty raise, but she's in the middle of cooking ratatouille, or halfway across the world making a million-dollar deal with her Korean contacts. Or you try to set up something as seemingly simple as a dinner date and you realize that you can't find a mutually available time in the next month. Few women feel resentful about these inevitable facts of life—sad maybe, but not angry.

Other girdles are not so comfortably worn. About now you begin to notice that there are some friends who say they'll call you back as soon as they can, and two weeks later you're still waiting for the phone to ring. You stew for a while and then decide: the hell with it—you'll call her back. The voice at the other end is saccharinely apologetic. But by her tone it is clear that she's forgotten about you, or at the very least, returning your call isn't high on her list of priorities.

Many women often say, "It's hard for me to let on to my friends how dependent I feel sometimes. They all seem to have it so together." I doubt that most women have it that together, but somehow women get the impression that everyone has their autonomy act more in line than they do. How is it that dependency, which used to be considered a normal, feminine trait, is now viewed as a kind of dirty word? In part, it's because many women share the fear that any expression of dependency automatically means a reversion to the old symbiosis. More likely is that many women are unprepared to grapple with a friend's dependency on them. There's a whole literature devoted to the "role strains" pressing on the working wife, and the suggested remedy often is to mobilize a number of strategic support systems.[12] Consequently, there seem to be an increasing number of women who need to be mothered but haven't much energy to do much mothering.

Of course, learning to rely on your own internal resources is all for the good. But the feeling that many women have that they can't really let their hair down with their friends also creates a feeling of alienation. It's the feeling: If she *really* knew me, she'd reject me. So why take a chance and let her know me?

WHEN A FRIEND'S IN NEED

The shades of gray are most pointedly felt in what women feel they can expect from their friends in a crisis. "A friend in need" has always been the slide rule by which true blue has been measured. The problem is that aside from lifelong friendships, all the other rules of friendship we used to take for granted are undergoing such an upheaval, we may not be sure of what we mean to our friends. Or they to us. And because obligations go hand in hand with how close you feel to someone, there's lots of room for confusion, disappointment, and ill will.

CARA JOHNSTONE told me, "If you would have asked me a number of years ago about barriers in women's relationships, I probably would have said, 'What barriers? There are no barriers between true friends.' "

Cara is now aware that this is a clouded vision. But you couldn't have told her that six years ago when she first met Irene.

Like many women, the original forum for their friendship was their place of work. Both had jobs as assistants for a mail-order company which dealt in fashions for the women who didn't fit the mold that women's bodies are all supposed to come from: the under five-foot woman, the strapping six-foot woman, and the zaftig woman. Both were extraordinarily talented, moving from assistant to full-fledged buyers in a matter of ten months. Still, both felt the corporate situation stifled them—how, they wondered, can creativity blossom within a structure where you spend more time writing interoffice memos than developing fashion lines? After many long discussions, they found a solution: They decided to write a book together on the side: *Fashions for Figures that Aren't In This Year,* they called it.

During the next six months they spent almost every spare moment together—working, laughing, exchanging ideas for their proposal, finding an agent. Six months later they got a bite—a ten-thousand-dollar advance from a major book company. Hearing the news, they jumped up and down like nine-year-old schoolgirls.

"I was incredibly attached to her," Cara told me. "We spent our days in the same office, our lunches together brainstorming on the book, the evenings calling back and forth with this or that idea. She was my alter ego—we both had our own strengths and together we were dynamite. I loved every minute of it. I loved her," she added. "She was so strong and together, and I would often find myself trying to model myself after her."

Two years later their book was in print and Cara was pregnant. She wanted to be home with her baby but couldn't afford not to work—financially or psychologically. After much consideration, she decided to quit her job and do some fashion consulting on the side.

All in all, it was a positive decision, but her friendship with Irene underwent a dramatic change. No longer did they have the day-to-day forum which guaranteed that they would see each other. And Cara was too involved with her infant and consulting responsibilities to even contemplate the idea of another project. They went from seeing each other five times a week to having dinner together once every two months. And while they spoke regularly, it wasn't the same.

"There was something missing," Cara remembers. "I can't put my finger on it exactly, but the friendship just seemed to be on a different level than it was before." She's right—something was missing: the intensity and closeness that often develops when friends are an integral part of each other's everyday lives. Just like the little girl who revels in the feeling that she is central to her mother's life, Cara and Irene had been central to each other. And that kind of attachment feels so good and nourishing that anything less seems bland by comparison.

Intellectually, of course, Cara, like most of us, understood that there was nothing to be done about the situation. But on an emotional level she began feeling more and more distant from Irene's life. It wasn't just that she wasn't seeing Irene or hearing from her as often, but that Irene had seemed to develop a whole other network of friends. "I know this sounds silly, but I was jealous. It was the feeling that before, we had been best friends and confidantes, and now I was just another person in her life. And I felt very lonely."

Her feelings were not unique or silly at all, I told her. Many women who are opting to work at home feel as if the rug of their support systems has been pulled out from underneath them. In fact, that the friendship was maintained to any degree at all is in and of itself a major accomplishment, with the majority of those relationships fading fast because they are neither geographically nor personally in tune with the woman's new life. As for making new friends in the neighborhood— well, they're not too easy to come by either, particularly in the suburbs, where the requirement for friendship is often availability for coffees and tennis.[13]

Cara compensated for her feelings largely by ignoring them. "Well," she thought, "so I'm not Irene's best friend, but we're still close." And every once in a while, she would receive a small token of Irene's affection: a swatch of exotic fabric that she had dug up in her travels and whose source she would share with Cara, or a little card in the mail which said things such as "Friendship is eternal." The friendship was different, yes, but it was not gone.

A few years later Cara's family moved so that her husband could pursue a job opportunity. The situation was only temporary—six months, in fact—but it was rough. Unused to living in the country, Cara found herself spending hours just getting the shopping done. And they were house-sitting in a home three times the size of their own. Cara couldn't wait to get home.

About a week before her scheduled departure, a week during which all of their belongings needed to be packed, the movers needed to be contacted, and the house needed a thorough top-to-bottom cleaning, the phone rang.

The voice on the other end was shaking. "Cara, it's Irene."

"My God, what's wrong?"

"It's my dad. He died this morning of a stroke."

Tears sprung from Cara's eyes. She knew Irene was as close to her father as she was to her own, and how devastated she would be if her father had died. "Oh, Cara, I'm so sorry. What can I do to help?"

The minute she said those words, she wished she could take them back. "Can I really just run off and leave everyone else to pack up?" she secretly asked herself. More conflicted was the thought, "Do I really *want* to?"

Irene had seemed to read her thoughts. "No, there isn't really anything. The people at the office have been wonderful. Jennie and Michelle have organized a kind of committee and they're taking care of all the arrangements."

Feeling as if Irene had taken her off the hook, they spent the next half hour talking, crying. It was hard for Cara—like most of us, thinking about death is not one of the more pleasant realities of life. "When's the funeral?" Cara blurted.

"Friday."

"I'll try to come," said Cara, "but things are so insane here with our moving back and . . ." Her voice trailed off.

"I understand."

"I love you."

"I love you, too."

For the next twenty-four hours Cara tried rationalizing herself out of going to the funeral, and with the upcoming move she certainly had some pragmatic ammunition. But inside, she was plagued with a stunning reality. "I wasn't the kind of friend I always thought I was," she said. "I always believed that real friends went out of their way for each other. I even ended some friendships when I felt that the woman was too selfish. And here I was doing the same thing." It was a dichotomy that plagued her.

But there was something else. "I kept thinking back to our phone conversation, about all these people who were there for her, and I realized that I felt left out of her new friendship circle and that I had felt that way for some time. And it just didn't seem I was such an important person to her anymore. Besides, I saw Irene as a person who could really *cope* with life. She'd always been able to handle whatever obstacles fell in her path. I really didn't feel that she *needed* me."

I heard the hurt in those words.

Still, she could not quite help but feel she had been a "bad mother," and when she moved back home, she tried to make up for the slight—visiting as often as she could, calling regularly. Then again, *did* Irene feel slighted? Certainly she didn't show it.

"One of my manufacturers offered me his house on the beach," she told Cara a month later. "Sam can't go. Wanna come?" That weekend they strolled along the beaches, talking about Irene's dad with tenderness and intimacy. It was, as Cara remembers, "like the good old days" when they worked together. She began to wonder if her guilt about not going to the funeral was really a projection of her own expectations for Irene. As much as Irene seemed to be holding it together, however, inside, she was falling apart. In fact, it was the first time Cara got an inkling of some of the insecurities that lay beneath the surface bravado of her friend's "having-it-altogether" veneer. Irene saw it, too, and decided to enter therapy.

A year later the two women were sitting in a restaurant. They were talking about—who knows what—when Irene suddenly turned serious.

"There's something I have to tell you."

"So tell."

Tears sprang forth. "I'm still hurt that you didn't come to my dad's funeral." Then a flicker of anger. "What the hell kind of friend are you anyway? You and Toby."

Shock. Toby had been a woman that Irene had known as long as she had known Cara. "You mean Toby didn't come either?" said Cara, trying to change the subject.

"The whole place was packed. My whole goddamned office was there. Everyone I knew was there. But her. And *you.*"

Avoidance. "What did Toby say about not coming?"

Irene shook her head. "She says she doesn't know why she didn't come."

"I know," answered Cara, truthfully. She explained how hurt she had been by what she saw as a decline in their friendship, how she had not felt truly important in Irene's life for a long time, how she felt Irene had so many other more "important" friendships.

"I don't believe this," said Irene with genuine surprise. "Those other people are friends, but not like you and Toby. I've always considered the two of you closer to me than any of the others."

"Oh, God," said Cara, salting up her fettucine Alfredo, realizing how hurt Irene had been, how betrayed she must have felt. She took responsibility for not coming, realizing that on some level the no-show was as simple as this: it was too damned inconvenient. Yet she could not help but wonder if Irene had something to do with it, that if, perhaps, she had let her know how much she was needed, she might have come.

"My therapist says I have trouble showing weakness and letting people know that I need them," Irene admitted.

"You should have said you needed me there," Cara said.

"And you should have *known* that I needed you," Irene retorted.

They both knew that the other was partially right.

They have spent much time since that day discussing what it means to be a friend these days—what it means for them to be friends to one another. Cara tells me that they've agreed on certain principles: You can expect a friend to drop whatever she's doing in a crisis. But you also have to make your needs clear and up front—it's not enough to say, "Would you mind coming over?" when you're feeling, "I need you here, *now!*" About other issues, they are less clear. Is it fair to expect a woman who has a child, like Cara, to be as available as Irene, who doesn't? Just how inconvenient is inconvenient—and by whose standards? Cara admits they haven't yet found the answers. All they can do is to keep the communication lines open to resolve any differences that come between them. That in and of itself, Cara says, has brought them closer.

They speak well, I think, for all of us.

WHAT HAPPENED between Cara and Irene is important not simply because of what happened, but why it happened.

The counterdemands placed on the "new woman" have made us susceptible to what sociologists call "role strain," an overload that comes from having to juggle too many responsibilities and expectations at once. But there is another kind of stress—role *conflict*—which comes from the demands of two or more roles that have conflicting interests. The costs of the stress are high. In this transition period, when we are struggling just to meet the demands of our jobs and our families, the extra burden of friendship, some researchers find, is enough to push a woman over the edge.[14] Friends in need are more than inconvenient—they may be the straw that breaks the camel's back.

The kind of connection women want from each other is another given. Valuing independence doesn't mean that, underneath it all, we still don't crave the kind of closeness we have been accustomed to. For all our liberation, women are saying things such as this:

"Recently, a close friend of mine had a two-week job on the Coast. I felt like she had abandoned me."

"When I recently called my friend, she said she couldn't fit me into her schedule for three weeks. I was damned insulted."

"One of the nicest things that's happened to me with a friend was having her call me at work. Her husband was out of town, and she was having a moral dilemma on her job. She was hysterical. I was terribly flattered that she had called me. She's so busy all the time, and seems to have her life so together, I was beginning to feel as if she didn't need me anymore."

"Sometimes when a friend calls me and I tell her that I'm too busy to speak to her right then, I hear this little hurt voice that's saying, 'Too busy? You're too busy to speak to *me?*' "

There is pain in these words—the pain of letting go of something cherished, of something needed. The routines of our lives may have altered the circumstances of our friendships, but from the voices of these women, what we expect from women deep down hasn't changed much: Be there when I need you. Don't leave me. Have time for me. When Cara says, "I felt Irene didn't need me," it sounds more like a hurtful slight than an excuse because she did not want to be inconvenienced. It is as if behind the voice of every liberated female, there's a little girl that's saying, "Where's *Mom?*"

The push-pull is all part of the transition we must make. That feeling of total involvement and connectedness to one another may feel good but is unrealistic given the new scripts of our lives. The difficulty is that most women are what psychologist David Gutmann calls "autocentric" in nature, which means we get a sense of stability when the things and people in our lives are available and stable; we judge what is meaningful by the amount of time we devote to any particular endeavor. What's the answer? To become, as Gutmann puts it, more "allocentric"—to get a sense of stability not from the constancy of the people around us, but from a stable sense of ourselves.[15] Our bonds with one another need to be more psychic than immediate. And we need to see these less intense relationships as satisfying, and not just making do with second-rate goods.

The anger which Irene feels but does not express is not a given, but nevertheless is a problem many women have. And these days we're not even sure when it's justified. Are we entitled to feel angry every time our friends disappoint us, or is this childish and immature? How much can you expect a friend to go out of her way for you, and you for her? Another question many women still have no answers to.

Of course, it would be a mistake to suggest that all women are confused about what it means to be a friend these days. The fact is, many women are strongly committed to coming through for their friends. One career woman, for example, tells me that her friend calls her from home to tell her she's sick with pneumonia. Her husband is out of town. In lightning time, she's at her friend's house mothering her—canceling an important business engagement without batting an eyelash. Sound like a superfriend? Not from the way she puts it: "I just pretend that I'm sick. Then there's no problem."

The flip side, of course, also exists. While we might not like the idea that some women aren't nurturing, the fact is, not all women are givers, and there are some who wouldn't lift a finger to go out of their way if your life depended on it.

But for every woman who can't give, and for every one who feels no conflict, there are hundreds of others who are in the process of working out the rules. It helps to think of it as going through a kind of transition —with the meaning of friendship riding the crest of the wave. Most of us are beginning to learn that there is no such thing as having it all. There is always some price. But we have yet to determine what that price is—and how the scorecard reads when we're done with the tally sheets. If there's one thing that can be said for sure, it is this: Most of us are trying.

FRIENDSHIP VS. SUCCESS

Whatever the problems for the working mother, they geometrically multiply for the woman who aspires to great heights.

Dr. Mirra Komarovsky, a renowned sociologist at Columbia University, tells me she has long been aware of the problems of successful women. "Relationships between women who are highly motivated to have a career can be very problematic. They don't have much time for talking. Their peers don't have enough time for psychological intimacy either. There is also a competitive aspect that keeps them from relating to one another as intimately as they might if they weren't so ambitious."

"The old male-male intimacy problem with a new face?" I asked.

"Exactly."

If women who aren't so ambitious have fewer problems along these lines, it's because they don't have to deal with the guilt of feeling they have betrayed their femininity. Psychologist Abraham Maslow speaks of a "hierarchy of needs," beginning with needs for food, shelter, and safety on the lower rung, continuing through the desire for belonging-ness and love to the need for esteem, and ultimately self-actualization.[16] This hierarchy is tailor-made for men, who are loved (and often chosen as marriage partners) for their devotion to their careers. For women, however, the same needs for self-actualization collide with our need to be loved, to belong. "Be smart, but not too smart," is the message we first get from mother, which is later reinforced within our peer group. Even in academic circles where girls are encouraged to achieve, there are certain unwritten rules and expectations that insidiously compromise self-esteem in order to achieve support and approval from others. "In my school everyone studies hard and wants to do well," says a sixteen-year-old sophomore who attends a specialized night school for extremely gifted students. "All the girls want careers. Even so," she hesitates as if to say the wrong thing might indict her, "there's this sort of law, I guess, that your friends are supposed to come first. What I mean is that, say you're studying for a final and your close friend calls you up, crying because her boyfriend has just broken up with her—it's expected that you'll talk to her and try to cheer her up, even if it means you may not do as well on the test tomorrow because you've spent three hours on the phone with her."

She goes on to tell me about an incident that happened about a year ago, the night before a history midterm, when her best friend called her up, hysterical, because her boyfriend had just enlisted in the Navy. An A student in history up to that point, she says she stupidly left her studying for the last minute, and with the added burden of having to console her friend, "barely got by on this one, by the skin of my teeth."

The girl had known about the exam, as they were in the same class, but nevertheless took the license to call with her troubles. "How did you feel," I asked, "when your report card indicated a grade far lower than you would have received had you not had to take care of your girl-friend?" "I suppose I felt resentful for a while; you know, grades are everything when it comes to applying to a top college. But at the same time, I understand where she was coming from. I mean, she really *needed* me, or else she wouldn't have called. . . . After all, what are friends for?"

The conflict between being a good friend, which for women translates into being there, and striving for success in a world where only a full-throttled commitment works, puts the career striver between a hard place and a brick wall. How do you meet the demands of friendship when it's already taking all your energy just to keep your career and marriage and children going?

THE FLIGHT FROM NURTURANCE

For some the only way to deal with the issue is to forgo not only friendships, but anything else that has to do with nurturance, for that matter, and head into working with a blinding laser vision. The super-achievers studied by Margaret Hennig and Anne Jardim generally waited until their careers were consolidated before they could even con-sider the idea of marriage and children. Few of them had any friends.[17]

Others marry and have children, but feel the split in their lives none-theless. "The only woman friend I have is someone who works as hard as I do," a woman who owns her own computer business tells me. "We talk whenever we can, but there's this tacit agreement that our relation-ship is on the back burner for a while. I mean, I barely have time for my husband. And my kids don't get much attention either, not only be-cause I'm not home, but because I'm wrapped up in my work so much of the time. How do friends fit into a situation like that?"

Later in the interview she goes on to tell me that she barely takes care of herself. "I run myself ragged, I get sick, and I'm back to work as soon as I can be. I have almost no fun. I know it's not a balanced way to live, but my feeling is that to be excellent at anything, you have to forgo the balance for a while."

Why do some women feel that they must choose between work or nurturance, that they can have only one or the other—to the point they don't even take care of themselves? The answer is both real and psychological. For a woman to succeed in the male world, she has to be not only as good as men, but better—in essence, more male than male. She is competing with men who can work all hours, and go off on business trips at the drop of a hat, because they have the support of their wives.

Psychologically, the resonance goes deeper. "The earliest message women get from their mothers says that it's not possible to be both nurturant and highly successful," says Dr. Flax. "Chances are she's seen her mother make all these sacrifices in terms of her work self in order to be there for her children. Or in the few cases where a mother was a real go-getter, the daughter may have perceived her mother giving up everything for her career, including nurturing her children. Either way, the message is, 'You can have either/or.' The result is that a woman who manages to integrate her work with her nurturing aspects experiences this as a betrayal of her mother. She's saying, 'Wait a minute; I don't have to do one or the other, I don't have to sacrifice the way mother did; I can do both.' That raises a terrible question of the way her mother lived her life. It's a betrayal for the daughter to do both, and betrayal ultimately leads to rejection. Therefore, many women feel that something horrible is going to happen to them if they manage to get the two together."

PREFERRING MEN

Other career-oriented women find they have friends, but most of them are men. "It's not that I don't want women friends," one high-powered woman confesses, "but I really don't feel comfortable with women who aren't at a similar professional level. And since there are very few women like that around, I've found that most of my friends are men."[18]

While her predicament is real, it may also reflect her need to stay clear from women, which, translated, means her need to keep her nurturant impulses under wraps. Then there's the possibility that women who become extremely successful do identify more comfortably with men. For a man it's accepted protocol to devote your whole life to your career. For a woman, even one who makes it in a big way, throwing herself headlong into a career may feel like an invalidation of her femininity. To say nothing of the judgmental eyes of other women. Her turn to friendships with men may be her unconscious way of saying, "Who needs to be reminded that I didn't turn out the way I was supposed to?"

Of course, there are a number of successful women who do find other women they can comfortably relate to. One finance tycoon who earns upward of a half a million dollars a year, for example, said that she blesses the day when she met her closest woman friend. Before that, as with others, her friendships had been with the men she knew. But, she admitted, "It just isn't the same as a close woman friend." Today, despite the fact that she spends most of her time traveling around the world, she calls her friend long-distance at least once a week, and the two talk for hours at a stretch. "My phone bills are ridiculous," she admits, "but the calls are worth every cent."

MOVING UP, MOVING ON

The real dilemmas, however, are not those of the women who've already become successful, but the women who are still working at it. A woman like this may very well start off having close women friends who are at approximately the same level of achievement. But what happens to those friendships when one starts moving up and the other one doesn't?

"ADVERTISING IS THE FORCE through which American culture shall once again enter the Renaissance," said the man at the podium.

"He must be joking," mumbled Lynn Steiner, reacting to the giggles of the woman sitting next to her. Exchanging wry glances, they got up and walked out.

That was the beginning of Karen and Lynn's friendship. While on the surface the two seemed like the odd couple—Lynn, a small-town girl; Karen, a daughter of Detroit—they felt the instantaneous connection that so many women speak of. Professionally, they shared the same field —Karen, a copywriter, Lynn, a jingle lady. Both were married and had kids. And both were as driven to succeed as Sherman tanks.

They were twenty-seven when they met, and had pursued other professions before. Karen had been a struggling nonfiction writer, Lynn, a struggling songwriter. But after a few years of the starving-artist routine, they had, each in her own way, come to the same conclusion: This is for the birds. It has often been said that advertising is the melting pot for frustrated artists. But the real truth is that many successful artists get their first breaks in advertising. That was the lure, the promise, that had attracted them.

Their relationship was based on a lot of things—fun, openness, and a penchant for fantasizing what it would be like to really make the big time. Plain old ordinary success was fine if that was all you could get, but deep down, each one dreamed about being a star. Of course, from the bleachers of their positions, the chances of that ever happening seemed remote.

Even more remote after Lynn was laid off. "They're canning the whole music department," she cried to her mother. "What the hell am I going to do?"

The typical reply: "I told you not to get involved in that cockamamie field. You should have gotten your Ph.D. in music—why, you could be a professor by now."

Like the good mother superior, Karen had different feelings about it. "You're terrific at what you do. Start your own business."

Those were words she later wished she had swallowed.

Lynn took Karen's advice, and three months later she had rented a small office, hired an office temp, and was ready for business. Except there wasn't any business.

"Hang on," said her friend, "It'll come."

And lo and behold, it did. Eight weeks later she was the proud contractor for one of the country's largest toy companies. The women celebrated over champagne. "To making it," they toasted.

Her career took off. Like a snowball, Lynn's success in landing the toy account brought another account along with it. Lynn began working like a fiend; even on the few short vacations she and her family took, her tape recorder and portable piano were close at hand. And she was on call—always. "When you're just starting out, you can't afford to miss out on one single opportunity," she rationalized. The truth is, that's a woman's fear—success seems so out of reach that even once we have it, we're sure it won't last or that it couldn't possibly be related to anything but luck.

What was great for Lynn's ego and her pocketbook, however, wasn't so terrific for her relationship with Karen.

"It was as if she was in another world—as if our friendship didn't matter anymore. I rarely heard from her, and when I'd call, she'd bitch and moan about how her mother was constantly calling her up at work and bothering her. I didn't want to say anything, but I understood how her mother felt. I also felt as if I'd been shelved."

To which Lynn replies: "Karen was acting like my mother. Neither of them seemed to understand that I didn't have the time."

A common rationale, perhaps, but inaccurate. We all have time. It's just how we choose to use it. As Angela Fox observed in her practice, "When a patient calls up and says she really wants to be in therapy, but she just can't fit in the appointment, you know and I know what she's really saying is that therapy is not a priority." The problem is that with all our scripting about success, it's pretty hard for a woman to say on the up-and-up, "Look, work is more important right now than our friendship." So instead, we blame it on time—as if the whole thing were out of control.

What is true is that women in Lynn's situation often need to invest themselves in their careers with a kind of tunnel vision—at least temporarily. It's not easy for a woman to be successful—everything in our psychological upbringing works against it. Which is why a woman may become so rigid, so seemingly one-tracked. That doesn't mean she's a cold, unfeeling bitch. On the contrary, chances are she's drawn to her nurturing side more than she wants to admit—which is why she has to defend so well against it.

It wasn't just the fear of being left that Karen was reacting to, but of being left behind. No doubt about it—she was envious. All along she wondered, "Will I be able to keep up? What's happening to our friendship? In my fantasy Lynn was going to be a rip-roaring success. She would be wealthy, travel around the world, hang around with the hotshots. And here I'd be ten rungs beneath her." Women have always used other women as a measuring rod for their own success. Which is why another woman's success can make us feel so utterly inadequate.

These feelings made it increasingly difficult for Karen to be supportive—how can you support something that makes you feel bad, that seems to be contributing to the demise of the relationship? When Lynn would call with a new idea, or more good news, Karen found herself looking only for the loopholes. "You're so tired," she would say. Or, "Have you considered what all this is doing to your family?"

"I felt terribly guilty about it," she tells me later. "I didn't want to hurt Lynn, but I couldn't seem to stop myself." That's because insecurity often leads to envy, and the ultimate aim of envy is to level, to equalize.[19] For reasons that should be obvious by now, one-up/one-down scenarios between women have unpleasant mother-daughter undertones.

From where Lynn was sitting, of course, things had a different ring. "I felt sabotaged. That's the only way to put it. I had expected Karen to be enthusiastic, and here she was putting up all of these obstacles, pointing out the roughest part of the situation. It was as if she didn't want me to be successful. She put a damper on the whole thing, and I resented it."

Why not talk it out? you might be wondering. Actually, Karen tried. "I feel left out, like I'm not good enough for you anymore, and it hurts," she told Lynn in one of their increasingly infrequent and strained conversations.

"I'm sorry you feel that way," was Lynn's reply. That was all. No explanation. No apology.

"It was insulting," Karen remembers, "as if she was saying, 'These are the facts of life, and tough titties!'"

To which Lynn replies: "I didn't know how the hell I was supposed to respond to that. What was I supposed to do? Stop working? Be less successful? I resented the fact that Karen didn't understand what I was trying to do. About the last thing I needed was her getting angry with me."

Lynn was on the defensive. She expected to get pats on the back from her friend, but now her experience is betrayal. She is a little girl again, filled with all the guilt about achieving and separating that was handed down to her by her mother. At the same time, she wonders, "Why the hell do I have to justify myself for becoming my own person?"

The dilemma is that while women like Lynn are in the process of shedding their old identities and want to see themselves reflected in a new light, women like Karen are saying, "Can a woman become successful without straining her friendships? And can friendship survive without regular maintenance, time, and energy?"

Sociologists report that even feminists live as if the conflict between being loved and being successful is axiomatic in women's relationships. While hailing the virtues of many traditionally "masculine" traits like independence and objectivity, they still can't get themselves to say that ambition, competitiveness, and skill in business are desirable character traits for women. In fact, they even view these achievement drives more negatively than women who don't identify themselves with the women's movement.[20] Even the feminist intuition seems to be saying that too much success for a woman comes with a steep price tag.

Which raises an interesting point: How is it that Lynn was managing to get by just fine without all that time—without, for all intents and purposes, the friendship?

The answer has to do with a concept called sublimation. "Sublimation" is the word used in the literature to describe what happens when you transfer energy from one area to another. High school boys, for instance, sublimate some of their high sex drive by channeling their energies into throwing a ball through a hoop. They get pleasure from the experience; their sexual energy has now found a safer, more acceptable outlet. When women plunge ahead in their careers, they are also sublimating—not necessarily their sexual energy, but their needs for intimacy. We are taking from one area and investing in another. That explains why a woman of the superachiever type can get along for such long periods of time without much intimacy—she is getting pleasure, that intimacy, so to speak, from her work and the gratifications it affords. The problem for Karen and Lynn was that Lynn was transferring her energy into her work, and was getting a lot of psychological goodies from it, while Karen was not.

While the problems might be clear, the solutions are not so easy to come by. On the optimistic side, there is always the possibility that women can sit down and work out their differences. More often, however, they do not live happily ever after.

Unless, of course, a twist of fate intervenes.

The rest of the year passed uneventfully. Karen continued to feel slighted, and Lynn pursued her new business with her usual drive. Then, two months into the New Year, Karen received a frantic phone call at work. Lynn's words were only barely intelligible amid the muffled sobs, but with questioning, Karen was able to interpret the gist of the situation. Lynn's major client moved to another jingle company, taking two other accounts along with it. The wheels of prosperous Lynn Steiner Music had come screeching to a halt. "Can you talk now?" Lynn pleaded.

"I was really a basket case," Lynn recalls. "It was in the middle of the day. My husband was out of town, and the only person I felt close enough to tell was Karen. I knew she was working, but I figured I'd take the chance."

It was in Karen's response that we see the hurt. "It was really clear that Lynn was in terrible straits. Frankly, I'd never heard her sounding so distraught. My schedule was light for the rest of the afternoon, so I easily could have spoken to her. But I didn't. Instead, I made up this story that there was an important meeting, that I couldn't possibly talk then, that I'd have to call her back later. I guess I wanted to give her a taste of her own medicine, of what it felt like to be the underdog."

"I never knew *that*," said Lynn, shocked by the revelation.

"I know," said Karen. "I guess there are some things that are still hard to talk about."

The next few months saw a 360-degree turn in their relationship, with Karen being the one "on top," and Lynn the one in need. "It really turned my head around," says Lynn. "Karen was there for me, but she just as easily could have not been because of the way I had let my friendship with her slide when I was flying high. She was really a life-saver."

Karen viewed her role in a somewhat different light. "I realized that on some level I liked the fact that Lynn was in trouble. Not that I wanted her to fail, but I liked knowing that she needed me. And I liked knowing she was not tied up twenty-four hours a day, that she was available. Not exactly constructive feelings, are they?"

Lynn had her own share of guilt to reckon with. "It occurred to me that I really hadn't been fair to Karen, that I wasn't being a real friend. Real friends don't suddenly disappear when they become successful. They do everything they can to share their success, to bring their friends along with them."

Then why hadn't she? I wondered.

She shook her head. "I can't put my finger on it really, but it has to do with the feeling that you never have enough to begin with, that you are cheated somewhere, so you become stingy about sharing what you don't feel you have enough of for yourself with anyone else." The voice of the little girl who never felt she got enough love from her mother, precisely.

Today Lynn is back on her feet, and in the interim Karen has received a promotion. They have spent a long time discussing their relationship, the difficulties that might occur. And they are both asking themselves the question "Can a woman be successful without becoming like a man?" They tell me that they haven't totally answered it. But the fact that they can now talk openly about their jealousies and feelings tells me that they are halfway there.

Karen and Lynn were lucky; both grew a little from their experience. But what might have happened had there not been the temporary moratorium on Lynn's success?

One common scenario is that Karen would have continued to withdraw from the relationship to exorcise herself of her feelings of competition. "Oh, I don't see Lynn anymore," she might have said when people asked. "Success just went to her head." Not an ideal solution, perhaps, but the fact is, it can be very uncomfortable to be around someone who makes you feel inadequate. One cosmetic millionairess learned the lesson long ago. "Everyone always talks about the woman who drops her friends when she becomes successful. That's a crock. They drop you. You're lucky if by the time you've reached your pinnacle you have any of the old friends left at all."

Then there's the possibility that Karen may have made Lynn feel so guilty that Lynn would feel no choice but to let go of the relationship. As one woman put it, "There's this feeling of jealousy that comes through. It's an unspoken kind of ostracism that makes you feel, 'What the hell do I need this for?'"

Of course, the "underdog" is not always to blame. Tickled by the glitz of success, Lynn may have found Karen an unpleasant reminder of her past struggles, and as a result, may have disengaged herself from the friendship. "If I ever become really successful, I'm going to drop all my middle-class friends," a close friend of my parents once announced in her presuccess days. Today her name is known in social circles all over the country and her daughter's name is a household word. My parents haven't heard from her in twenty years. While it's not pleasant to think about it, women can be snobs.

WOMEN, FRIENDSHIP, AND THE MALE ACHIEVEMENT ETHIC

Whatever the resolution, the bottom line of the conflict seems to be this: Can a woman be successful without becoming like a man?

Most of us would like to say unequivocally, "Yes!" But given the patriarchal setup of our society, it's not always so easy; there is still sufficient bias against women that it is reasonable for women to feel they have to work harder, prove themselves more fully, be more like men than men.

The short-term result is that many women have latched on to the male model of success. The tendency is as old as the women's movement itself. "As women began to be perceived by themselves and others as being capable of rational, intellectual thought . . ." writes historian Nancy Sahli, "they perceived this capacity as being on a higher status scale than that of the emotions."[21]

That women want to use their capabilities for "rational" thought, as Ms. Sahli puts it, is of course to our credit. That we do this in the context of shelving our nurturing impulses, agreeing with men that matters of the heart are less valuable than those of the brain, obliterates what many have begun to perceive as women's greatest strength—our "different voice," as Carol Gilligan calls it—the voice of caring, of attachment, of love.

"In my office I've noticed a new norm," a high-powered manager in the computer business tells me. "It's how much like a man a woman can be. The big thing revolves around having a child and how quickly you can drop the baby and get your ass back to work. One woman had her child and was back at her desk two weeks later. She doesn't even talk about the baby. She works sixteen hours a day. She's considered a star, a role model. That's the realm of competition these days. That's what it means to be a success."

Women as these are split off from their internal workings as women. They have absorbed the worst aspects of the male achievement ethic while denying the positive aspects of their femininity. That's not to say that a woman cannot combine a career with family life. But when she feels she must cut off her feelings in order to "make It," when she refuses to challenge the idea that achievement and nurturance are incompatible, she makes the same mistake many men have made.

"Moral nihilism is the conclusion . . . of women who seek . . . to cut off their feelings and not to care. . . ." says Dr. Carol Gilligan. "Construing their caring as a weakness and identifying the man's position with strength, they conclude that the strong need not be moral and that only the weak care about relationships."[22]

When we refuse to allow each other to grow, when we hold back from actualizing ourselves, we stagnate the development of the whole female gender. But when we replace our femininity with the callousness of the male achievement ethic, we do a disservice to the whole human race.

Chapter 8

FRIENDS AND DIVORCE

OCTOBER 24, 1974. The fog drifted over the bay, a common sight in the Santa Cruz hills. As I pulled into my driveway, I was ebullient: Our women's therapy groups had full registration, new clients were floating in by the day; the counseling center that Claire and I had conceived of six months ago was taking form. We were going to make it work.

I was so excited I hardly noticed my husband's maudlin mood.

"I have something to tell you," he said, seemingly oblivious to my up-tempo spirits.

"Can't it wait a minute?" I asked, becoming more irritated by the moment, wishing that I had stayed at the office, or maybe gone out to dinner with Claire.

"No," he said. "I want to talk to you *now*. Sit down."

"Well?"

"I'm leaving," he said with his eyes toward the floor. "I want a separation."

I heard the sounds, but the words did not register.

"I'm packing some things now and staying somewhere else tonight. I'll come pick up the rest of my clothing tomorrow."

I should have seen it coming. The last year of our relationship had been a constant battle between two people whose lives were moving in completely different directions, who could find no way to bridge the gap. And in my heart I knew that I was largely to blame for the growing chasm, refusing to go to social events important to his career, informing him in no uncertain terms that I wanted to have nothing to do with the corporate life in which he was becoming increasingly entrenched. If his exit was infuriating, it was only because he had mustered the courage to say it first.

Nevertheless, I was unprepared for the speed of his departure. Within thirty minutes of his announcement, he was gone, and with him, three and one half years that we had spent trying to build a marriage. My first impulse was to call my mother. Instead I called Claire. "How do you feel?" she asked in her typically therapeutic style after I had told her what had happened. I was unable to answer. I felt nothing.

The months passed, and the only strong reaction I had to my husband's leaving was an overwhelming feeling of relief. Claire and I began spending more time together away from the office—going on hikes and boat rides, sunning in my backyard—during which time she continuously commented on how well I was keeping it all together. The truth was, I was too busy to think about it. I had Claire, who often included me in plans with her new boyfriend. I came and went as I pleased. I was enjoying my freedom.

Besides, I had already fallen in love with someone else.

It was only after that relationship, too, was ended, that I started to come undone. The departure of my husband was temporarily glossed over by his replacement, but when my lover walked out, I had nothing left but my own feelings to deal with. I was terrified. Alone. Feeling as if I were falling into a bottomless crevice. For the first time questions such as, "What will I do?" "What's wrong with me?" and "Who will take care of me?" crept into consciousness, the last being the most pressing despite the fact I was more than able to fend for myself financially. Within a week I was having acute attacks of anxiety; within two, I completely fell apart, curling up on the sofa like a fetus and crying and shaking for hours at a stretch.

It was during one of those attacks that I began to understand the depths of terror and loneliness that propel people to commit suicide. I had never contemplated killing myself; nor did I then. But the empathy with which I was able to comprehend the terror out of which such urges are born frightened me. I was three thousand miles from home, from my family, my sister, my friends. I picked up the phone and called Claire.

"I need you," I remember telling her between sobs. "Please come." It was the first time I can remember ever uttering those words so directly, so honestly to another woman.

"Can't it wait?" she said, obviously not comprehending the desperation, the urgency. "Jeff and I think we found an apartment, and we want to go look at it."

"Claire, I'm really in bad shape. I don't know what I'll do. I'm afraid. Come *now!*" It did not occur to me that I might be infringing on Claire's plans, that her desire to look at an apartment with her boyfriend could take priority over me. She had been my best friend and colleague for nearly two years. I had never asked her for anything. I felt a right to my needs, to my neediness.

Two hours later Claire showed up, with, much to my amazement, her boyfriend. I was taken aback by her lack of consideration, her inability to understand. She, too, had gone through a divorce. But I was too far gone to consider sociability, and poured my heart out. For a long while Claire didn't respond, although I could not help but note a distinct look of contempt on her face. After finishing my monologue, eyes red, still curled up on the couch, Claire looked at me and said in a voice as piercing as ice, "You need help."

It was downhill after that. I collected myself in time, slowly piecing my life together with the delicacy of gossamer. But Claire and I had stopped talking. Except for perfunctory remarks or the strained communication necessitated by our working together, few words passed between us. In our one and only discussion of the issue, Claire told me that she had frankly been shocked that I had fallen apart so completely. She had felt betrayed by the image of strength and confidence that I had projected when my life was predictable, safe—when I had someone to take care of me. Having watched me succumb to my inherent dependence, she no longer had any interest in being my friend. She was not interested in being friends, she said, "with someone who needed to be taken care of."

One morning I walked into work and was greeted by Claire's chilling stare. "We just received a call from the state government," she said in a monotone. "They've just changed the ruling about our eligibility to accept Medicaid patients. They've bumped us off the roster."

I was stunned. Over the past eight months we had built up a large

Medicaid practice, which now comprised more than half of our clientele. But the ruling that only licensed psychiatrists and psychologists would be eligible was definitive; it was no longer sufficient to receive supervision from these professionals, as we had been doing in the past. Numbers rolled into my head: the rent, the insurance, the car, the food. How was I going to pay for them? At the same time, I was not about to throw in the towel after two years of struggling to get where we were because of one setback. I was too invested in my work, the institute, the development of my own autonomy.

"Well," I said with a deliberateness resembling the old confidence which had first attracted Claire to me, "we'll just have to make a go of it with cash-paying clients. I think we have enough experience and exposure to do that."

"I'm not interested in doing that," she shot back. "I'm not interested in working anymore with you." How easy of her to say. After all, in addition to the institute, she also had a growing, and increasingly profitable, private practice.

I was devastated. She had rejected me, and now she was virtually taking control of my life, my means of survival. Had I been prone to violence, I think I would have killed her. It took all the self-control I could muster not to spit in her face. My body shook with rage, and my eyes were blind with the desire for vengeance. And it was at that moment that I understood the depth of passion with which one woman can hate another.

And so our relationship ended with the abruptness and intensity with which it had begun. A survivor at heart, I eventually put my life back into some semblance of order. To support myself I took a temporary job as a typist, a skill which I was most grateful to have acquired. Six months later I was offered a research position in New York City which eased my financial distress considerably. Pulling myself together emotionally was more painstaking and time-consuming, but eventually I felt myself become whole again. In retrospect, I believe I was all the more stronger for the experience. I had been through a crisis, was left to fend for myself, and had come through it all. Divorce, painful as it may be, often triggers psychic growth and development.[1] It was during that period that I did some of my most painful and eventful growing.

Still, to this day, the feeling of humiliation lingers. I have forgiven, but I have not forgotten. Above all, what I have carried with me is the message that while it is fine to show another woman strength, it is not okay to show a woman need.

LOSS OF IDENTITY

At no other time does a woman need her female support system more than during a life crisis, such as divorce.* As women, we have been raised to get our primary sense of validation through our attachments. We define ourselves, in large part, in relationships to others: mother, wife, daughter, sister, friend. Retaining aspects of the early relationship with mother, our sense of self is experienced as continuous with others, as connected to the world, which is why we identify with each other so.

When we divorce, a large part of our identity is pulled out from under us. We may not know who we are. For years we have been an extension of a husband, a Mrs. Somebody. Now we don't even know what to call ourselves. It is little wonder that so many women, years after the fact, still carry their husband's names. "It's to avoid confusion for the children," they say. Yet how much of keeping our old namesakes is a way of clinging still?

Women going through a divorce backslide for a period of time. Even autonomous women will feel a sense of disconnectedness, of isolation. It's like moving; all the things that are usually in place, that give us a feeling of continuity and attachment, are lost. "It was my idea to terminate the marriage," one forty-one-year-old public relations assistant tells me. "Even so, I have to admit that I have never been so frightened in my life. Having work helped. But the fact is, I had gotten married right after college, so this was the first time I had been forced to live on my own."

"On my own." What words could be more frightening to a woman whose whole sense of self is enmeshed in her attachments? Our boasting of autonomy may temporarily seem something of a farce—words spoken with no real gumption behind them. Living with a man allows us the license of such an illusion. Without the illusion to support us, our facade of strength comes tumbling down.

*NOTE: While the focus of this chapter is divorce, many of the dynamics discussed are equally applicable to other life crises.

Men, of course, are traumatized by divorce, too. There is no way to get around the dissolution of such an intense emotional bond without concurrent feelings of grief and loss. But in general, divorce, at least in the early stages, involves more problems and is perceived as more traumatic for women than for men. Given the connection between our attachments and our feelings of self-esteem, women are more likely to view divorce as a personal failure. Women also suffer far greater economic losses, with two thirds of all women saying that their incomes following divorce are significantly lower than before. (This is true of less than one fifth of the men.)[2] More importantly, many women tend to lack one critical resource which their male counterparts possess: autonomy.

It is important to say that, despite the emotional havoc that is wreaked on women during the early stages of divorce, in the long haul, divorced women tend to do better than their male counterparts, with men reporting far higher rates of mental disturbance than women.[3] But first, women must get past the initial crisis. And given women's difficulty with separation, this is no easy hurdle.

ADULT GROWING PAINS

Divorce is not unlike an adult version of separation—individuation.[4] For some women, those who have maintained or developed a sense of themselves outside of their role as wife (and mother), it is simply a matter of breaking old ties that no longer work, of going through a period of grief and mourning not unlike what a child goes through upon losing an attachment figure. Nor is divorce equally traumatic for all women, with 13 percent of women reporting the experience as "relatively painless."[5]

But for others, for whom marriage has served as a shield against having to develop any measure of independence, take away that shield and what you've got is a woman who, for the first time in her life, has to go through what most men resolve when they are children. When it comes to differentiation, many a woman is still in part a young girl in an adult body.

Dr. Paul Bohannan, who has tapped into the similarity between separation in the early years and the dynamics of divorce, terms this adult replay the "psychic divorce." What it requires, he tells us, is that we separate ourselves from our spouse, that we literally wash that man right out of our hair. The difficulty for women, however, is that this ultimately means becoming more autonomous—not an easy prospect without a stockpile of autonomy to begin with.

Says Dr. Bohannan: "The psychic divorce involves becoming a whole, complete, and autonomous individual again—learning to live without somebody to lean on—but also without somebody to support. There is nobody on whom to blame one's difficulties (except oneself), nobody to shortstop one's growth, nobody to grow with. Each must regain—*if he ever had it*—the dependence on self and faith in one's own capacity to cope with the environment, with people, with thoughts and emotions." (Italics mine.)[6]

Most men have that sense of separateness, that sense of self.

Many women do not.

Naturally, the struggles surrounding divorce stretch beyond the emotional upheaval. There are legal and economic problems, custody battles, adjustment difficulties for the children.[7] There are also social problems. In a society that tends to organize itself around being partnered, single women, generally viewed as a social liability (as opposed to men, who are always potential husbands), are left in an awkward position.[8]

But it is the trauma of learning to be alone, of standing on our own two feet, that is the most devastating. For the vast majority of women who have not successfully broken the early ties with their mothers, the divorce crisis hurls them back to the time they were struggling with the same issues when they were two. The idea is that what was left undone in the past will be completed, that they will reexperience the early struggle with a better resolution. It is a regression in the service of progression.

But the red carpet showing us the way does not magically unfold before us. A woman who has been dependent all her life doesn't wake up one morning and say, "Today's the day to get my autonomy act together." Even if that's her ultimate goal, she may not have the vaguest idea of where to begin, or how to take the first step without falling flat on her face.

Which is where the need for our women friends comes in. Just like the two-year-old who needs a strong, reliable mothering figure to whom she can run back to while learning to explore the great big world on her own, women going through divorce need such a "mother," too. Whether she is twenty-two, forty-two, or sixty-two, if she has never negotiated her independence before, she needs someone who will help her overcome her fear of the water so that she may ultimately learn to swim.

Tempting as it may be, returning to mother's arms is usually not a good idea. A discussion with Natalie Garfield, a therapist who specializes in mother-child relationships, illustrates the point. "I have this one patient who was just divorced and who has a lot of difficulty in terms of separation. For example, she recently told me that she had coffee in a coffee shop for the first time by herself. She's thirty-three years old. She then went on to tell me that she went to dinner at a friend's house, and called her mother to tell her where she was. In fact, she tells me that her mother checks in on her every day. This woman is very pleased with the nice new relationship she has with her mother, who, she says, is being very supportive, but the daughter is really feeding right into her mother's needs for dependency. The reason she's supporting such unhealthy behavior of the mother and the mother is supporting the regressed state of the daughter is because it feels good to both of them. Of course, this woman is in therapy and we are dealing with her problems with separation here. But many women in similar situations are not in therapy, so they just plug right into their own mother's patterns and reaffirm them on both sides."

To run home when you're thirty-three and feeling needy, feeds into the unhealthy symbiosis that mother herself might need. It was in those arms that clasped so tightly about us that our conflicts and fears about separation were born in the first place.[9]

Which leaves us our friends. Women friends hold out the kind of potentially firm support and intimacy we need, a reliable source of nurturance without the symbiotic strings. They also afford us the opportunity to reexperience our anxiety about separation and get past it.

Unfortunately, the converse is also true. If a woman has never truly separated from her mother, and if her friends are unable to provide her with support during this adult replay, she may, like the young child, become more frightened about being on her own than ever before. She may run to marry the first man that asks. Even if she manages to steer her way through the crisis, a part of her will remain a fearful, dependent child. She will feel mistrustful of other women. Worse yet, she will not truly trust herself.

That's why not having another woman's support during the divorce crisis can be so devastating. And why having it can be so uplifting.

THE MOST POIGNANT STORY I've heard on the subject comes from a woman I shall call Nina. The glowing support she received from her friends—particularly her best friend, Nancy—attests to the strength of women's relationships, epitomizes the best of what women have to offer.

When I met her, Nina was forty-two years old and the head of her own flourishing home-style catering business. Nina had to schedule our interview at nine in the evening because the recent surge in clients kept her working from seven in the morning until six at night. The three-hour interlude was the time that she religiously set aside for her two sons, David and Ben, sixteen and thirteen, respectively. Closing the door to the den in her spacious ten-room home, she admitted, "I feel guilty having to schedule time for the kids in such a regimented way, but otherwise I'm afraid I'd never see them." Her face was tanned and her hair fell in long, untamed curls. She was dressed in pink overalls, boldly striped socks, and saddle shoes. Except for the lines of age around her mouth and above her brow, she could have passed for twenty-five.

Nina was doing very well financially, but things had not always been so. She had always had a comfortable amount of money, but it had not been earnings wrought of her own accomplishments. Married at twenty-three to an investment analyst, and conceiving shortly after, she had lived out the traditional female role to a tee. "Of course, there were a few odd jobs along the way," she added. "I worked part-time as a clerical assistant for an insurance firm. I also had a job for a while at the health food store on Main Street. And," she smiled, as if remembering the good old days, "for five years I was an absolutely *dynamite* Tupperware lady."

Her marriage, as she described it, was "innocuous"; not exactly good, not really bad; not really much of anything. But she had her friends, she had her children, she had her Tupperware. "I was walking around in a state of semiconsciousness."

When one of Nina's friends suggested, four years ago, that they join a consciousness-raising group, Nina went as kind of a lark. She thought it would be fun—a way to meet new people and get out of the house one night a week. She was completely unprepared for the impact the group would have on her. "It was like opening my eyes for the first time. Looking back, it seems absurd that I didn't realize how growth-stunting my relationship with my husband had been. But the more I discussed it with these women, the more I came to realize that I had given up my own potential as a person to be a 'good' mother and a 'good' wife.

"Part of it was my problem; in many ways I married someone just like my mother, someone who was critical and unsupportive as she had been. But a lot of the responsibility fell on him, too. The truth was, despite his boastings that he was a liberated man, he was very conventional at heart."

She stopped and ran her fingers through her thick hair. "The truth is, he didn't want an equal partner . . . he wanted a mother."

These revelations were difficult and painful for Nina. She had been raised to believe that a woman's raison d'être was to serve a man—to be a good wife and mother. Although she had once had professional aspirations, her dependency on her husband had chipped away at her spirit. Worst of all, before attending the group, she had believed that she had everything a woman could want. She believed she was, in the face of it all, content.

With the support of the group, Nina slowly began opening up, both to herself and her closest friend and confidante, Nancy. "She knew every single heartbeat along the way," Nina recollects, "from the minor dissatisfactions to the major problems with my marriage." What so impressed Nina was that breaking down her own barriers encouraged Nancy to respond in kind. It was almost as if they had each stood on the edge, each deferring to the other to make the first move. "It was a moment of revelation to me that when I complained about my husband, she complained about hers. That's what made it okay—it opened a floodgate that probably led me faster to my divorce and eventually led Nancy to hers. There was so much affirmation—yes, he doesn't do this; yes, I'm entitled to that; yes, I deserve more than I'm getting. Another thing that happened was that another good friend wrote me a letter saying how concerned she was at how difficult my marriage was. That was a major influence. I mean, it was in *writing*. Here she was not only saying that she thought there was something wrong—she was telling me that she was behind me 100 percent should I decide to get out."

While all this support was indeed comforting, it initially produced some anxiety, too. While acknowledging that she was not happy, Nina was still not sure if she was ready to make the break. She had lived the

Great American Woman's Dream—a big house in the suburbs, two kids, two cars—and had covered up her drives for achievement with the cushion of her material comfort.

Her decision to leave, as it turned out, was not entirely in her control. Having sensed his wife's unease, and finally admitted to being involved in an affair, Nina's husband announced, seemingly without warning, that he wanted a divorce. Nina was terrified, but she agreed.

As before, her close friends came to her rescue. "The feeling that I got from them was one of immense support. I didn't see any of them as having any selfish motivation. They were there for me; they were available to me. Especially Nancy. I could call her anytime of the day or night to cry. I could ask her to come over because I was too upset even to talk on the phone, and she would spend hours with me, talking it through, helping me to understand what was happening. When I really began going off the deep end, she would come by the house every day to check up on me. One of the most important things that I remember was crying profusely, saying to her, 'I need you.' That was the first time I had ever said I needed a woman. That was an enormous breakthrough for me and an enormous breakthrough in our relationship."

I listened to the gush of love and support with more than a twinge of envy. Having had the opposite experience, I wanted to believe the support Nina received from her friends, from Nancy in particular, resulted from the fact that she was, albeit unknowingly, far more independent than I had been going into my divorce. If her friends were willing to come through with such stunning loyalty, it was because she simply had not been as needy as I.

"Do you remember feeling very lonely and afraid, kind of lost in terms of your identity?" I asked.

"My feelings were more intense than what you're describing. Desperate. Terrified. Panicked. Alone. Those words describe the feelings more accurately. Intense pain that would then burst open into fear. I can remember the time that I realized I wasn't going to be living in my old house anymore, and it felt like the biggest sword was going through my heart and just bursting it. I didn't know how I was going to live through it. I was on the verge of a breakdown."

The irony, it seemed to me, was that the same qualities that precipitated Claire's rejection of me seemed to draw Nancy and Nina's other close friends in.

"My friends were not threatened by my dependency on them at all," she said. "In fact, I think they experienced some relief, some pleasure even, at seeing someone who had been so controlled, who didn't have a crack, fall apart and have their guts laying all over. It gave them a chance to be like a mother to me. Before the divorce they never had the opportunity. In retrospect, Nancy even said that she was somewhat awed by the intensity of the whole thing. I had always assumed that she had already gone through something like that, or that she was above it, or beyond it. That wasn't so. Instead, she felt that she needed to go through something like that for herself in order to grow. That I was able to face those kinds of feelings and express them, was seen as something courageous—something that evoked her admiration, something to model herself on."

Nina and I had both gone through a life crisis. Both of us had felt utterly and completely alone. Nina, however, aroused sympathy and support. I, rejection and disdain. What accounted for the difference?

Dr. Arthur Miller, a psychiatrist who has studied the reactions of friends to divorce, believes the key to the issues is to what degree a friend's divorce sparks some kind of emotional conflict. Time and time again, he has found that the friend flees because the divorce evokes some conflict in herself. "A friend's response to divorce has to be seen in terms of whether or not the idea of divorce, the reasons for it, the way it is carried out, and the emotional results threaten the friend's psychological defenses against anxiety. How the person reacts in the face of the divorce can be seen as a response to a threat."[10]

Dr. Miller goes on to say that the perceived threat can be either real or psychological; that is, we may feel anxious about a friend's divorce because it breaks up our friendship circle or because it dredges up some unconscious fear. Sometimes a bit of both are operating at the same time. But as a rule, the more present the unconscious element, the more likely our response will be seen as "irrational."

If the struggle for the divorcing woman is to regain a sense of sure footing, the task for the friend of the divorcée is to figure out just what it is she is reacting to, and hopefully transcend it. And as always, the easiest feelings to access are those that are closest to consciousness.

Let's look first at women's responses in terms of the reality of the relationship.

SHATTERING THE GROUP BALANCE

Again and again from friends of divorcées, a common plaint is heard: "I loved her. I loved him. I didn't know whose side I should take." The feeling of having to choose, and of having to juggle our allegiances back and forth from one partner to the other is obviously a very real issue. Those of us who spend the majority of our time socializing in sets of two have become so accustomed to dealing with the male and female of the pair as an intertwined unit, we cannot see them as separate. Anything that intensifies the split, the need to choose (using friends as a sounding board for bad-mouthing the other spouse, fighting with one's own spouse about who is "right" or "wrong"), increases the desire to run away from the situation altogether.

Then, of course, there is the possibility that our allegiance to either party may come undone. Particularly for women who are not especially trusting of relationships with women to begin with, seeing friends in the throes of splitting up may launch a little red flag: If she couldn't make it with him then how can I possibly expect her to be loyal to me? The fear may be triggered at the time of separation or long before. "A friend of mine recently confided that she's been having this affair for the past six months," one woman tells me. "It destroyed me. Not that I felt judgmental about extramarital sex. It was more the feeling that if she could do that to him and could look him straight in the eye, then God knows what she might do behind my back." Disillusioned about a friend's trustworthiness to her husband, she wonders about her ability to maintain strong allegiances as a friend as well.

If it comes as a rude shock when the seemingly most content of couples admits that they have been miserable for the longest time, it may be an even ruder shock to learn that your husband's feelings for your woman friend had more than a twinge of innocent sexual innuendo. Suddenly, the same man who had always derided our friend for being too much of a nag, or too aggressive, develops this avid concern about her fate after hubby leaves the picture. The same woman whom we pitied in her marital misery now arouses jealousy more than sympathy. A twenty-five-year-old, strikingly attractive woman admits that her best friend's husband has been a gem since her divorce, at the expense of her friendship. "I can call on him for anything—if a pipe is leaking, if my necklace falls behind the sink, if there's a mouse." The problem is that while he is so gallant toward her, for his wife to get him to do the same chores is like pulling teeth. "She's become extremely jealous," says the divorcée, adding, "If I were in her shoes, I think I would be, too."

A woman does not have to be in the bloom of youth for such jealousy to emerge. Studies of widows, whose average age was about sixty, show that even among the more mature population, jealousy runs rampant. Were the wives jealous of them when their husbands were around? the researchers asked. Over one third of the respondents answered yes. The authors go on to tell us of one widow who, upon visiting a friend in California, was admonished that when she returned home, her female friends would abandon her. The respondent was shocked. "Are you out of your mind?" she retorted to her friend. "I have very dear ones, they're of twenty-five years standing. I just didn't find them, you know." To which her friend responded, "If you were (a) ugly, (b) a stupid personality and icky, then they would stick by you. But let me tell you, you will be a threat, and you will lose most of your friends." The widow was so incensed that she nearly struck her friend from across the luncheon table. In the end, however, she was forced to admit that "everything she said was true."[11]

SEEING THE LOOPHOLES IN OUR OWN MARRIAGE

The reason behind this threat is that marital discontent is contagious: If Susie's been miserable all these years, maybe I've been, too. But what if the thought of leaving our own relationship is too frightening to contemplate?

"She called and told me he just walked out on her," this suburban housewife recalls in a hushed voice that reflected her utter shock. "He told her that she wasn't the woman he'd married, that when they'd met, she had been a dynamic, working woman, and now all she's done is stay home, make babies, and get fatter. I was personally devastated. I mean, can you imagine waking one day and seeing your husband pack his bags, when meanwhile you didn't know that he was miserable? It was like hearing that someone you love has a terminal disease; you want to reach out, but a part of you pulls back because you're afraid it might be contagious."

The fear of contagion is no empty threat. There is evidence suggesting that, indeed, divorce is catching, that when one couple within a social circle breaks up, others are likely to follow in tandem.[12] It's like a keystone effect—remove the critical block, and the rest come crashing down.

While one woman may react by withdrawing, another may become downright abusive. Particularly if she is in an unhappy situation that she is unwilling to extricate herself from, seeing a friend bailing out arouses feelings of shame and inadequacy:[13] "If she's doing it, why aren't I?"

A woman who had never worked a day in her life dropped the bomb over lunch. "I'm leaving Tom. The truth is, I've been miserable with him for years. No matter what it takes, I'm getting out."

The revelation hit her friend like a thunderbolt.

"You've been married for fifteen years, and you mean to tell me you just now realized you're miserable? Besides," she added, going straight for the jugular, "how is someone like you going to support yourself? You'll end up living on welfare."

To the contrary, she ended up working *for* welfare after passing her civil servant's exam. Her new lease on life motivated her to lose twenty pounds. She never looked or felt better. The healthier she got, the more abusive her friend became. "She herself wasn't happy," the newly liberated woman tells me. "Her husband has been having affairs for years. He treats her like a slave. Seeing me was like an embarrassing slap in the face. I did something about my predicament. She didn't."

Rescuing a friend in the throes of divorce means getting involved. It means getting into the shoes of what the divorcing person is feeling. The woman who is not ready to deal with conflicts in her own marriage has no other choice but to stay as far from her friend as possible.

Not surprisingly, women who are economically dependent are most prone to such vulnerabilities. Over the years, the concept of alimony has increasingly lost favor.[14] Close to 75 percent of divorced women work,[15] as compared to approximately 50–60 percent of married women.[16] For women who enjoy financial dependence, particularly those women whose husbands support them in style, the thought of having to make it alone in the big, bad world, is too terrifying even to contemplate.[17]

The problem is compounded for women who have invested a lot of their energies in keeping a doomed marriage together. Calling this the "overturned canoe syndrome," social psychologist Carol Travis found that some people work so hard to preserve their failing marriages that by the time divorce inevitably erupts, their batteries have gone dead. "Imagine a person paddling a canoe through choppy water, struggling to stay afloat. Suddenly a large wave overturns the canoe. The person *could* swim to shore, but is so depleted from the previous struggle that she sinks."[18]

IF THE IDEA OF WATCHING a friend divorce is scary to some, however, it is also a green light to others. For women who are unhappy in their marriages and are ready to meet the challenge, a friend's separation can go a long way in fostering her own decision to leave. It is almost as if she can vicariously go through the process with her divorcing friend, moving her own development along at the same time. For Nina's friend Nancy, this is precisely what occurred.

"Before Nina began telling me how miserable she was, I had never stopped to think about how I really felt in my marriage," Nancy recalls. "Having her open up opened me up, too. Looking back, I think that the reason I was so encouraging—sending the letter, checking up on her constantly to make sure she was doing okay—was not only a way of helping Nina get out, but of helping myself. In a funny way, her pain gave me strength." And courage. Nine months after Nina separated from her husband, Nancy hopped on the bandwagon and left hers.

These are the more "rational" reasons women turn from their divorcing friend. Let's turn now to the unconscious elements.

THE NEED TO RESCUE

Perhaps the most poignant of these issues concerns the issue of rescue.

We all know women who appear to mobilize their energies as soon as something terrible happens to their friends, who are at their best when a friend is in need. My mother is one such woman. Tell her you feel fine, and the conversations last ten minutes. Let her know that you're sick or depressed, and she's happy to nurture and tend for as long as your little heart desires. Sometimes even longer.

"I never expected so-and-so to come through for me the way she did," is usually the way such rescue is experienced. "Why, while I was married and out of trouble, we weren't even that close at all. Then I got divorced and fell apart, and there she was."

What is it that propels such women to be at the forefront of bailing their friends out of trouble and misery? According to the patients Dr. Miller has seen in his practice, the motivation is largely a result of having a parent who was suicidal, depressed, or otherwise emotionally imbalanced. Particularly prone to the rescue syndrome are those who feel, consciously or unconsciously, responsible for the parent's suffering. Devoting oneself to making the other feel better, Dr. Miller observes, is largely a way of ameliorating the guilt. While seeing a friend who is depressed or suicidal is threatening to some, for women who need to be the "rescuers," the circumstances suit them perfectly.[19]

Jane Flax sees the motivation to rescue from a slightly different perspective. She, too, has found that women prone to rescuing have mothers who are problematic. But the motivation to rescue, she believes, arises less out of guilt than as a way of preserving one's autonomy, or in some cases one's sanity. "Women put all this energy into rescuing their mothers, and later, their friends, in order to rescue themselves. Because a woman feels that to become different from the mother is a rejection of her, she feels she either has to be like the mother or get her out of whatever mess she's in. In the case where a mother was particularly needy or suicidal, for example, that can be a heavy burden to bear. I had one patient whose mother was a manic-depressive, in and out of mental hospitals for years. The daughter put all this energy into rescu-

ing her. It was as if, until the mother was sane, she could not be sane."
This particular mother, Dr. Flax goes on to tell me, did not respond to
her daughter's attempts to bail her out, and her daughter has become a
manic-depressive.

It is important to distinguish genuine support from the compulsion to
rescue. Lending a helping hand to someone we care about is a normal
and positive reaction to a friend in need. Feeling that we are not only
responsible for taking care of our friend, but that our efforts should
carry such weight as to forestall her suffering, however, is indicative of
rescue.

Whichever of these motivations is more prominent, being rescued
generally helps the divorcée through the period of crisis.[20] Provided
there are not other demons that lurk beneath.

TRAPDOORS

Working through one's problems by rescuing a divorcing friend, while
having an underlying neurotic element, actually works to the good of
both the woman who is giving the support and the one who is receiving
it. It matters little if someone joins the Salvation Army in order to work
through issues within oneself or not: The point is that good is being
done.

What is often overlooked is the fact that helping someone is often not
in the other person's best interest but in one's own. Take, for example,
the woman who zealously supports the breakup of her friend's marriage. On the one hand, she might simply be mirroring her friend's
underlying wish to extricate herself from an unhappy situation, providing her with an extra bit of ammunition to make the break. But what of
the woman who pushes her friend onward and outward because she
actually gets pleasure out of seeing her friend miserable?

A thirty-eight-year-old woman who initially patted herself on the
back for her staunch support of her closest friend, who had recently
separated, later admitted: "I'd like to say that I was there for her out of
the goodness of my heart. But there was another part of me that got a
certain pleasure out of seeing her unhappy. She has always been more
successful than I have, and this was a way, I suppose, of feeling that I

was better off than she was. It was a way of alleviating some of the rivalry."

Arthur Miller sees the acting out of such competition in his practice all of the time. "It is a balm to one's wounded ego and self-esteem," he tells us. It is also a good way of producing a reservoir of guilt, which rescuing helps alleviate.[21]

Then, of course, there is the possibility that what is being acted out is our earliest wish to separate our parents so that we may have Mom all to ourselves. "Nora's divorce gave her back to me," says one single woman about her best friend. "When she was married, it was him first. Now it's me she comes to."

OVERNURTURE

While there is always an element of rivalry and the desire to be central in our friends' lives, by far the most twisted pattern of rescue is seen in what I call overnurture. Supporting a friend during a crisis generally helps her in her efforts to find herself. Caretaking beyond the point that she needs to be taken care of, however, is another story. In fact, there is good reason for suspicion when a friend becomes oversolicitous, overly protective of her fledgling friend. What may, on the surface, look like good old-fashioned mothering may, at its roots, be not so good symbiosis.

Smothered with love. That's how Donna's concern felt to Jacqueline after she had recovered from the initial trauma of her separation. Having initiated the breach, a step which proceeded from her analysis, which indicated that she had symbolically married someone just like her mother, Jacqueline found the realities of being alone those first few months were more difficult than she had imagined. And at the slightest whimper, and frequently without her asking at all, Donna was there to her rescue—soothing, calming, tending.

The attention was wonderful at first, and Jacqueline felt fortunate to have such a supportive friend. But as the sores began to heal, there was something disquieting about all the mothering that she now felt was being thrown her way. In fact, she began to feel downright stifled by it all.

"I'm going into business for myself," Jacqueline proudly announced two months after her separation.

"Keep your job," her friend insisted. "You need something secure, something stable in your life." Her friend's assessment shattered her own dubious feelings of balance. "I decided maybe she was right, maybe this wasn't the time."

But according to Donna, two months later wasn't the time either. Nor was it, from her perspective, the time for Jackie to date any one man too seriously, given what Donna had recently started calling "Jackie's innate vulnerability to rejection." Why couldn't she just relax for a while and let Donna take care of her?

The more time that passed, the more Donna started looking like a doting mother rather than a friend. She called her midday at work and promptly at ten every night, "just to make sure I had come home safely and I was feeling all right." In fact, Jackie began realizing she had been in tip-top spirits for months, which on some level didn't suit Donna at all. "It was as if everytime I started looking healthy, she would begin dredging up old wounds. It was as if she liked me being dependent on her; she liked continuously taking care of me."

Then and there, Jacqueline put her foot down. "If you call me up one more time at ten o'clock, if you buy me one more self-help book, I never want to speak to you again!" Her resolution was more liberating than her separation. "It was like I had finally been set free, like I had gotten a two-hundred-pound weight off my back."

As for Donna's part, she felt hurt, used, and unappreciated. The friendship was never the same again.

"Withdrawal, indifference, or a critical attitude of friends can add to the divorcée's suffering," says Arthur Miller. "But an overly solicitous, infantilizing approach, often pursued to exploit the rescue for (her) own emotional purposes, can be emotionally crippling or delay the convalescence from the divorce."[22] Like the mother who stands in the way of separation, the goal of such a woman is to keep her friend attached.

From the other side of the fence, it is important to say that some women encourage this kind of shepherding, only to reject the caretaker once they have regained their health. As one woman who had been badly burned put it: "I wasn't the one who called her—she was constantly calling me. There were so many times when I wanted to hang up on her, but didn't. Then when she got over the hump, she stopped calling me altogether." That such insensitivity exists between women friends is not a pleasant revelation. Indeed, from my experience, it arises more out of insecurity than the desire to hurt or manipulate. Women such as these tend to be dependent at heart, while at the same time despising this basic truth about themselves. Their neediness, once expressed, is something they need to forget about, to repress, if they are to maintain this false illusion of themselves as independent. Hence, after being nursed back to health, they want no reminders of who they were not so long ago. If they cannot tolerate seeing their old friends, it is because they are afraid to see their old selves.

DISAPPEARING ACTS

What of the woman who runs away from the neediness, who reacts to her friend as if she had a communicable disease?

Examining the cases of patients who fall into this pattern, Dr. Miller has found a common pattern. Almost invariably, the woman who flees from her friend's cry for help was originally attracted to her now divorced friend because her friend possessed certain qualities that the woman who runs out wished she herself possessed. But when the divorce occurs and the divorcée falls apart, she shatters the image her friend had of her. Disillusioned, her friend turns away.[23]

For many women the particular quality that often attracts them to a friend is autonomy. This is particularly true of a woman who feels unsure of her own autonomy. (And how many aren't?) Attaching herself to a seemingly more independent friend gives her a sense of independence via association. "If she can be independent," she tells herself, "so can I." But what happens when this ego ideal cracks, when rather than being the strong one, her friend becomes an emotionally bumbling child right before her very eyes? For the woman who is insecure in her own competency, it is an alarming reminder of her own vulnerability and susceptibility to dependence. If she were rational about the whole thing, she might chuckle at her assumption that every other woman in the world is more independent than she. But rationality is often sidestepped by her own precariously balanced autonomy. In this battle for self-preservation she looks at her friend and thinks, "This could be me."

Looking back, this is precisely what happened between Claire and me. Let's go back to our story—this time with an eye not only to the history of the friendship, but to the background which Claire brought to it.

Sitting in a large convention hall which was filled with sex therapists-to-be, a bloated, balding man with a red face had the floor. This afternoon's session was devoted to what the program called "sexual alternatives," but which in the outside world would be considered sexual perversions. We had just heard from a married man who spent his weekends devising plans to get away from his wife so that he might dress up as a woman. "A little strange, but innocent enough," I told myself. "After all, he's really not hurting anyone."

My tolerance for freedom of sexual expression, however, was pushed by the present speaker. From New York, his method of attracting prospective "customers" was via the underground newspapers. And his bag was S & M. He went on to cite a number of pleasures he and his willing victims got from their sexual games.

I sat there in horror. The vivid depiction of these scenarios turned my stomach. Even more disturbing were the cheers elicited from the audience to the tune of "Far out" and "If it feels good, do it!" Freedom to sexual expression was one thing. This struck me as just plain sick.

After the man finished his "seminar," the resounding applause gave way to a floor open to questions and comments. One woman commented that while she herself had never had any sadomasochistic tendencies, she felt that as long as the "victims" were consenting adults, no sexual aberration could be considered wrong or dirty. I raised my hand. "I don't think it's a matter of moral judgment at all, but of psychological judgment. And my own inclination in dealing with a man who can have orgasms only by having needles stuck into him would be to send him for psychiatric help." The room hushed and then broke out into a wave of attacks on my statement. I clearly did not make many friends that day. But I did make one. It was Claire.

After the session was over an attractive woman a few years older than me caught my arm. "I want to tell you that I really admire you for having the guts to stand up to that crowd and tell them what you think," she said. "You spoke my sentiments exactly."

And thus, our friendship, which eventually blossomed into a business partnership, emerged.

My gutsiness was only one of the traits that Claire admired in me. Five years her junior, I already had a master's degree and was self-supporting. While married, I did not appear overly dependent on my husband, never letting the marital relationship interfere with my friendship with Claire or with business. I was assertive and full of energy, believing that if a woman wanted to do something, all she had to do was go out and do it. The therapy institute we started together was largely based on that premise. In Claire's eyes I appeared to be the epitome of independence and self-assurance. For Claire, who espoused libertarian ideals like a Maoist rocking on the Red Book, I symbolized everything Claire both was and was striving to become.

"Having you," she once said with her usual penchant for analytic interpretation, "is like having a good mother."

Her own mother was a subservient woman who kowtowed to her immovable Catholic father's every whim. Raised in a small rural town in the Northeast, her upbringing had been stifling and restrictive. The rule of thumb for women in her family was that a woman's place was in the home, making babies and being a sideline to her husband's career. A woman's dependency on a man was something that was considered not only normal but desirable.

Not to Claire. At a young age she knew that she wanted a career, and studied hard and long in college to ensure her entry into a good graduate school that was, hopefully, as far away from home as possible. At twenty-two she married a professor, only to divorce him two years later. He "stifled her autonomy," as she put it. No better were her parents, who not only disapproved of her career in psychology, but blamed her for the divorce, which to them had been nothing short of scandalous.

Seeking to escape her ex-husband and the fetters of her parental stronghold, Claire moved to Santa Cruz—three thousand miles from home. At the time I met her, she was working on her Ph.D. and was a member of every feminist group in the area. She was not blind to the relationship between her strong feminist leanings and her lack of separation from her parents, particularly from her mother.

"I cannot speak to her for weeks at a time, not see her for months at a stretch, and all it takes is one phone call, one damn visit to hook me into the old pattern," she confided one night over dinner. Not surprisingly, her jaunts to the East Coast became increasingly less frequent.

Despite the miles between them, Claire's mother's voice rang through loud and clear. At the age of thirty Claire was living with a man, yet insisted on doing everything in her power to keep it from her mother. She kept her own separate phone number, "for mother only." And when her mother came to visit for two weeks, any sign of her lover was hustled out the door, including him. "You're being ridiculous," I told her, while helping turn her apartment from a den of sin into a convent. "And you," she told me, "do not know my mother." Nor, I suspected, her power over Claire.

Our friendship flourished, as did our business. Any inclinations I may have had toward dependency that may have lurked below the cool veneer were not apparent to anyone, including Claire. It was not that they weren't there, as my reaction to my separation indicated. But with the security of a husband by my side, they remained well hidden. Claire had once remarked that I was one of the very few married women she had met whose marriage did not interfere with her female friendships. What she did not know was that if I had endless amounts of time to spend with her and to devote to my work, it was because both these activities were preferable to being with my spouse.

Then came the fated October evening on which my husband announced his plans to leave. That night Claire had been at her most supportive, lifting my spirits and boosting my ego. "You were too good for him," she told me. Perhaps a classic line, but one you never tire of hearing when you're down in the dumps. Over the next few months she continued to stay at my side, taking great pride in "how well I was doing, given the circumstances." It occurred to neither of us that my "strength," my "ability to cope," had less to do with my inner resources than it did with the fact that I had found another man to fill the void.

Then came the "breakdown." Suddenly, independent, having-it-all-together Eva, who had been the model of strength, looked more like a clutching, desperate child. That I felt perfectly entitled to such temporary madness, viewing it as a painful and transient period from which I would emerge the stronger, did nothing to assuage Claire's horror and disdain for this psychological wreck. It was as if she had discovered some chronic and malevolent defect in my character, one which she wanted to have no part in dealing with. At the time, all I could think was that she was a bitch; that she had cruelly betrayed me. If I had listened a little more closely to what she said, I would have known what

I know now: I had touched a raw nerve: her own dependency, her own vulnerability, her own feelings of helplessness.

That she completely avoided me, dropping our friendship like a hot potato, was only one symptom of her distress. More telling was the sudden emergence of the psychosomatic symptoms Claire began presenting. If I were not the idealized tower of strength, neither was she. Suddenly, Claire became overtly nervous and distraught, a sense of distress which blossomed into a chronic, free-floating anxiety. She returned to therapy. For the first time in her life, she was popping Valium like vitamins just to get through the day. As I was slowly working my way back to health, Claire was, bit by bit, starting to come undone. I had been the good mother gone bad. I had failed her. Now it appeared she was failing herself.

"When a woman friend falls apart, she's no longer being the good mother for her friends," says Dr. Flax. "This reawakens the friend's unconscious anxiety that every woman is going to inhibit independence like the mother. And because the investment is so great in getting this good mother in the first place, it unconsciously arouses tremendous anxieties in the other person, whose hopes of finding that such a good mother is really possible are shattered."

When a woman like Claire, who is uncertain about her own autonomy, comes into contact with someone in dire need, she can't step back from the situation because she is too wrapped up in it. Like the adolescent who searches for role models and who turns away from friends when they fail to provide such models, the idealization has undergone a revamping. The inevitable feeling is one of betrayal and irrational mistrust.

"I've lost my faith in you; I don't know who you are," Claire had said weeks after her scathing rejection, in our why-can't-we-be-friends-anymore conversation. "If you can fall apart like that, who knows what you're capable of?"

"If you can fall apart because I fall apart, who knows what *you're* capable of?" would have been the appropriate response if I had known then what I know now—which I did not.

DEMANDING WIFE, DEMANDING FRIEND

It's important to say that a friend who runs away from the neediness doesn't always have something screwed up in the autonomy department. To the contrary, quite often a woman can become so needy and clutching she scares everyone off. What would we expect, for example, from a woman who is continuously demanding and dependent upon her husband, driving him to the point of such distraction that he ups and leaves? More often than not, the dependency just gets transferred as she dumps a garbage truck filled with unreasonable expectations onto her friends. And just as it sent her husband running for dear life, it sends her friends running in the opposite direction, too.

Take Marisa, for example. Her friends had always known she was the nagging type, ordering her husband around like some kind of servant. They were also not unaware of her complete and unqualified dependency on him, a symptom which presented itself in nervous attacks when she did not know where he was every minute of the day. That she managed to have good friends despite these drawbacks was not really surprising. As long as her needs were met by her husband, she didn't need to impose on her friends.

After he left, however, the tables turned. Marisa became morbid, hysterical, and constantly demanding. She felt perfectly entitled to call her friends up at any hour of the day or night for consolation. At first, they tried to be helpful. After a while they began thinking like her ex-husband: All they wanted to do was get her off their backs. Marisa accused her friends of being unloyal bitches. As she watched them fall by the wayside, one by one, she decided to move back in with her mother.

Women who reject women like Marisa are not bitches—they are survivors. Even under the most dire of circumstances, no one likes feeling suffocated. It is reasonable to expect a friend to come through in a crisis. It is not reasonable to expect her to disrupt her whole life, to tend to her like a mother. Even the best of mothers, upon watching their child fall for the first time, will check to look for bruises, perhaps giving the child a hand so that she may regain her balance. As for doing the walking, well, that's up to the child.

SUPPORT VS. ABANDONMENT: THE PSYCHIC AFTERMATH

Let me emphasize that most women, in one way or another, manage to muster some female support when they are divorcing. While old friends may be rejecting, there is a strong network of women who have experienced the trauma of divorce and who greet the newly divorced with open arms. In addition, such formalized organizations as Parents Without Partners are growing by leaps and bounds.

Nor is the termination of earlier friendships always precipitated by friends. In a number of instances, the divorcing woman herself may drift away from her previous relationships. If her friends are married, she may feel like a fifth wheel. There is a lot of truth in the old adage that "misery loves company." Seeing a woman who is a glowing mother and wife can often exacerbate our own feelings of loneliness.

Most often, however, it is the divorcée who is rejected and not the other way around, and when this is the case, for whatever the reason, having a critical friendship fall through can be devastating.[24] Because of the psychological power women have over other women, it is shattering to us in a way that it wouldn't be if a man didn't come through. In Djuna Barnes' novel *Nightwood,* the protagonist explains how the intensity of being rejected by a man differs from that of being abandoned by a woman:

A man is another person—a woman is yourself, caught as you turn in panic; on her mouth you kiss your own. If she is taken away, you cry that you have been robbed of yourself.[25]

What gives the abandonment such psychic freight is that it comes at a time when a woman already feels abandoned. First, her husband leaves. Now her friend abandons her. "The rejection of a woman when she is divorcing can constitute a psychic trauma," says Angela Fox. "It's like being abandoned by your mother when you need her most."

Fox goes on to say that a woman whose own mother loved her enough will be more resilient to the rejection because she is on more secure footing. The woman who did not receive good enough mothering, however, may never get over it. "If the abandonment replicates the original abandonment by the mother, there's a good chance that woman will fall apart. Even with therapy, she may never really recover from it."

Being abandoned during divorce also goes a long way to explain a woman's feelings about separation. In order to successfully differentiate, one needs the presence of a reliable mothering figure—someone who gently encourages separation while remaining available should the experience of venturing into the unknown become too frightening. The mother who rejects the child for separating, or is not around when the child comes running back in fear, causes that child to retreat, to be forever fearful of venturing on its own, to remain in a stifling but necessary symbiosis. Like the child, the woman who cannot find the support she needs will also retreat. Perhaps she runs home to mother. More likely, she throws herself into the arms of the first available man. Reinforcing what happened with mother long ago, the rejection retains an inflated sense of power and proportion, reaffirming our deepest fears: Autonomy invariably leads to rejection.

On the other hand, when we have friends who are willing to stand by us and support our growth, we replace the early message about differentiation with a healthier resolution. We learn that we can fall apart and come out ahead. We learn that we can be nurtured for our autonomous selves, because our autonomy speaks well both for us and for other women. This assurance is one of the most powerful things a woman can give to another woman. It turns the old symbiotic ties around and moves us forward. "Women's relationships have the ultimate power of recapitulating the mother-daughter relationship with a healthier outcome," says Dr. Flax. "The message most girls get at eighteen months is that separation is something bad, something that breeds rejection. When the damage is undone later on by a woman's being rescued by other women, it is an incredible boost to the woman's self actualization and growth."

NEW SINGLES, NEW PERSPECTIVES

Most importantly, what happens between women when they are divorcing affects the quality of their feminine alliances after divorce. For women like Nina who receive the kind of support which makes separation exciting rather than a tiptoe in the dark, a tone of warmth and dynamism is infused into their friendships. They brim with renewed faith in women and in themselves. Indeed, if I had to select a time when women's friendships were most loyal and least ambivalent, this would be it. With illusions about men in the past, and with an open door to grow and explore in the future, women can offer each other the ultimate in support.

"I can directly tie my pleasure in women to my divorce and the support I received from them," says Nina, in retrospect. "Before that time I did not take that much pleasure in women. It just wasn't that enjoyable spending time with them. Most of that had to do with the fact that I wasn't sharing myself when I had a man. The other thing was that I didn't have a strong sense of myself as a person. How can you be responded to and share yourself if you don't even know who that self is? Forming close ties with women after I separated was fascinating. It was something I realized I wanted to do with hours of my time. It was like a whole new world opening up. I think I always used to take women for granted. But since my divorce I have been looking at the role women play in my life and feeling the value of them for even so small a thing as talking to women about waiting for a man to call and asking myself, 'What is it that you're really waiting for? Three hours spent with this man? Will it be more enjoyable than the three hours we are spending together right now?' I'm starting to look at time and pleasure and evaluate the worth of women in the true sense of the word.

"Something else has happened, too," continued Nina. "I had never been particularly interested in talking about 'things women talk about.' They just didn't interest me that much. I had a very condescending attitude about that and denied myself of that kind of pleasure. But now I can talk to an eighteen-year-old-girl about hair and enjoy it."

One of the advantages of being a divorced woman and having other divorced women as friends is that there is an abundance of good role models from which to choose. Many of Nina's friends had been financially dependent on their husbands before the marital split, as had Nina herself. All of them had had to struggle to learn to fend for themselves. They were forced into independence, if not by will then by proxy. Secure in their own sense of themselves, women learn that autonomy doesn't have to be an either/or thing. Talking about babies and home decorating and clothes doesn't mean that you also can't talk about careers, politics. Giving in to one's "feminine" wiles does not mean you will revert back to the hausfrau, whose greatest source of excitement is the afternoon soaps.

Another reality that divorced women who have grown from the experience share is a realistic assessment of men and marriage. They are beyond the fantasy and idealization that single women cling to. They lack the motivation to collude about the less than perfect virtues of marriage.

Says one thirty-nine-year-old woman who has been divorced seven years, "I think the way divorce changes you most is that you come to realize how much more important women are to you than men. When I was divorcing, my women friends were wonderful; they stood by me every step of the way. That feeling is so uplifting, and it has carried through to this day. I have a lot of men friends, and a number of lovers, but it's women who are my anchor. Compared to women, I find men emotionally immature, and I think I know men pretty well. I mean, I have so many men that I've been friends with or been in relationships with. The bottom line is that with men I've always felt like the emotionally strong one—like I'm the one who's always doing the emotional giving. But with a woman, you can be yourself—weak and strong. You can vent all your emotional insecurities and not feel that they will be judgmental of you, or that they would think of that as a weakness. They live through it with you. You see a part of yourself in someone else's struggles and successes. It's like a mirror image. I think that we've all been raised to believe that that's something you can get from a man. That's what you try to do when you're married. But the truth is, once you've seen both sides of the coin, you know that's something only another woman can provide."

That is not to say that women are never let down by other women. In any relationship there is bound to be disappointment. What is striking, however, is that there is more of an acceptance among these women, taking the good with the bad, of not having all their expectations met without feeling devastated by it. In an interview Jane Flax attributed this to giving up the fantasy of the perfect mother. "One of the primary things that women have to resolve in order to become autonomous is the fantasy of the perfect mother, the mother who can do no wrong. Being divorced goes a long way in doing that. Many women thrust all their emotional needs onto their husbands when they marry. Inevitably, they are disappointed. That disappointment conveys an important message, which is that if a man cannot be a perfect mother, maybe nobody can. So when they turn to their women friends after divorce, they are more willing to accept mothering that is by no means perfect, but that is simply 'good enough.' "

Being accepted and learning how to accept, coupled with the knowledge that men are not the be-all and end-all of a woman's existence, gives these women's friendships the intimacy and intensity of adolescent friendships, but with the added hindsight that comes from having been around long enough to know that one does not dispense with one's female friends to secure the adoration of a man. "Women are now a priority in my life," says Nina. "I want to be able to go to the movies with them on Saturday night. I want to be able to giggle hysterically while we maneuver to get a man to pay attention to us. It's a conscious choice not to let men get in the way. In fact, seeking out men is more of a bond between myself and friends than it is divisive. We bemoan our fate of not being with someone. We say, 'Oh, yeah, let's go to this party, maybe it'll be good,' or 'Let's devise a scheme to see about this guy or work on how to get that guy who is interesting to one of us.' Even if there is a conflict about a man, we can always manage to work it out. For instance, I have this situation with one close friend, where, it's uncanny, but we are always interested in the same man. It continues to happen. But we're both committed to making sure that a man doesn't come between us. We're more important to each other than a man neither of us knows really well, and we've always been able to come to some understanding."

Which is not to say that Nina or women like her do not think about getting married again. They do, although every woman I have interviewed says that the man they would ultimately choose would have to be accepting of their women friends. "One of the major things I want in a man is someone who thinks my relationships with women are wonderful," says Nina, "a man to whom I can say, 'I'm going away with

Miriam for the weekend,' and he would say, 'That sounds fabulous.' You see, I haven't given up on men altogether. Thinking about going to Brazil with my friend Phyllis sounds wonderful, but going to some romantic island with a man that I'm in love with sounds wonderful, too. They feel like two different things, two different life experiences. I like pizza and I like ice cream. I wouldn't want to have to choose."

Beyond everything is the impulse to grow. Having been supported in differentiation gives women the courage to take new risks. Breaking the symbiotic ties with mothers and husbands frees women to come into their own, to keep on growing. "My relationships with women now are very dynamic," concludes Nina. "They're founded on growth and support—whether that has to do with a man, with kids, with career, anything. It's funny. When I was married, I didn't think a whole lot about developing myself. Now growth is the bottom line for me."

And what of women who at the time of their divorce experienced the pain and humiliation of rejection by their women friends? What are their friendships like? One woman who found herself friendless during her separation ("What friends?" she said bitterly when I asked her about what role her friends played after her divorce) puts her feelings this way. "I always used to think that women were more trustworthy than men, and in some ways I still want to think that. But it's difficult when you've been so hurt, so let down. Now I have to admit I approach my relationships with women much more gingerly."[26]

I feel the fear myself. Indeed, after Claire, it was years before I felt comfortable enough to even approach having any kind of close relationship with a woman. There were acquaintances, naturally, but my guard was always up. The image of being the competent, autonomous person which I had unconsciously projected to Claire became quite deliberate. It was my way of averting the fear, of precluding rejection.

With time the wound has begun to heal. I no longer feel so susceptible to hurt as I once was. While I have never had oceans of friends, there are now a few women in my life that I believe I can count on unequivocally should I need them.

Yet, as for totally letting the barriers down, for expressing need—that still remains out of the question.

Chapter 9

OFFICE HOURS

SUSAN Mahoney clearly remembers the early stages of her professional career as an editor. She was one of the few secretaries in her company who aspired to greater heights. A bright, ambitious woman who never questioned her desire to move up the professional ladder, she nevertheless experienced tremendous conflict in her desire to forge ahead, a conflict, she says, that was triggered by the resistance of her less ambitious female coworkers. "I was always very clear about the fact that I wanted to be an editor," she recalls, "and began working as a secretary because that was considered the first step. I didn't get involved in other women's lives, in discussing their personal affairs. I was not a part of the women's gossip, of their network. There was simply too much I wanted to accomplish. And for the whole two years that I held that position," she adds, "I also had no one to go out to lunch with."

Now, ten years later, Susan is a senior editor and experiences different but related difficulties. "There are some women on my staff that I get along with very well. They have goals similar to those I had when I was in their position. We relate on a friendly basis, but those ties are never too personal, and never at the expense of our professional goals. But there are other women, women who say they want to get ahead but

who give off mixed signals. On the one hand, they work hard. At the
same time, they seem to have this dire need to have this intensely personal relationship with me. For instance, one woman, who was obviously having a lot of personal problems, came into my office before an
editorial meeting and broke down in tears, telling me the nitty-gritty of
the problems she was having with her live-in boyfriend. I sympathized
with her, and told her I was sad to learn she was feeling so badly. At the
same time, I had to cut her short because of this meeting and I guess I
didn't encourage her to come and confide in me like that again. I suppose I think it's inappropriate for a boss to play shrink or for an employee to expect that of her boss. The last thing I wanted to do was
appear callous, but I did want to set limits. Anyway, word apparently
got around, and the way this woman painted the picture was that I was
totally insensitive. From that day on, some women in my office think
I'm a real bitch."

NOWHERE ARE THE CONFLICTS between nurturance and autonomy as
blatant as in the world of work. Women, even aspiring women, like
Susan in the story above, find themselves enmeshed in the struggle
between achievement and affiliation. Before entering the working world,
we believe that men's domination is at the heart of our problems with
getting ahead—it is the men, we convince ourselves—who keep us
down, preventing us from actualizing ourselves. Yet any woman who
has worked long enough in the realm of other women, knows all too
well that it is not our conflicts with men, but with women, that arouses
our greatest fears. It is not men but women who hold the key to our
independence with an iron grip.

The working world may be dominated by men, but the issues that are
at the forefront when women work together are women's issues: affiliation vs. professionalism, jealousy and role confusion, nurturance and
autonomy. Men's concerns are professional—getting the job done, being competent, moving up. Many women share these concerns, but they
are interlaced with more relational desires—that of liking and being
liked, sharing and not sharing, inclusion and isolation. In the nine-to-
five of a man's world, we are wrapped up in the female sphere still.

To work, to make one's way in the world, is to be separate. A man
achieves his adult status when he gets his first job; for him, working is a

rite of passage. For a woman, work signifies independence and separation. And on some level there is nothing she fears more.

Mother never saw us as separate; she was threatened by our moves toward independence. Afraid that we would be different from her, that with a sense of ourselves we would no longer need her, she squelched the pride we took in our achievements. The working woman faces many such mother figures every day in her endeavors. No matter how driven, how ambitious she may be, working with women rearouses these basic conflicts: putting success first feels like some sort of betrayal of the whole female gender.

When young girls ignore the rules of competition, the imprinting begins. "Let me have another turn," little Janie cries, although she's been beaten fair and square. "All right," says the other little girl, long resigned to the fact that being nice is more important than winning. Such encounters form pivotal experiences in our lives, reinforcing mother's negative association with achievement. The pattern is repeated through later stages of development: the adolescent girl who forfeits her own grades to spend all night talking to her friend who's just been dumped by her boyfriend; the college woman who does not join the sorority of her choice because her friend has not been accepted; the working woman who feels conflicted about vying for the promotion because she does not want to lose the network of the secretarial pool. Even the feminist message that says "Go for it; be successful" has a powerful undertone: "—as long as it is not at the expense of nurturance."

By the time we enter the working world, we have been well schooled in the relational sphere, making the rules of patriarchal bureaucracy all but alien to us. Our primary experience with one another has been with nurturance, connectedness, relationship. We have encouraged one another to deny our competitive impulses. We do not know how to interact with other women in terms of prescribed roles—to give and take orders, to form bonds based on achievements. "The basic feminine sense of self is connected to the world," says Nancy Chodorow. "The basic masculine sense of self is separate."[1] The rules of patriarchal bureaucracy are rooted in a structure defined by separation, differentiation, compartmentalization—everything success is—and women intrinsically are not.

The conflict between what women need and what work demands creates tremendous tension in the working relationships between women. Because our own success is staked in the success of other women around us, we have a strong investment in fostering one another's autonomy. At the same time, our need for relationship tugs at the heels, throttling us back within more acceptable "female" limits. The split between forming personal relationships or being excluded completely that Susan Mahoney speaks of reflects our underlying difficulty with independence. We have not yet figured out how we can be competent and caring, successful and a good friend, too. "This is a culture that has two poles," says Jane Flax, "independent and separated at one and fused and merged at the other. Women's difficulty with independence has to do with running the risk of being isolated, of being rejected."

Small wonder that women like Susan Mahoney say they find it easier working with men. If men are not the ideal, at least they have come to some sort of resolution about their drives toward achievement. "With men, it's clear what their goals are. But with women, it's often difficult to tell what they really want—friendship, achievement or what?"

OUTSIDERS ON THE INSIDE

My own guess is that women who work do want to feel a sense of accomplishment, but they may lean toward the social aspects of work when they discover it's still a man's world.

Men know that they will be given a fair shake based on their job performance and competence. But what does the average female office worker have to look forward to? She is likely to be given more routine tasks than her male counterpart and to be paid less. Any promotion will come more slowly. Her image will be scrutinized more than her competence, her behavior more than her skill, her clothing more than her achievements.

Men tend to be disturbed by a woman's presence in a work situation, and she can expect to be treated as some kind of annoyance best ignored. She will be seen as carrying the weight of women's collective disability, and will find that less work is both offered to her and expected from her. If she is competing with a man for a job, the odds are she shouldn't hold her breath.

Even if she has the same probability of being hired, she can look

forward to some kind of clerical work, while a man with identical quali-
fications will be groomed delicately for management. And should she
move up the ranks, she can expect identical work to be evaluated less
highly than her male counterpart's.[2]

The job of the working woman is to turn this opinion around.

The problem is not only the obstacles imposed by men, but that for
the whole of our upbringing we've lived by different rules—women's
rules meant for women's work. We are "outsiders on the inside," standing at the doorstep of the real world but lacking the key to get in.
Psychologist Barbara Forisha, an expert on women in business, says it
all: "Models of successful behavior in the work world are masculine;
women do not 'fit.' "[3]

WHAT DOES BUSINESS WANT?

What does it take to make it in business? What qualities are at the
forefront when a boss hires a new employee?

"Women who want and manage to achieve a high status experience a
'cold war' and must have the psychology of long-distance runners to
endure the loneliness that comes from rejection by their colleagues,"
says psychologist Constantine Safilios-Rothschild.[4]

"You must be cool, unflappable, unemotional, keep your mouth shut,
and be prepared to violate those rules when and if necessary," says Jo
Foxworth, president of her own advertising agency.[5]

A vice president of a firm of financial analysts says, "I expect the
same thing from people who work for me as from myself: dedication,
commitment, and efficiency. I generally let people set their own deadlines, and I expect that once they've done that, they stick to it. I don't
care if it takes them thirty seconds, or five weeks, twenty-four hours a
day. Whatever it takes to get the job done is what I require."

Responsibility. Unemotionality. Drive. Dedication. Nowhere is there
the mention of nurturance. Indeed, none of the women or men I interviewed mentioned nurturance as a desirable quality in the workplace.
To the contrary, it has been suggested that too much caring is more of a
detriment than an asset. One major mail order firm, for example, cites
being too friendly with one's employees as good cause for a poor work

review. Not surprisingly, those indicted for such an "offense" are over-whelmingly women.

Other company heads complain not about the nurturance per se, but about women's inability to keep professional confidences. "One of the things I have to tell the women who work for me over and over again is that information is power," a female vice president for a sales promotion firm tells me. "I hate to say this, but women just divulge too much. What might appear as healthy camaraderie in domestic endeavors can be a real detriment when you're working on high-level negotiations. Women don't know how to negotiate too well, particularly with other women, because there's always this dynamic of wanting to bring things down to a more personal level. That's great at the club, but it's disastrous in business."

WHAT DO WOMEN WANT?

While work structures are organized around independence, rationality, and self-reliance, women's psychic structure is founded on attachment and emotionality. "Cathexis" is a technical term which refers to a process of taking in. According to Freud, our sense of ourselves is formed by absorbing energy from a love object and internalizing that energy as our own—a kind of human osmosis. This is what fuels the ego to grow.

The psychological propellants given to little boys and little girls, however, are as different as rocket fuel and unleaded gasoline. From the outset a boy's burgeoning feelings about exploration and accomplishment are rewarded by mother's effusive praise. The female baby, on the other hand, gets her strokes for remaining attached. The result is that men are driven by their ability to master; work is more highly cathected. A woman's power source, however, is derived from her feelings of connectedness; work, in and of itself, is not sufficient to get her motor running.

The evidence of how such disparate experiences shape achievement motivation has been revealed by research findings. Focusing on the potential springboards for the desire to excel, one study has questioned whether children strive to achieve because of an internal standard of success or because they want to receive praise from others. The children studied ranged in age from four to eight.

The results indicated that boys who are academically successful are motivated to achieve because they want to feel good about themselves. In contrast, girls used achievement as a way of securing love and approval; affiliative needs as opposed to achievement needs were what correlated most highly with academic success.[6]

Simply put: Take away the element of approval, and girls' motivation to achieve is severely dampered.

The difference can be seen in the variable responses so often heard between women and men. "I hate my job," says the woman, "but I love the people I work with," implying that her personal relationships are enough to compensate for the day-to-day drudgery. "I hate my job," says the man, not thinking to include how he feels about the people he works with as a primary criterion. Men see their work and the people they work with as distinct entities. Women view these two facets of work as more or less one and the same.

SCENES FROM AN OFFICE

Given the fact that most working environments are patriarchally structured and not particularly nurturant, how do women cope?

In large part, by bringing the mountain to Mohammed. That is, by doing men's work in a woman's way. Women are far more likely to form close relationships with one another than their male counterparts with whom they engage in intimate and sympathetic conversation. Our greater needs for affiliation lead women to open up with a rapport and honesty unprecedented in relationships between male colleagues.[7] Men tend to react to coworkers solely in terms of roles. But women's lives are more fluid and malleable—their ego boundaries more permeable. Our early attachment to Mother leads us to define ourselves as continuous with others, as connected to the world. Asking a woman to completely separate her personal life from her work is like asking a man to separate his feelings about himself from his achievements.

Beneath the businesslike veneer of even the most successful woman lurks the quicksand of intimacy and affiliation. In their book *The Mana-*

gerial Woman authors Margaret Hennig and Anne Jardim noted that while friendships for men are a valued outcome of the job, an asset used to further their careers, women view friendship as a prerequisite for interaction.[8] Without those liaisons, women have difficulty functioning. Their work is disrupted; job efficiency comes plummeting down.

The fewer emotional tributaries flowing outside the workplace, the more likely the job is to become a woman's pool of nurturance. In a study of employed men and women, single women cited interpersonal relationships at work as a source of gratification more than married women. In fact, these liaisons were more important to them than a sense of accomplishment. Married and unmarried women did have one thing, however, in common; in both cases they were far more likely to mention their friendships at work as a source of pleasure than their male counterparts.[9]

Such findings as these can be read in one of two ways. The first is that our ability to form friendships despite the competitive tenor of most working situations is a testimonial to our ability to defy patriarchy, a form of resistance against the impersonality and cutthroat quality so typical of men's working relationships. More importantly, feminine alliances provide women with a kind of good-old-girls network, the female counterpart to the good-old-boys network from which most women are inevitably excluded. "Women, because of their minority status," write sociologists Barbara Goldman and Barbara Forisha, "are isolated from their male peers; the informal work groups and support groups are not open to them."[10] Hence, the need for support systems among women.

Yet the authors' statement assumes that women's networks grant license for achievement, that they propel women forward. Unfortunately, they often may not.

WORKING OR MOTHERING?

While strong relationships with female colleagues may feel good, they also may impede growth. It's true that support networks and collegial relationships that are geared toward professional advancement can be one of a woman's most valuable assets on the job. But all too often, work-related friendships are an expression of our preference for being well liked as opposed to being competent. Of course, women aren't necessarily the villains. It's easy to understand how the desire of men to keep women down can zap the motivation out of even the most ambitious woman. Discouraged professionally, we go about making our mark in the best way we know how—by being "nice." Whatever the source of the dilemma, making interpersonal relations a priority only provides fuel for those who are dead set on believing that women aren't too competent to begin with when it comes to "serious" business.[11] To say nothing of our efficacy on the job.

"A woman's role when she is at work is not to be someone's mother, confidante, or friend," says Jane Flax. "It is to perform. The result is that women feel very conflicted in working situations with other women. There is always that pull to return to the intimate female sphere, which in most cases compromises job efficiency. There is no way you can be effective when your primary goal is to obtain nurturance. Nor can a woman be truly competent if she is continuously concerned with whose feelings she hurts."

Today we tell our coworker our problems. Who is to say that tomorrow she won't be in a position to use that "privileged" information against us? Saying that we do not want to be like men, we are empathic and nurturant. But what happens when our own success is staked in making another woman feel bad?

The conventional wisdom which proposes one not mix business with pleasure does not need to be swallowed whole in order to see the pitfalls in forming intimate relationships with women at the workplace. Take, for instance, the following example. Two women, who have become friends, are assigned to work on a joint project. Woman A is industrious and creative, and puts her all into making a good show. Woman B, however, does not meet up to her share of the collaboration, riding on the shirttails of Woman A. Woman A feels both angry and used. She also knows that unless she speaks up, she will not receive the recognition due her. What does she do?

Two voices are trying to speak at once.

The voice of the caring, nurturing mother says, "Your friendship comes first. Whatever decision is made must be done within the context of your emotional commitment to this person." The voice of the businesswoman says, "Business is business. You must do what's best for yourself professionally, even if it is at the expense of other people's feelings."

Most women are more comfortable with the first voice than with the second. Although many women may be eager to get ahead, they have not yet learned to separate their professional life from their emotional life. They do not know how to sit down with a friend, who is also a colleague, and say, "Look, I'm unhappy working with you. It is professionally unsatisfying, and I feel the need to make a switch." What experience have they had to negate the idea that professional rejection, as painful or necessary as that might be, is not an indication of personal rejection as well?

Some women can do it. Most cannot. When we take women's propensity toward nurturance—to put feelings a step and a half ahead of everything else—and then add the implicit independence and rationality that working situations demand, it is very evident that few women are integrated enough to accept professional rejection from another woman without also hearing the perennial source of her greatest anxiety: "You don't love me anymore."

"The conflict often gets acted out unconsciously," says Jane Flax. "Sometimes a woman will come across as completely loyal. For example, she'll talk about how important her friendships are, how she would never do anything to jeopardize them. At the same time, the same woman can butter up the boss and be ready to stick a knife in her friend's back should she need to. The problem is that women are often unclear about what should take priority in working situations. There's no implicit agreement that business concerns will take precedence over affiliative concerns. Either she's a friend or a businessperson. She doesn't know how to be both."

The more intimate the ties, the more the voices of separation and dependency, nurturance and autonomy, are likely to clash head on.

TOO CLOSE FOR COMFORT

Again and again from women I have interviewed, one refrain is heard: "Do not mix friendship with business." The collective sentiment comes straight out of the voice of experience. Working with other women is difficult enough, given our propensity to attend to the needs of others. Working with friends only intensifies the problem. From what vantage point can we separate our professional roles and aspirations from our emotional entanglements?

"This summer I asked a close friend to do some research for me," says a thirty-one-year-old freelance writer. "She had just lost her job and I thought I could help her out. It was a disaster. All sorts of problems befell her. Her car broke down. Her kid got sick. She twisted her ankle. The upshot was that I had two days to write this article as opposed to two weeks. If she hadn't been such a good friend, I never would have put up with it; I would have found someone else. But I didn't have the courage to tell her she was fired. It would have destroyed her. Probably our relationship, too. But I'll tell you one thing," she added as an afterthought. "I'll never put myself in a position like that again."

Such situations are par for the course. Women are always lured into a mothering role with other women, and with a friend the pull is like an electromagnet. The difficulty is that mothering is not a work function, but a parenting one. If the dictates of being a good mother or friend keep a woman from functioning at her peak, she is standing in the way of her own growth. And the woman who takes advantage of a friendship, using the interpersonal foundation of their relationship as an excuse to act less than professionally, impedes the growth of us all.

But the problem of working with friends is bigger than this. With every friendship comes a hidden agenda, a transferential element that unconsciously plays out old mother-daughter scenarios. Adding work as an ingredient to the batter is like throwing a double portion of yeast into a loaf of bread—the bread rises higher, but prick it with a pin and you have a flat loaf.

One of the struggles a woman named Brie, a patient of Angela Fox's, is having these days is figuring out a way to fire her professional manager. Her feeling is that her friend-turned-manager has misrepresented her as a songwriter and undermines her talent. Although it has become clear that their professional relationship is no longer viable, Brie has spent seven out of her last eight therapy sessions rehearsing the break at the rate of fifty dollars an hour.

Dark clouds had portended the storm from the start. "There were certain clues from the very beginning about how this manager saw Brie as a songwriter, how she wanted to package her," says Ms. Fox. "It was inevitable, given the situation, that she was going to feel cheated, and on some level she recognized it." Nevertheless, she bound herself contractually to this woman, propelled by a force she did not as yet understand. Consciously, she wanted to believe her manager would lift her career to new heights. Unconsciously, she was motivated by a desire to repeat her negative relationship with her mother.

Neurotic transference, uncontrolled, sabotaged her career. Listening to recordings of the songs her mother-manager had handed over to record producers, Brie wanted to wretch. Her songs, born of heartfelt emotions, had been electronically transformed into synthesizer bubblegum music. For the privilege of "having some guy who sounded like he had a toothache" croon away, she had forfeited the publishing copyrights to some of her best material. To boot, her manager had finagled a way to skim fifteen hundred dollars more than Brie right off the top.

"The underlying dynamics," says Angela Fox, "couldn't have been more obvious. All the characteristics this manager possessed were those that Brie's mother had possessed, arousing the same feelings—you're ripping me off, you don't think I'm a worthwhile person, you represent me other than the way I am—all those things were true about her mother. Her mother had misrepresented her to the world. Her mother never approved of her writing when she was young, continuously telling her she was wasting her time. Her mother was highly critical of her." In essence, Brie's mother had cheated her, ripped her off, just as the agent had done.

Having come to these insights herself, Brie's dilemma is far from over. In every transferential situation there is always a certain degree of wish fulfillment, a desire to recapitulate history in the hopes of a more propitious resolution. Daughters who reject their mothers (as Brie had by leaving home at seventeen) experience the concurrent desire for Mom to turn around and beg them to stay, with the promise of doing better the next go-around. When Brie musters the grit to fire her manager (which is difficult in and of itself, as one does not "fire" one's mother), similar desires are likely to loom. The degree to which Brie's therapy has been successful will largely determine the outcome.

"The child in her will be pulled toward trying to revise the situation, particularly if her manager is upset and promises to reform; it was the child in her that chose the manager in the first place. If, however, she's grown during the analysis, her decision will be governed by the part of her that is an adult, that has achieved a separation from her rejecting mother."

Of course, women friends working together is not always an augury of disaster. The desire to work through old sores in the hopes of resolving them is not only at the root of all our friendships, but is a driving force in sustaining them. So long as the "mother we choose" has our best interests at heart, we may well be able to push past the conflict and grow from it.

More often than not, however, such relationships are filled with demons. Even if the decision to collaborate is not cut out of a neurotic mold, resolving issues of contention becomes a guilt-laden affair.

Take, for example, the story of a forty-year-old hat designer. A year ago she had hooked up with her closest friend in the hopes of getting a mail-order business off the ground. Six months after the two women began working together, little money had been made, and the designer began to feel her talents would stand a better chance with someone else. Had this not been her closest friend, she probably would have come right out and said she wanted to terminate the relationship. Instead, she sidestepped the issue altogether and began working with someone else without even telling her friend. Her friend eventually heard of the new merger through the grapevine, bringing their long-standing relationship to a painful end.

It comes as a rude shock when our best friend not only rejects us, but does it "behind our back." The difficulty is that we have no precedent for separating without the concurrent fear that rejection is not far behind. Like the eighteen-year-old who suddenly leaves home with not even a note, the only way we have to resolve such a conflict is to run away from home.

THE POLITICS OF FRIENDSHIP

Andrea Carter was an ambitious girl who began her professional career as an interviewer for New York Telephone. At twenty-four she had packed her bags and moved halfway across the country in order to experience life in the big city. Within a month of the move, she had found an apartment and had landed a job. The only thing missing from her life was friends. "I desperately needed some contact with people, some friends."

At work she met a woman whose predicament duplicated hers entirely. "Danielle and I were the two new girls in the department. We were about the same age, even around the same size. We were both living away from home for the first time." Naturally, they became friendly with each other. "We didn't know too many other people in the company. So we arranged our coffee breaks together, went out to lunch together. It became almost a daily thing."

Andrea and Danielle shared their pasts, their apprehensions about the present, their hopes for the future. Both women wanted to move up in the company; both harbored middle-management aspirations. As a result, much of their conversation revolved around issues at work. "We were primary support systems for each other. A lot of what we discussed had to do with coping with difficulties on the job, learning the ropes, coping with our boss, who was a very nice woman but could get very hyper and drive you nuts."

One day, six months after the two women had started work, Andrea was called into her boss's office. "You're an extraordinarily talented young woman," her boss had said, "and you should be in a position commensurate with your skills." Andrea was offered a promotion.

"I had mixed emotions, feeling proud and excited, but not knowing what to tell Danielle. One thing that was very important to me was that we maintain the friendship." The next three months were spent trying to bridge the gap between their newly divergent positions. The two women continued to lunch together, although less regularly. They did not discuss the ramifications of Andrea's promotion, sweeping it under the rug in the hopes that the issue would simply disappear. It did not.

"It was very embarrassing," recalls Andrea. "We began to have less and less to talk about. When we were in similar positions, we could talk to each other about problems at work, support each other, complain to each other. But in my new position there were a lot of things I couldn't discuss with her. There were some projects I was working on that she wouldn't understand. There were other things that involved certain management decisions which affected Danielle and which I didn't feel free to divulge. That made things kind of tough. She's still back in the old department, on the old job, and I'm not."

Not surprisingly, women like Andrea Carter who find themselves having to jettison old friendships for the sake of upward mobility, experience a fair degree of guilt.

"I couldn't help but feel I had done something wrong," says Andrea in retrospect. "I don't like to think of myself as using people. And what is it that you're doing when you drop a relationship simply because it's no longer convenient? I always thought of myself as very loyal. Now, frankly, I'm beginning to wonder."

It is not simply guilt that we feel when putting ourselves first, but fear —fear that if we take care of business first, we will lose other women's love. "A bitch," says Pat Rotter in the preface to *Bitches and Sad Ladies,* "is someone who can finally say, 'I come first. I am the most important person in my life.' "[12] But for women the cost of being a bitch is rejection. Andrea Carter may say that what she feels is guilt, but underneath it all is the real terror—the fear of abandonment.

In her study of women in top positions, Jane Adams found that few women, even women who were successful by anyone's definition, felt comfortable with the political aspects of their jobs. "Many women put competition, corporate gamesmanship, and manipulation in the same desk drawer, shut it, and label it 'negative.' "[13] Which is why so many of these women chose to keep their personal lives completely separate from their professional ones.

Women are not so naive as not to know that to get ahead professionally, relationships must be consciously plotted, strategically manipulated as a means to an end. Nevertheless, most women try sidestepping the issue in the hopes that it may conveniently disappear. To politicize something as emotionally loaded as a friendship with another woman is to consciously say that there is something more important than nurturance. It is to say that we can live without intimacy with other women. It is to take the risk of being the bitch.

INTIMACY AS WEAPON

The flip side, of course, to the woman who feels guilty about discarding friendships when they are no longer professionally advantageous, is the woman who uses privileged information to fulfill her own professional ambitions. While self-disclosure may give us a feeling of connectedness, in the business world information is powerful ammunition.

Until last year Wendy Norris, now thirty-three, had been a freelance copywriter. Although she enjoyed the flexibility of self-employment, the demands of living project to project had begun to wear thin. She wanted some security. She wanted to know where her next paycheck would be coming from. She wanted a "regular" job.

Through her connections Wendy learned that a major advertising company was looking for someone with her skills. Her portfolio was impressive, and she quickly passed through the initial interviewing process. Eventually, she reached the woman who was to be her potential boss.

"She was the type of woman that everyone was afraid of," Wendy recalled. "She would walk around and everyone would shake in their shoes." Wendy was a strong woman herself, however, and asserted herself from the start.

"Do you know how many hours you're going to have to work?" the boss had said.

"It's my understanding the job is basically nine to five," responded Wendy.

"Wrong," corrected the vice president. "You're going to have to be on call always. We work weekends here. We work around the clock."

Wendy considered these demands for a moment and replied squarely, "If that's what you need, this is not the place for me. I have two children; I have a family life. I think I can make a positive contribution to your company, but I will not spend my entire life working."

As a result of that interview, Wendy was hired. "I think I was the first woman that ever took the risk of standing up to her. And she respected me for that."

That interview had set the relationship between the two women on an even footing. Her boss treated most of those under her with a certain contempt, but Wendy's limits about what she would not tolerate could not have been clearer. "I wasn't going to be spoken to in the way she spoke to the others. She tried once or twice, and I let her know straightaway that such behavior was unacceptable."

Wendy's strong sense of self-assertion earned her boss's respect, and it was not long before she received a promotion to senior copywriter. Her talents were also well recognized, and before long, Wendy was receiving more than her fair share of clients. While she stuck to her guns about leaving work at a reasonable hour, she felt like a rubberband being pulled in ten different directions the entire day—constantly overextended, constantly in demand, constantly on the verge of snapping.

A year after Wendy joined the company, Wendy's husband began having serious problems with depression, leaving her to cope with the majority of the household and child-rearing responsibilities, as well as her job. Indeed, Wendy was about on the verge of a breakdown herself.

Sensing her distress, her boss called her into her office. "Wendy, you seem overwrought," she said. "You have a serious problem. Maybe you should see a psychiatrist." To which Wendy responded that she already had.

"Well, dear," she had said out of what Wendy wanted to believe was genuine concern, "why don't we talk about it. Maybe I can help. Everyone needs some help once in a while. I'd like you to be able to trust me."

Wendy proceeded to fall apart. "I ended up sitting there for two hours pouring my guts out to her. I told her everything about what was happening at work and at home. As it turned out, it was the biggest mistake I could have made.

"When I fell apart, she started treating me differently. Then she started trying to use me, trying to talk to me the way she had talked to all these other people, and because I was feeling vulnerable, I didn't have the energy to fight it. I'd given her the weapon to turn on me, and she used it. She became extremely nasty. Knowing that I was in a very weak position, that I was feeling very beaten down, made me that much more vulnerable. Just like the strength I had shown her before fed on itself, the vulnerability fed on itself. If there's anything I've learned, it's that in a working situation, never let women see your weaknesses. *Never.* They will use it against you."

It may sound, from the tone of the above story, that the problems that befell Wendy were simply a case of female naiveté. But actually, that's the smallest part of the drama. In truth, far more disturbing things were going on for both Wendy and her boss, and for other women who find themselves in similar predicaments—elements of sado-masochism.

While it's unpopular to think of mothers as outrightly sadistic, the fact is that more than a handful of mothers can be accused of persecuting their children, of overcontrolling them. It's also a basic psychiatric tenet that such victimization is an overcompensation for one's own fear of being controlled. Finding others to victimize, one wards off one's own anxiety of being victimized by others. Freud calls this the identification with the aggressor. It's why the battered child so often grows up to be a battering parent.

I don't know Wendy's boss's history. But somewhere along the line I would suspect she herself had been tyrannized. Now it was her turn. Controlling those who worked for her with her wicked tongue and condescending attitude was her way of ensuring those same devices would never be used against her.

When the two women began working together, Wendy's assertiveness precluded such control. And while her boss was attracted to Wendy's outward strength and assertiveness, we might also suspect she was unconsciously terrified of it. Temporarily, she obliterated the fear by winning Wendy over to her side. Then came the opening—Wendy's breakdown. She grabbed on to the control panel like a leech.

While it feels better to point the finger at the boss, Wendy was 50 percent accountable for the tyranny. True, women are more prone to open up to one another than men. But given what Wendy knew of her boss, it was clear from the outset that she was not only giving her boss the ammunition, but the gun. She saw the trap, but nevertheless walked straight into it.

One does not have to delve far to see the unconscious roots out of which her decision was wrought. "My mother was a very unreliable person. She was the type of woman who'd say she'd pick me up and then do a no-show. One minute she could be very kind and understanding, encouraging you to open up to her, then the next moment she'd use that information against you." By breaking down in front of her boss, Wendy was not only replicating the early scenario with her mother, but was hoping this time it might have a better resolution. Unfortunately, as is often the case, it did not.

What is so interesting is that the dynamics of sadomasochism has, at its roots, the underlying fear of separation. Says Erich Fromm, "Both tendencies [sadism and masochism] are the outcomes of one basic need, springing from the inability to bear the isolation and weakness of one's own self. I suggest calling the aim which is at the basis of both sadism and masochism: *symbiosis*. Symbiosis, in this psychological sense, means the union of one individual self with another self . . . in such a way as to make each lose the integrity of it's own self and to make them completely dependent on each other. The sadistic person needs his object just as much as the masochistic needs his. Only instead of seeking security by being swallowed, he gains it by swallowing somebody else. In both cases the integrity of the individual self is lost."[14]

BACKING DOWN FROM INDEPENDENCE

This brings us to an important point. If what Fromm says is true, then what we are really doing by overly divulging is reenacting our relationships with our mothers. We say we want to make it in a man's world, but when we rush into the office to tell our colleagues the intimate details of last night's pickup, or spend our time in intimate exchange, to whom are we remaining true? Is it any wonder that so many women claim that working hasn't contributed one iota to their autonomy? It's a replication of the old symbiosis.

If women have been slow to learn the lesson of not divulging too much, it is because it goes against their desire for fusion. We say that we're just following our natural inclinations, but in truth, those inclinations don't do much for independence. If anything, it's privacy that fosters separation; keeping highly personal issues out of our work relationships is a direct statement about a woman's desire to focus on the job at hand, to separate.

If any suggestion that we are keeping each other down raises our hackles, it is because the truth makes us uncomfortable. And while most women overtly condemn such ploys as the one Wendy's boss used, the fact is, we load ourselves with an explosive which is just as volatile. It is called rejection.

A twenty-seven-year-old merchandising executive says, "At least once a week my phone rings at nine-oh-five and my boss says, 'Do you have a few minutes?' and calls me into her office. I go in and there's always one point of reference that's business-oriented, but that is resolved in three minutes flat. The rest of the time is just a monologue about her family problems, situations, weekend experiences. Endlessly, personal calls are taken with me sitting there, so I've ended up knowing everything that is going on in her life, with her daughter, her husband, her daughter's teacher, the housekeeper. I've always been friendly with the women I've worked with, but I've never felt the need to develop intensely personal relationships that I see some women having. It just makes me uncomfortable in a work situation. But over time it's become clear that intimacy and self-disclosure is something my boss expects, as much as she expects high sales figures.

"There is only so long you can sit and listen and say nothing, or give gibberish. When someone is pouring out her heart, there is definitely something comparable expected back in return. So despite my feelings, I've been hooked into this disclosure thing, like it or not. You know," she says, with a look of resignation, "I just can't imagine a male boss coming in first thing in the morning and saying, 'God, I had this awful fight with my wife! She's been a real pain lately, and I really can't stand it, and what should I do . . . blah, blah, blah.' "

Does this sound like appropriate behavior? More to the point, does it sound like a boss whose main concern is getting her job done?

The more we divulge to our coworkers about our intimate lives, the more we reinforce the old psychological script we played out with mother—if I tell you all, you will never abandon me. If I share my vulnerabilities, promise that you'll always love me. As long as we define our working relationships by our attachments, we continue to perpetuate the idea that women cannot develop significant relationships without this mushy, intimate disclosure. Dependency is continued.

The struggle to learn how to deal effectively with women in a work environment, to find an appropriate balance between the drive for affiliation and the need for efficacy on the job, is the task that all women in the labor force must face. To ask women to divorce themselves completely from their emotions is unreasonable. Yet to become too wrapped up in the realm of emotions, to ignore the political framework in which most work situations are ineluctably bound, is not only to be counterproductive from a purely economic point of view—it provides fuel for every man and woman who believe that women should not be leaders, that women's place is in the home, that women are something less than first-rate employees.

Some women I've spoken to are already well on their way to finding that balance. "I've always had wonderful relationships with the women I've worked for," one paralegal assistant told me. "And we've remained friends even after I stopped working with them. I think that's because we've always had a sense of where work leaves off and where friendship begins. I don't expect to be treated differently at work because we're friendly, and my bosses haven't given me special favors either. Which isn't to say that we don't do the things other friends do for each other *after* office hours," she added.

Others say that they are uncomfortable when their relationships with coworkers and particularly with bosses are too intimate, but they simply don't know how to get around it. They're afraid that they will be shuttled out of their boss's good graces and that they might even possibly lose a promotion if they do not respond to intimate disclosure with some confessions of their own.

Angela Fox couldn't disagree more vehemently. "It takes two to get involved, and if a woman senses that her boss wants to hook her into an overly intimate relationship, she has to be very careful not to give her an opening. If the employer opens the door and pours out her personal life and she's met with a closed door on the other side, chances are the employer won't go to step two."

As for losing out on a promotion, Ms. Fox thinks "that's ridiculous. People don't get promoted for sharing their personal lives. I think it's part of women's insecurities that they feel they have to play out these old roles in order to be accepted." She then goes on to tell me about a patient of hers who is an executive for a large retail outlet and whose job is to promote a new department. She has been given no staff, virtually no money to work with, and no corporate support. Not surprisingly, the department is failing, a fact which filled this woman with anxiety. As she was pouring out her heart about her problems, Ms. Fox interrupted her and asked, "Let me ask you something. How do you think you would handle this situation if you were a man?"

"It was as if a whole new world opened up to her," Ms. Fox told me. "If she were a man, she said that what she would do is go to the top-echelon executive, rip open the door, and present a plan about what kind of promotion for the department was needed, what kind of advertising was needed, and what kind of budget would be required. She would have said, 'Look, you're interested in this department? This is what we need to make it go.' The whole picture of how she would be working if she were a man was so different from the way she was behaving as a woman."

In a nutshell, many of our problems on the job are self-imposed, and if we're to overcome them, we're going to have to take a good hard look at our own needs to be liked, to nurture, to do men's work in a woman's way. And we will have to start putting ourselves in men's shoes to understand how we can make it in a league that men have dominated for so long, and to face the fact that for women getting ahead in the working world is a new ball game.

Chapter 10

BOSS-EMPLOYEE CONFLICTS: THE SAGA OF ARLENE NIELSEN

EVERY weekday morning Arlene Nielsen walks briskly from her two-bedroom condominium located in a Dallas suburb to her new silver Honda Accord. It is seven forty-five and Arlene is on her way to the forty-story building which houses the electronics corporation for which she works. She is an attractive woman of thirty who keeps her slender figure through exercise and "diet, diet, diet." As she waits for her car to warm up, she greedily devours one of two prepackaged granola bars, stashing the remainder in the glove compartment for consumption during lunch.

Arlene loves her work and the material comfort her middle-management position affords—the car, the condominium which she shares with her husband, the Harve Benard suits and Anne Klein dresses that have become a standard part of her wardrobe. Arriving at work forty minutes later, she checks her appearance in the rearview mirror, grabs her briefcase, and makes her way to the fourteenth floor, on which her department is located. Walking confidently through the large, neatly organized space, she greets her seven employees with a warm, toothy grin. They seem pleased to see her, and her presence has a settling effect as the four women and two men retire to their individual niches and get down to work.

There are, of course, routine problems to deal with: One employee is absent. Who will do her work? The computer system has been out for the past half hour—what should take priority until it is working? One employee asks if she can leave early to attend her daughter's class play. Arlene's desk is already stacked with messages and interoffice memos, the morning mail soon to be added to the heap.

Arlene doesn't ruffle. After three years she has become accustomed to the pace, the responsibility, the people. She is self-assured and has learned to develop an even temper which serves her well in her managerial position. It is a trait that took her a long time to develop and only now has become part of her autonomic style. For, as many women in supervisory positions discover, there are few adequate role models available. For women who are moving up the professional ladder, there are few resources or mentors from which one can draw in order to learn the kind of androgynous orientation so necessary if one is to be a competent woman in a position of power, without simultaneously losing one's femininity altogether.

LEAVING THE HELPING PROFESSIONS

Arlene was twenty-seven before the idea of entering the corporate ranks had occurred to her. She held a master's degree in speech pathology, and for the first five years of her professional life had worked with severely disabled children. Five years of caretaking had burned her out. "It takes a special kind of person to work with the disadvantaged and still come home with a smiling face," she admitted honestly, "and I was not one of them."

Bright and still young enough to make the switch, Arlene set out to get a corporate position. She wrote well, and with the help of some friends, pulled together an excellent résumé which highlighted her organizational and administrative abilities. She followed every lead, accepted every interview. Three months later, her efforts paid off. She was offered a low-level management position in a major electronics firm. Her job was to monitor data collection and coding for a large survey-research project the company was conducting. Not a huge salary, but it did get her foot in the door. "My primary purpose was to learn as much as I could as fast as I could and move up."

Indeed, her boss, whose name was Sylvia, was well equipped to teach Arlene the technical aspects of her department. A master technician who had an inherent flair for systems management, Sylvia was reputed to be one of the most adept organizational wizards in the company. What she had to offer, unfortunately, was largely canceled out by her lack of compassion, empathy, humaneness.

THE ANTIFEMALE FEMALE BOSS

"Dragon Lady." That was the unofficial title that Arlene and the other women in her department had given to her boss, a woman who breathed fire but was as cold as a dead fish.

"The first word that comes to mind when you ask me to describe her is 'abrasive,' " said Arlene. "She had worked her way up to middle management and was set up with all the strappings of power, with all the right symbols, and she wore those symbols like badges. She was totally absorbed in getting ahead, and had absolutely no empathy for anyone—particularly for women. It is as if she had taken the worst from the male image of what a tough executive is supposed to be like, without having any of the nurturing characteristics typically associated with being a woman. She was even more closed-minded than the male managers. She was a real bitch."

"Even her way of dressing was pathetic," she added. "She'd wear these low-heeled, kind of square-toed leather shoes, almost like loafers, but a little nicer; suits that were well made and expensive, but square in shape and very unflattering to her figure. Little shirts that buttoned up at the neck—almost like a man's cotton pinstriped shirt, but a woman's duplicate; short hair; thick glasses. When she'd take the glasses off, you could see she was very, very attractive. She had nice hair, a pretty face, and a good figure. But she deliberately made herself look like a schoolmarm."

Looking down at her own flattering but professional silk dress, she added, "There's no reason for it. Women can be businesslike without looking like a man. They don't have to defeminize themselves to be competent."

While Arlene tossed off that realization lightly, almost as a fact of life that anyone who has been around long enough would know, it had been a recognition that was earned through blood and sweat. While more and more women are blazing the career track, the pressure on them to prove their competency is enormous. Out of one side of its mouth the American public may be saying it would vote for a woman President, but out of the other it says that a woman must be equal to or more competent than an equally qualified male.[1] Women in management positions also frequently find themselves without female peers—as many inroads as women have made, there are still more of us on the bottom than in the middle or on the top. The result, says broadcaster Charlayne Hunter-Gault, is that unless a woman is particularly strong, "she is going to be under an enormous amount of pressure to behave the way they [men] do: to have lunch with them, to drink as many martinis as they drink; in the discussions, to lead them and use logic the way they do."[2]

The biggest hurdle of all is that women in supervisory positions have a dearth of role models to turn to, in part because until recently few women had the wherewithal to advance to the upper echelons, and in part because women who have succeeded without the support of other women may have the attitude, "If I made it without any help, so can everyone else."[3] Feeling as if they've paid their dues, and angry that no one was there to show them the way, they kick up the dust and cover their tracks. They do not want to mentor other women. Even if they do, the role model they present is so negative, many women have no interest in having them as mentors.

Sylvia was such a woman. Notorious for her antifeminist platform, she had made it quite clear that any relationship to being a woman was purely coincidental, an unfortunate twist of fate. To the contrary, she had severed all possible ties with the female gender, judging women more harshly than men and with a kind of critical eye that comes from a defensive bitterness in which one's own firmest fears are planted. It was for that bitterness that Sylvia was best known, and for which Arlene most resented her. "Intellectually, I could understand where she'd come from, how difficult it must have been for her to get where she was. But to work for someone like that, well, that's another story altogether."

One afternoon, approximately six months after Arlene had been hired, one of Arlene's coworkers, Suzanne, learned her son had split his head open playing punchball in the school yard. The child was rushed to the hospital.

"I have to take the rest of the afternoon off," Suzanne had said to Sylvia, doing her best to maintain a measure of calm in the face of her growing hysteria.

"I'm sorry. We're backlogged today, and I can't get anybody to fill in on such short notice."

That was the price tag Sylvia put on work—either drop everything and everyone else or don't work for me.

"Look, Sylvia, my son's been hurt, and I have to go to the hospital to be with him."

"Your son is not my concern," she responded coldly. "If I had to give time off every time someone's child had a toothache or got hurt, half the department would be running out at any given moment. You have a job to do, and I expect you to do whatever it takes to get it done."

Knowing Sylvia's track record for firing women at the first opportunity, Suzanne panicked. She could not leave her son alone, but also could not afford to lose her job. Fortunately, Arlene and her other coworkers had been cross-trained and came rushing to Suzanne's aid. Forfeiting their lunch hours and remaining at the office late, they picked up the bulk of Suzanne's work, allowing Suzanne to be at the side of her son while satisfying Sylvia's demand to meet the deadline. It seemed an optimal solution.

Nevertheless, the incident infuriated Sylvia, who reacted like a villain who had been foiled. Using the only weapon she had, she recorded the incident on Suzanne's review: "Attendance problem. Personal life interferes with productivity at work."

"She could have given her the time off," said Arlene, who was turning red around the collar despite the fact the incident had occurred more than two years ago. "The company is structured to allow for those kinds of emergencies. You can have a doctor's appointment. You can have work done on your car. You can go to school to your kid's parent-teacher conference." But company policy, in this case, did not jive with Sylvia's way of looking at things, particularly when it came to problems specifically associated with women—like kids.

"She was always saying that there was no room in her life for children—either her own or those of anybody else she worked with.

Frankly, I think she would have been more cooperative if Suzanne's car had broken down." Arlene shook her head, and then added with more than a twinge of disdain, "What kind of person, what kind of woman could be like that?"

The answer is, a bitter and insecure one. For while women who establish themselves professionally reap many rewards in terms of money and status, the costs of success for women remains high. Professional women, in particular, are likely to discover somewhere along their career track that business life and personal life are difficult to harmonize. In fact, Hennig and Jardim's study of twenty-five highly successful women suggests that the typical pattern for them is to defer friends, marriage, and children until they are in their late thirties or early forties.[4] Without the advantage of a "wife" to take care of the shopping, the laundering, the emotional caretaking, aspiring women frequently find that the only way to reach their professional goals is to forfeit their relational ones.

Sylvia Tanner had indeed sacrificed. For while she kept her personal life as far from the office as possible, there were certain facts of her existence which were common knowledge. For Sylvia the facts were these: She was in her mid-forties, had never been married, and lived alone. She was successful professionally but had not had the benefit of female role models to show her how one could be a successful woman professionally without sacrificing everything else.

It is a psychiatric staple that individuals, when confronted with an emotionally explosive situation, turn that situation around and reject the very thing which they are most conflicted about. Sylvia could not, one would suspect, live with the terrible pain that the costs of success had incurred. What she could do was convince herself that such feminine needs as nurturance and children were frivolous at best, at worst some kind of deformity. In this way she evaded her own painful dilemma. What looked like bitchiness was really a protective shield from her own pain.

"What women like this feel is that they have to suppress all their own nurturing capacities and needs for nurturance," says Dr. Flax. "They suppress half their personalities. And it's so painful and so difficult for women to do that, given their basic need for connectedness, that they are forced to use very defensive methods to maintain this kind of rigid, uncaring personality. For them to admit the pain of completely forgoing their female identity, to admit what they've gone through, would destroy them. It's just too threatening. So they become the worst, the nastiest, the most disgusting bosses. They don't know how to deal with authority. So, of course, women under them hate working with them."

Indeed, Arlene did feel resentful. From that day on, the day of the wounded-son incident, when it had taken all of the energy she could muster not to spit in Sylvia's face, to the time when she was promoted, Arlene steered as clear of Sylvia as possible. While she was angry at herself for not speaking out, she kept her mouth shut for the sake of her professional future. Inside she stewed. She looked at the other women in her department, many of whom lacked the skills or the ambition to move up, with empathy and pity. She thought, "If ever I'm in a supervisory position, I'm going to do my damnedest not to be like that."

When, three months later, Arlene was promoted by her division head, she remained true to her word. Her official assignment was to manage a newly formed research division, but her negative experience with Sylvia left her with a carte du jour of her own: "Don't let anyone get mad at you." "Be a good-mommy boss and eventually everyone will cooperate with you." "Don't be like Sylvia." These were the principles guiding Arlene's behavior those early managerial days.

"It was important that people working for me saw me as competent, of course," Arlene recalls. "But at the time, being liked was equally important." She paused for a moment, putting her hand under her chin. "Probably more important."

As is often the case, that need is the source of many women's gravest problems.

THE GOOD-MOMMY BOSS

Her first week on her new job, and already Arlene was beginning to feel the pressure of her inexperience. Not only was she new to the technical aspects of the department, she was assuming a superior position to six employees, almost half of whom had daughters close to her own age. Would they resent her? Would she be able to win their approval? Could she live up to the expectations of the woman who had promoted her? The uncertainty of the situation was enough to rattle any newcomer, and now, only four days after her ordination as manager, a critical member of her staff had called in sick. Not yet a week had passed and Arlene was beginning to feel as if she were slipping behind.

"Who else knows how to operate the IBM computer?" Arlene had asked the group of three women newly under her wing, women who had not only worked together for the past five years, but who were twice her age.

"Sorry," said the spokeswoman for the threesome. "No one but Jim knows how to program that computer."

"That's strange," Arlene had thought to herself. In every other department at least two employees were cross-trained for every position in that department—a managerial strategy designed to avoid precisely the problem Arlene was facing now that one of her staff members was ill. But who was she to challenge the word of these women who would certainly know better than anyone else about what had gone on in the past?

Besides, she already felt like a babe in the woods about to enter the lion's den—something like a camp counselor who is assigned to a bunk of ten-year-old girls who have spent all of the last five summers together and who get no greater pleasure than driving the poor newcomer to her limits of tolerance.

Gritting her teeth, Arlene spent her first weekend on the job finishing off the work she had been told no one else could do. Not exactly a good way to start off on the right foot, she knew, but it sure beat putting her foot into her mouth. She would, she promised herself, cross-train her employees first thing next week in order to be prepared for any further unforeseen catastrophes.

At four in the afternoon, after six hours of grueling work, Arlene decided it was time to familiarize herself with the work stories of her employees. Skimming down the pages of evaluative material, she suddenly froze. At the bottom of Gertrude's chart three words stood out like day glow in the dark: "Cross-trained—IBM computer." So had read Adrienne's chart, and Judy's—the same women who denied knowing anything about the workings of the blessed machine.

That was the kind of resistance Arlene was to face during her earliest supervisory days, particularly from the older women. She had not expected instantaneous cooperation, of course, but in the back of her mind she had anticipated the real problem to come from the two men on her staff. To her amazement, they not only accepted her but did everything they could to help, giving her tips, showing her the ropes, never once seeming to question who was in charge.

"Their attitude was strictly business," Arlene recalled. "They were young and didn't seem to have any hang-ups about having a young woman supervisor. Whatever conflicts they may have experienced took the back burner to their own career advancement. It was as if they were doing something for me in the hopes that I might someday return the favor."

Actually, Arlene was fortunate—if she had fallen into the norm, she wouldn't have had the men pulling for her either. A recent survey of two hundred managers discovered that men often not only resent working for women but insult and harass them. And putting more women into positions of power only makes the problem worse. According to researcher Carol Weiss, as the proportion of women managers in a particular office increases, so does men's fear that they will lose out to women in promotions. Kaleel Jamison, a Cincinnati consultant who runs seminars dealing with conflicts between men and women at work, offers another explanation. "Having a woman boss can bring up old childhood traumas of mothers or elementary school teachers telling you what to do." Men, she says, "also fear that working for a woman will hurt their careers. They recognize that the most powerful jobs are still held by men, and they worry that their status will diminish if they're assigned to a woman."

But if men give female bosses a hard time, so do women. When Kane Parsons and Associates conducted a phone survey, 39 percent of women nationwide said they preferred a male boss, to only 16 percent who said they preferred a woman (43 percent said it made no difference). The reason? "Men are fairer and more understanding . . . women are petty, envious, power-mad and too aggressive."[5]

Obviously, the three older women working for Arlene held these sentiments, spelling trouble from the start. They had been in their present positions for over a decade and had gone through a slew of female bosses around Arlene's age. One boss had wanted things done this way. Another had wanted things done that way. They had been through every possible permutation their rote jobs would allow. Who was Arlene, this woman who was no older than their daughters, who had not run a department before, to tell them what to do?

Hoping to win them over, Arlene adopted a helpless, daughterlike stance. "I was very sensitive to the fact that they were much older than me. It wasn't an issue of competition—they had absolutely no desire to be promoted. At the same time, I knew if I appeared too authoritative, I would threaten them. I think my rationale was that I could get them to cooperate if I made them feel as if, on some level, they were really the ones in charge."

Playing it weak, Arlene admitted, also helped her cope with her own discomfort in relating to these women. After all, she told herself, what daughter tells her mother what to do? And what mother tolerates being bossed around by her daughter?

On some level, of course, the women were not oblivious to Arlene's superior position. In fact, a lot of their resentment came out in typically childlike fashion. Much as children do from time to time, they were testing "Mommy's" limits.

"Why are you coding all that information into the computer?" Arlene had asked Adrienne, whose job was to keep record of the checks coming through the department.

"Things have always been done that way."

"But I've looked over the system thoroughly, and there's no reason to code all that data."

"Look," said Adrienne defensively, "I've always done the accounting this way, the person before me has done it this way, and the person before her has done it this way. Now you're telling me to do it differently?"

Arlene backed off. She knew the details Adrienne insisted on coding were unnecessary, that she was wasting lots of valuable time by doing so. She also knew that when there's an employee-employer dispute, the employees stick together. And the last thing she needed was to have these older women, these mothers, gang up on her.

"I remember feeling really on the spot. I could have insisted she do it my way, and risked arousing her wrath, or simply let the matter drop." She let it drop. Repressing any actions that might be perceived as unfeminine or nonnurturing, especially anger, she continued to hope to lead these women through the desert via gentle, nonauthoritative leadership. At the first bristling of her employees' dissatisfactions, she did all in her power to appease them.

She never did mention the computer incident.

ROLE CONFUSION

Arlene's biggest problem, ultimately, was not with the older women, but to the woman closest to her in age. To some extent, the generation gap helped establish a certain distance between Arlene and the three older women, as did the sex differences with the two young men. With Paula no such boundaries existed. And while Arlene did not consciously recognize it at the time, she was in dire need of an ally. The men were supportive, to be sure, but Arlene did not feel she could really sit down and talk to them. The flak she received from the older women made her uncomfortable. She had not been in her position long enough to have developed a support network with the other managers. She was lonely. Unconsciously, she turned to Paula to fulfill her need for contact.

Arlene allowed certain liberties in her relationship to Paula that she would have not permitted even with the older women. One of those liberties was personal exchange. It seemed to happen innocently enough, with Paula dropping little scraps of information about how she was having difficulty with her husband and her three-year-old son, the kind of information one might come to know anyway simply by working together over a period of time. But it did not take long for those innocent exchanges to blossom into twenty-minute diatribes each morning, during which Paula traced her problems every heartbeat of the way. What began as a need for camaraderie turned into a one-way street which bore striking resemblance to the mother-daughter situation. And in it, Arlene was undoubtedly the mother.

"I think I had wanted someone to help me," Arlene admitted, "but instead I ended up taking care of her. I didn't like it; I resented being Paula's mother. At the same time, I felt sorry for her."

So sorry, it eventually obliterated her efficiency as Paula's superior. "I kept thinking about the women in the old department and how terrible Sylvia had been to them, how I didn't want to be the kind of boss Sylvia was. In some way I felt I had to compensate for her insensitive approach. So when Paula did something wrong, I couldn't find it in myself to criticize her. I would say to myself, 'She tries so hard, but she's having so many problems, how can I tell her she's sloppy or disorganized?' It just seemed to stick in my throat. So anything I said to her was always couched in a way to make it look as if it were somehow my problem. 'You know I'm crazy. I'm a nut, but this is driving me crazy.' And even when I presented it that way, I would end up dwelling on it because I didn't want to hurt her feelings."

"The most common response to the conflict between female role and organizational comfort is the attempt to maintain the major female role imperatives of caring for people and performing the task as it should be performed," says Patricia Kosinar.[6] All too often, however, women like Arlene are unable to polarize themselves sufficiently from the interpersonal web to effectively enact their role as supervisor. Rather, they become emotional arbiters, perennial caretakers whose primary concern is keeping everyone happy-faced—often at the expense of the job at hand.

"To forfeit productivity in order to protect the feelings of one's employees is not a supervisory function but a parenting one," says Angela Fox. "When a woman fails to enact her role as the one in charge because of her concerns about her employee's feelings, she's acting out a very neurotic theme of dependency. A woman's function at work is not to be someone's mother. It is to perform." The price Arlene paid for being a "good mommy" was professional incompetence.

LOSING AUTHORITY

It had been two months since Arlene had assumed her new position, and with each passing day, her authority was diminishing. The initial animosity of the older women had seemed to subside, largely due to Arlene's efforts to appease them. And while Paula continued to be a drain, it was apparent that she had a special affection for Arlene. There had been at least one goal Arlene had managed to achieve—she was definitely not like Sylvia; she was well liked.

The sticky part was that the women no longer took her seriously. In contrast to the men, who continued to take the initiative, the women did the minimum amount of work possible. Picking up Arlene's insecurity with her role, they had already pegged her as an ineffective manager —nice, but ineffective.

One Friday afternoon Arlene received an interoffice memo informing her that the new deadline for departmental budgets was being moved up by a week. Arlene panicked. How was she going to get her lackadaisical staff to take on the added responsibility? "Drop whatever you're doing," she told them, "and let's get moving on that budget." But Arlene's authority, in and of itself, was no longer sufficient to motivate the women. Two days later none of the women had even lifted a finger to complete the task at hand.

"Doesn't what I say count?" she had wanted to yell. Instead, true to style, she chose a more palatable approach. "I'm very disappointed in you—I was counting on you all to take responsibility for yourselves." An ineffective but nurturing mother trying to coerce a naughty child.

Begrudgingly, the women finished the assignment.

There were other telltale signs as well, particularly with Paula. "She really began taking advantage," said Arlene, shaking her head almost in disbelief that she had allowed such a situation to fester. "For instance, another one of the supervisors came into my office to talk to me about the upcoming budget meeting. It was obviously a hushed conversation. Nevertheless, Paula came in with ostensibly an interoffice memo or something in her hand. I got pretty annoyed. It was clear that we were having a private conversation. To make matters worse, when I didn't respond to her, she just stood there while we finished our conversation. She was going to be one of the girls listening in on the discussion. It happened, obviously, because she felt on a friendly basis with me," said Arlene in retrospect, "so on some level she felt she had a right to be there."

However, despite the fact that Paula was obviously acting inappropriately, Arlene was unable to send her away. "I knew if I said anything, she'd be terribly hurt and angry. I frankly didn't know what to do. So I did nothing."

Arlene began to realize that she was losing her ground as any sort of authority figure, that she had tied her hands with inappropriate role relationships with the women who were supposedly working for her. To the contrary, her mixed messages about authority gave her employees the power edge. By playing on and taking advantage of Arlene's need to be loved, she had been hooked into a mother-daughter battle in which the mother's apparent vulnerability gives the daughter the psychological upper hand. While technically the boss, emotionally Arlene was at her employees' mercy. It was a case of what psychologist Judith Bardwick calls "the weaker inhibiting the stronger."

"Especially if she is sensitive to what it feels like to be rejected and emotionally coerced," says Dr. Bardwick, "the more powerful woman is likely to deny her resentment of the other's dependence, to respond with support and to withhold negative judgments. This is more likely if the weaker woman expresses her pain in inescapably feminine ways, because they are more likely to trigger nurturance responses. In this way the weaker may inhibit the stronger."[7]

LEARNING TO BE THE BITCH

It was the supervisor who had been in Arlene's office the day that Paula intruded who was the first to point out the dilemma. A few days after the incident, she and Arlene went out to lunch. Arlene confided in her the difficulties she was having with the women, about how she was unable to get them to cooperate, how afraid she was of hurting their feelings. It was a risky move, she knew, as one does not admit professional failure lightly. But given that this woman was in another department, which in no way competed with Arlene's, that she even had a different boss, Arlene decided to take the chance. Besides, what other alternative did she have?

The supervisor, who was a woman close to Arlene's age, but who had been in a position of authority for three years, looked Arlene straight in the eye. "Bullshit," she said, firmly but gently. "What you're really afraid of is that if you tell them what to do, if you assert yourself and act like a boss, they won't like *you* anymore." Arlene's eyes opened wide; her face flushed with embarrassment.

"Don't feel bad," said the supervisor reassuringly. "Every woman I know has been there."

"The hardest thing about supervising other women is that sometimes you have to be the bitch," Arlene was to say two years later. "You are going to have to tell people to do the things that they're not going to want to do. You will occasionally have to hurt their feelings. And they're going to resent it. What you have to learn is to live with the resentments, to experience those lonely times when you know everyone is angry at you—when everyone thinks you're nothing but a bitch."

Arlene's response is classic among women in supervisory positions. They don't want to be bitches. They don't want to be like Sylvia Tanner. They do not want to be incompetent either. The problem is, with few role models to act as lanterns in the dark, they're not exactly sure how they're supposed to be.

What Arlene was sure of, however, was that she did not want to fail at her job. Her first six month's review was drawing near. And Arlene could not help but notice that the woman who had given her the promotion had been acting coolly toward her of late. She knew she was either going to have to shape up or ship out. "It was really quite simple," she said, "It was their ass or mine."

Digging herself out of the dilemma she had created wasn't easy. A boss who over time is unwilling to assert her authority and establish appropriate ego boundaries can become so normal that no one can conceive of her as ever truly wielding power. That is why the lack of a firm structure from the start can so disable a female boss. While rigidity and unemotionality may taint a woman as a bitch, motherly, nurturing behavior taints her as a titular head, the kind of mother who continuously must use the threat, "Wait until your father gets home." Arlene's position of authority, despite the fact that she had corporate policies such as insubordination to support her, was insufficient to elicit an employeelike response. Arising from her own need for approval, she all but forfeited the power that her title assigned her.

"When women find their female employees are not responding to them appropriately, there's often something wrong in terms of real power," comments Angela Fox. "Whatever her title, the person under her does not really believe she has the power to hire and fire. Somewhere, she's sending off a mixed signal. Because the woman in the superior position is the role model, she must not only have her own boundaries clearly defined—she must be willing to exercise her power. Any ambivalence in that situation triggers off the immediate response of Mother not being good enough, or being powerless in the relationship. Men perceive themselves as having real power and they follow through on it. Many women do not."

Arlene had never stopped to question her own feelings about power. She had not recognized that given the role confusion in the mother-daughter relationship and between women in general, merely pinning on the label "boss" was not enough to give her authoritative standing. That is, until now.

"I began to see that the problems I was having with the women were largely my fault. In many ways they were like little children who were taking advantage of the baby-sitter. They didn't believe that I was in charge, because I didn't act like someone in a position of responsibility. I was responsible for the mess everyone was in, and it was my responsibility to bail everyone and myself out.

TAKING CHARGE

One Monday morning shortly thereafter, Arlene walked into her office at 11 A.M. Her alarm had failed to go off and she was two hours late. She found the men, as usual, figuring out what needed to be done, and going about their business doing it. The women, on the other hand were kaffeeklatsching around Paula's desk. In the two hours of the workday which had passed, they had accomplished little more than making the coffee.

"There's a deadline for one of the publicity campaigns that you've all been made aware of. We're behind as it is. It appears that you've done no work this morning, which means that you'll all have to find two hours each to make up for that time."

Freeze.

"What the hell's gotten into her," Arlene heard one of the women say as she went begrudgingly to her desk.

"Must be her period," offered Adrienne.

That afternoon Paula came into her office, requesting she be given amnesty from the two-hour work decree. "You know I can't stay late because of the situation at home," she said.

"Do it on your lunch hour," Arlene said assertively while silently quaking inside.

"But you know that's when I visit Johnny at the day care center," Paula pushed.

"You'll have plenty of time to be with him when you're out of a job."

Arlene knew that she was overreacting, that given her past performance, her new leaf would be viewed as all but schizophrenic. And internally, she struggled every step of the way with her impulse to be more empathic, more understanding, "more a mother and caretaker than a boss." She had skills to learn, problems to overcome if she was ever to master the art of supervision. She had created a mess, that was plain. Knowing the best way to undo the damage was not so obvious. Given the situation, she felt she had no choice but to be less understanding, more assertive, "more like Sylvia," at least temporarily.

Arlene also began to recognize that not only had she been doing herself a disservice, but she had cheated those working for her. A boss's feelings of powerlessness get transmitted downward, leaving the subordinates little option but to respond in kind. By not setting herself up as a role model, a woman who could effectively handle authority, she was sending her employees the same kind of message Sylvia had sent her: Women do not know what to do with power once they have it.

Nevertheless, the change was slow—a painstaking process of trial and error. "It was a constant struggle to ward off the feeling that by being authoritative, I was being nasty, that I wasn't being a good-mommy boss. But then I thought to myself, 'Does a good mother let her children run haywire?'" Also helpful was the continued support she received from the supervisor who had pinpointed the difficulty in the first place. "I think I learned more from her than anyone else. She had more experience dealing with people and suggested wonderful ways of handling situations. What helped the most, though, was knowing that I wasn't a total failure, that I wasn't alone."

Once the initial shock had passed, Arlene began to reap the rewards of her labors. The older women became more responsible, more supportive, confirming the fact that women are more amenable to a boss whose emphasis is on getting the job done than to a supervisor who is an emotional caretaker.[8]

"One of them even told me that she was glad to see that I was getting my act together, that I had opportunities as a young woman that she never had, and it was my responsibility to take advantage of them."

In turn, Arlene learned to delegate responsibility without sounding like a schoolmaster. "There are ways of asking people to do things that makes them respond more positively. One of these ways is to ask nicely. It's inappropriate to say, 'There's something that needs to be done. Would you mind doing it?' But you can say, 'It's getting backlogged over there, and it's very important you help out.' That way you make people feel valued and important." That way, Arlene also knew, was only available if there was an implicit understanding that the one who's doing the asking has the ultimate authority to enforce the request.

THE FIRING SQUAD

The only one who did not respond to Arlene's cues was Paula. To the contrary, she began overtly defying her, coming into work late, leaving early, taking advantage of her absentee leave. "That's when I realized how out-of-hand I had let the situation become. And I knew that I was going to have to put a stop to it."

The decision to let Paula go was, in Arlene's mind, the most difficult thing she has ever had to do. But at the time, she felt she had no choice. She had given Paula a verbal warning, followed by a written memorandum, followed by probation. Still, Paula refused to accept the limits of her new relationship to her boss. And the more assertive Arlene was, the more resentful Paula became.

"It would have been much easier had she been a man," Arlene told me. "With men the issues are always clearer from the start. It's a lot easier to say, 'Listen your work isn't very good,' or to try and whip him into shape or let him go if he doesn't work out. With a woman there's all this guilt, and with Paula there was the added guilt that the situation was more my fault than hers. It's like having to send your daughter away to boarding school because you failed to set appropriate guidelines when she was growing up."

Arlene was also concerned with the political ramifications of firing Paula. Firing a woman sends an instant message which reaffirms the view that women are less competent than men. Any one of a hundred incidences might boomerang if given the chance. As a result, many women will do all in their power to try and bail out even the most inefficient female employee.

But in Arlene's view her relationship with Paula was beyond surgery.

One Friday afternoon, Arlene called Paula into her office. "You've had a verbal warning, a memorandum, and have been on probation. Your work and your attitude, nevertheless, have not changed for the better. I see no other choice than to give you your termination notice."

As if what Arlene had said were spoken in a foreign tongue and had not registered, Paula looked her straight in the eye. "Look," she said mildly apologetically, "I understand that I've been goofing off from time to time. I'll try to improve."

"Be assertive, be assertive," a silent voice prodded Arlene. Aloud she said, "Look, Paula. I don't think you understand. I'm not asking you to do better next time. I'm telling you that there is not going to be a next time."

Tears started streaming down Paula's face. "I'm speaking English at last," thought Arlene.

"But you can't fire me," Paula whined. "You know all the problems I've been having. I need the money. I've got bills to pay." Her pleas were becoming more frantic. "Please, Arlene, just give me another chance."

Arlene's immediate impulse was to give in, to try to make the situation work. But in her gut she knew the relationship was doomed to failure. "I just knew I had to end it."

Arlene stood up and told Paula that she was firm in her decision, that she wasn't going to change her mind, that she was sorry but could not spend any more time discussing the issue.

Paula, who had finally gotten the message, exited in a huff, turning around only long enough to say, "And I thought you were my friend."

THOUGH THE DETAILS of this story are unique to Arlene Nielsen, and the resistance of her female coworkers perhaps extreme, the problems she encountered on the job are recognizable to many of us. The obvious and not so obvious discrimination that women in power positions face are primary issues for every woman who wants to get ahead. Women may be entering traditionally male occupations at an unprecedented rate, but the fact remains that they still have to overcome the obstacles of bias and discrimination, both from men and women. "Assertive" behavior from a male boss may translate into "aggressiveness" when it's from a woman. The number of support systems for women on the job that are currently emerging[9] are only beginning to compensate for the good-old-boys networks from which we've been virtually shut out. And women are still punished more for sexual liaisons formed at the office,[10] as every Mary Cunningham knows, suggesting that the old double standard is alive and well.

At the same time, Arlene's struggles cannot be traced *only* to the difficulties of a competent woman in a man's world. While the patriarchal working environment establishes a framework ripe for problems, it also epitomizes the conflict between nurturance and autonomy, dependency and differentiation, femininity and masculinity. Beneath the obvious constraints of the working world, there are buried the profoundly difficult dilemmas in women's relationships, in terms of both their mothers and the whole female gender.

Arlene Nielsen was experiencing the role confusion that every woman I have spoken to experiences, a muddled state of affairs that arises because mothers view themselves as extensions of their daughters and vice versa. More than that, however, her dilemma highlighted some basic struggles that women are presented with these days. Where is a woman's place in business? Can a woman combine work with marriage and children, and still do well at both? Should a woman offer another woman custodial care? In what way should or shouldn't a woman utilize her innate talents as a woman to move up the corporate ladder?

Arlene's difficulties arose not only because she was a woman working in a world dominated by men, but because she was a woman in varying relationships of power with other women. For as Arlene and other women in supervisory positions have discovered, wielding power over men is a far easier psychological task than managing other women.[11] While men may resent the woman in charge (in Arlene's case they did not), they nevertheless are usually willing to accommodate themselves to the power differential in the interests of their own careers. They are not interested in developing inherently intimate relationships with the women for whom they work. If women have fewer problems establishing appropriate boundaries with the men they work with, it is because the men establish those boundaries themselves.[12]

Women's relationships, on the other hand, are always infused with a kind of internal tension, a push-pull that has at its roots the underlying role confusion in the mother-daughter relationship. How does a younger woman get past the psychic barrier of telling women twice her age what to do? Given her connectedness to other women, what precedent has she had for fostering a separation between her roles as woman/mother/daughter/friend/coworker? And of course, how does she deal with the potential ramifications of exerting her authority? More simply, how does she live with being the bitch?

We might guess that the more clearly defined the roles, the less conflicted the relationship. But given women's strong identification with one another, assigning the label "boss" or "employee" is often insufficient to ameliorate the confusion, just as being a "mother" or "daughter" does not always translate into clear-cut delineations between the two.

The permeability of women's ego boundaries may, in fact, be one of the reasons that female mentors are so rare. The closer the relationship, the more room there is for mother-daughter transference. And the more such confusion exists, the less likely that the relationship between mentor and protégé will be a positive one.

According to psychologist Judith Bardwick, women who are involved in a mentor-protégé relationship are likely to "operate on both a task-related, objective level and a personalized, intimate one because they have learned to increase their self-esteem through the security of knowing they are liked. I think the female mentor is, to herself and her protégé, simultaneously the objective teacher, the intimate friend, and the ambivalent mother."

At the same time, given women's propensity for intimacy, acting as a mentor to another woman can be a tricky affair. "As men must outgrow their mentors, the protégé woman must relate to and then separate from the authority figure," says Dr. Bardwick. "The difference, when the relationship is between women, lies in the protégé's need to identify with the already successful woman and create the intimacy, the 'best friend' relationship, that she has learned will sustain her through stress. It is very difficult to create autonomy through intimacy, that is, through dependence.[13]

For whatever the reasons, women like Arlene, who are ready to recognize their deficiencies as supervisors, often travel the road toward success alone. And indeed, it is a formidable task, for they must do it in the face of opposition from men who view them as outsiders and women who view them as traitors.

However they meet the challenge, they are likely to find that there are certain givens.

EGO BOUNDARIES

Women who work for other women want rules, if only to help them establish their own vulnerable ego boundaries. And because the boss is in the superior position—logistically, because her role gives her authorization for authority, and psychologically, because she is in the mommy role—it is up to her to set the precedent. Psychologist David Gutmann, who has studied extensively the effect of ego boundary differentiation on men and women, discovered that the ability to separate emotions from the objects around them was a signpost of health in American men. For women in the domestic sphere the opposite was true. "In the female domestic world diffuse ego boundaries may be a necessity and precondition for mastery and contentment. Firm ego boundaries could lead to alienation—to a rupture of empathic bounds with one's family and with the pleasant self-confirming cycles of domestic and neighborhood life." But what goes in the confines of our domiciles can be maladaptive in the regimented and well-boundaried world of work. In fact, Dr. Gutmann tells us that diffuse ego boundaries are "often a precondition for male pathology."[14]

When a man responds in a working situation with his emotions first, when he fails to establish appropriate role behavior, he is said to be ineffective. When a woman fails to establish appropriate role relationships with her employees, we say she is merely being a woman, with the underlying assumption that maybe she is not meant to be in a man's world in the first place.

More importantly, by not establishing appropriate boundaries, women not only forfeit their own authority, but do a disservice to those in their charge as well. By not providing those boundaries for the women who worked for her, Arlene failed to provide an adequate role model for them, much as Sylvia had done for her. Had she been less concerned with being "nice" and gaining approval, she could have been a pivotal person in fostering their growth. Separation means providing a situation where a person can master her own impulses and explore her own potential. When a mother sees her child acting inappropriately, she is not doing her a disservice by correcting the child's behavior. Being a good-mommy boss goes far beyond being empathic; it involves showing your employees those areas in which they can improve. True differentiation allows a woman to criticize as well as praise.

"A woman who is truly in charge says what needs to be said," says Angela Fox. "Not providing appropriate guidelines does not help women to grow; to the contrary, it keeps them attached."

Ms. Fox continues: "From a purely economic point of view, being overly sensitive to the other person's feelings and identifying with the other person is not productive. It does not get the job done. That's not to say that a woman should not consider her employees' feelings at all. I think a good parent company is an appropriate model. Certain kinds of supervision, noncritical remarks, and positive feedback are all more productive than a negativistic approach. In other words, a good-mommy boss is likely to have more productive workers than a bad-mommy boss. But a good parent company also provides an awful lot of boundaries, a structure which is very clear-cut. You have to go through A and B in order to get to C."

ACCEPTING POWER

While bosses like Sylvia Tanner come across as power-hungry, bosses like Arlene Nielsen are perceived as conflicted about their power. And regardless of whether in actuality they have the power to hire and fire, that powerlessness is inevitably transmitted to those in their charge.

"My supervisor is the typical example of a woman who isn't able to feel comfortable asserting authority," one clerk-typist tells me. "Her primary function is to make peace between the girls. She's everybody's friend, the one everybody goes to and says, 'I have this problem' . . . from a hangnail to no sex the night before. Don't get me wrong. She's a good-hearted person, but I've had it up to here with her sweet-apple-pie routines. She'll hire somebody less competent with a better sob story than somebody who is competent without a story. In fact, I don't think she really considers whether somebody is competent or not. I've completely lost respect for her."

If a boss is conflicted about her own authority, what can she expect from those who work for her? Giving a woman a powerful position is meaningless unless she is willing to exercise that power. For a long time Arlene, like many women, was not.

The fear is that if we allow ourselves to experience power, we will become like men, and women will no longer love us. Why else would a boss compromise her efficacy? If we give up our sensitivity but once, we will become everything we have resented men for being. The typical image of the male corporate figure is someone who thinks about nothing else but his career. He doesn't give a damn about feelings. Most women do not want to be like that; it's not what we've fought for.

In truth, however, power can be a positive force in getting a job done. Even in the mother-daughter situation, a mother's authority is viewed as positive if it is in her daughter's best interests. The adolescent, for example, who is feeling the peer pressure to sleep around but in her heart of hearts is not ready, is grateful when mother puts her foot down and says, "There's no way in hell I'm letting you go away for a weekend with your boyfriend without supervision." Her mother's help in setting limits is the first step in learning to establish those limits on her own.

So it is also in the work setting. "Theoretically, power and love go together," says psychologist Barbara Forisha, "and the biggest uses of power are accompanied by interpersonal concerns and compassion. Power without love turns into domination, and love without power becomes manipulation. Thus, to use power for accomplishment rather than destruction, power must be joined with love or interpersonal understanding."[15]

THE NEED FOR BALANCE

Powerful, but sensitive to power; empathic but firm; boundaried but flexible—these are the characteristics of the effective supervisor. She can be understanding without allowing her emotional concerns to run wild. She sets goals without sounding like a drill sergeant. In the search for the proper balance she takes the best from male and female strengths. As one female manager who was quoted in the *Wall Street Journal* put it, "I care, but I don't take care of people."[16]

Studies on what makes a woman an effective supervisor lead over and over again to one conclusion: In order for a woman to maintain her self-esteem and actualize her talent as a professional, she must integrate her feminine characteristics with her more newly learned "masculine" skills. Women are not men. To expect women to close off half of their personalities is not only absurd but counterproductive.

Sociologists Barbara Forisha and Barbara Goldman summarize it well:

"Where women have been taught to be nurturant, to be attractive, to be well liked, men—workers—have been taught to be strong, to take risks, and to achieve. Female role learning is not functional in an organization, and this creates conflict, to which there are several resolutions. One is to ignore the conflict and uninhibitedly adopt the values of the male role. Another is to avoid it by refusing to accept those values at all, by taking a job, or an attitude, which presents no conflicts. A final resolution, the most difficult, is to integrate both sets of values. For women moving beyond the traditional jobs, and the traditional solutions that go with them, the last is the only one to protect a woman's self-esteem and allow her to continue to develop."[17]

THE ANTIFEMALE FEMALE EMPLOYEE

Let me add a word in women supervisors' defense. It would be a mistake to suggest that all the difficulties in the boss-employee situation arise from the supervisory end. Even if a woman has reasonably resolved her feelings about power, there will be some inherent resistance to her authority. To take orders from another woman cannot help but be a reminder of long-buried feelings of powerlessness in relationship to Mom.

In addition, the sexual division of labor in most working situations replicates the sexual division of labor at home. "Work structures tend to be patriarchally organized," says Jane Flax. "Even when women hold high positions, they are generally under the auspices of a male boss. This gives women the feeling that women have no real power in the world. In addition, by being attached to a woman boss, you get less social esteem than being attached to a male boss. It's the sexual division of labor that duplicates the sexual division of labor at home."

A female boss without a proven track record begins ten steps behind a comparable male. Study after study suggests that women consistently underrate the work of women. In one piece of research, women were asked to rate paintings that were supposed entries in a contest. When male names were placed under the paintings, women rated them more highly than when the identical paintings were attributed to female hands.[18] Another study, which compared women students' reactions to course descriptions which gave no information about the credentials of the instructors aside from their sex, evidenced a similar finding. Women not only rated the courses taught by women more negatively than those supposedly taught by men; they were less willing to enroll in them. "In summary," suggest the authors, "the results of our study provide good support for the assertion that if they have no information about a target's competence, women judge the work of other women more negatively and behave differently toward it than they do toward comparable work of men."[19]

If you're in a supervisory position and you're smugly thinking to yourself, "Aha, I knew it," let me add a final word. The same study showed that this pattern was reversed if the female's competence was established. In fact, women were *more* amenable to enrolling in seminars taught by women than by men if the instructor's competence was clear. History may give us the notion that men are more valuable than women, but we will be more than willing to accept a woman's authority if it is reasonable, appropriate, and provides us with a positive role model.

Arlene Nielsen believes she has become that appropriate role model. Over the years, she has managed to find a happy medium which allows her to have an interpersonal relationship with her employees without forfeiting her authority. The women who work for her do not find it odd or confusing for her to delegate responsibility one moment and share a giggle the next; her relationship to them is warm, caring. At the same time, they do not consider Arlene their friend. Secure in her own position, the women under her have only to follow her lead.

Still, a hint of times long past remains. "I think I'll always find it more difficult to work with women than with men. It's such an emotionally loaded situation. With women either below you or above you, you're always concerned about striking the right balance. And with women on your level, there's always a problem with competition."

Chapter 11

COMPETITION ON THE JOB

IT was four months since I had last heard from Mira. The phone, which used to ring continuously as we brimmed with ideas late into the wee hours of the morning, now stood between us in our mutual state of disconnection. It had taken awhile before the reality that things had changed between us began to register; the phone calls she had never returned; my having run to the phone in anticipation with every ring; having hoped and having deluded myself into expecting that the next ring would be hers. For four months it never was.

We had started out as a team, Mira and I. Like Rodgers and Hammerstein, Lerner and Loewe, Sondheim and Bernstein—that is how we imagined ourselves, two great but as yet undiscovered songwriters who were going to bowl over the world with our treatises of love we had put to music. Our other work—her job as a teacher, mine as a researcher and sociologist—we believed to be temporary interruptions of what we saw as our true calling as songwriters. Not only were we convinced that we were going to make it: better yet, we were going to make it together.

I had met Mira six months after moving back to New York from a five-year stint in California, where I had been a practicing psychotherapist. We were both taking a songwriting class on the East Side, and while we had not exchanged more than two words, we knew each other through the array of heartfelt material that we presented in class. I loved Mira's work—it was astute, lyrical, and most importantly, it touched at some of the very emotions I was trying to express. It was less than a month later that we began our long and ebullient collaboration.

Writing with Mira was like dipping into a well that never dries up. Ideas emerged in a great stream from one, the other—or both simultaneously. We complemented each other in every way. If I was having a dry spell, Mira was invariably hot. If she was at a loss for ideas, I miraculously was brimming with them. There was never any question, there were never any arguments, about who wrote what line or who should get credit for what. "Lyrics by _____, Music by _____" is the way that copyright forms are structured. Ours always read the same way: Music and Lyrics by Mira Arnold and Eva Margolies. It was fifty-fifty all the way.

The two-year period we worked together was an absolute pleasure, and we became the staunchest of friends. We fought, but never for long, and always for the ultimate good of the project—artistic temperament, I think they call it. Even when we collaborated with other people, there was no jealousy or competition, both believing that that collaboration was to the benefit of our own. From the others we would take our newly found knowledge and incorporate it into our own work. Why compete with someone when you share virtually the same goal, when there is room for you both?

One of the people I collaborated with was a young man named Lenny, a bass player who had toured the country with some of the music business's most successful bands. Lenny had what Mira and I both lacked—professional experience—and I saw working with him as a chance to benefit from his experience, with the intention of ultimately transferring what I had learned into what I saw as my primary relationship with Mira. Working with Lenny was inspiring. But it was not fun.

When you are a songwriter who wants to succeed, it is par for the course to make the rounds—perennially going to publishers to display your lyrical wares and perennially being rejected by them. I was fortunate enough (or talented enough) to have made some inroads. Even publishers who could not use the material I presented were happy to send me to someone else who might. It was on one of those treks, made with tape in hand, that my relationship with Mira was to change.

I had, as usual, taped what I believed to be five of my most promising songs. Three of them (the first three on the tape) had been written with Mira. The last two were written with Lenny. I sat in the publisher's office with sweaty palms as he went through what songwriters call the brush-off—thirty seconds of listening to a tune, then belligerently pushing the fast-forward button to the next. Some publishers were a bit more verbal, summarizing their feelings in the catch-all phrase used for rejection: "Pass." After a minute he had dispensed with songs one and two and was on his way to fast-forwarding on the third. But when he got to the fourth, his expression changed. He did not stop the tape, but sat back in his chair and began humming. By the time the song was over, he was tapping his feet and knew the chorus by heart. The fifth song was met by an even stronger response. Then came the rush: "Who did you write these songs with? How long have you been writing? How would you like me to sign you as a staff writer? We'll pay you so-and-so much the first year, and double that the second if you work out." I should have been ecstatic; a part of me, of course, was. But underneath what was my first real success, the first time anyone ever offered to *pay* me for doing what I loved to do, was a gut-wrenching anxiety. I wanted the job, yes. I wanted to be a songwriter, yes. But what was I going to tell Mira?

In my naiveté, I tried convincing this publisher, who is now president of one of the country's largest recording companies, that the songs I had written with Mira were equally good, that my songwriting talent was triggered far more by working with her than with Lenny.

It was a move that was at best unprofessional and nearly lost me the whole contract. This man, highly esteemed despite his relatively young age, glared at me with more than an ounce of skepticism, as if to say, "Look, lady, you're in no position to call the shots. Take it or leave it."

I took it, but only after deliberating for days, and avoiding Mira's calls like I was dodging the draft. "You're being ridiculous," my husband would chastise. "She's a professional; she'll understand." Yes, of course she would understand, I told myself. After all, wouldn't I? Yet in my more honest moments I had to admit that I also would never forget.

Neither did Mira, not for a long time. That phone call was one of the most difficult in my life. Here she was, anticipating at worst that we had received yet another rejection. Surely she was not expecting to hear that our songs had been rejected but that I had been offered a contract based on working with someone else, that, given the exclusive nature of the contract, my other time commitments, and the requirement that Lenny and I produce at least two "acceptable" songs per month, my collaboration with Mira would have to take the back burner.

I tried explaining my position as best I could, as gently as I could. Mira tried empathizing with that position as best she could, as honestly as she could. She had understood, she told me. She would have done the same thing herself, she said, soothing my unnerving guilt. We hung up friends. But she didn't call for four months. I had betrayed the mother, and was paying for it like a bad child.

In time, we did manage to work through the rift between us. Mira admitted her jealousy; I confessed my hurts. We both discussed the dilemma of feeling one had to make a choice between the friendship and career aspirations and the almost inevitable feelings of competition that were bound to arise between friends who shared the same ambitions. Fate also lent us a hand: Six years later neither of us are actively involved in the music business anymore; thus, the tension of comparison between us has been removed. We are both relieved by the change. Yet we both know that under similar circumstances the same competitive feelings could fester once again. As for handling them better the second go-around—of that, neither of us is 100 percent sure.

When, at the 1982 U.S. Open, Pam Shriver beat her doubles partner, Martina Navratilova, ruining Ms. Navratilova's chance at winning the grand slam, Ms. Shriver broke down in tears. Naturally, she had wanted to win the esteemed title, but her joy had been dampered by the fact that she had beaten her partner and friend. The tears, it seemed, were wrought of both compassion and guilt. The next day the New York *Times* printed a picture of the two women walking solemnly arm-around-arm off the court.[1] Two women who are competing for world championships, and who are as much concerned about their friendship as they are about beating the other person out, was in the editorial eye, enough to make front-page headlines.

If women who can be partners and friends and competitors is newsworthy, it is because there are so few of them. One reason is because our upbringing stands against competition; society has preened us for nurturance, leaving us with crippling ineptitude when it comes to competitive endeavors. But most important is the fact that the competitive arena reawakens long-buried, unresolved feelings of competition with mother, the person who was at once both our greatest source of love and our most ardent rival. Competition between women has always had a kind of forbidden quality; it reeks of betrayal. The stereotypic view of competition between women being "unfeminine" or "unladylike" only scratches the surface of our deepest, most unconscious emotions: the guilt of feeling competitive with mother (and later other women), and the fear of retaliation and abandonment because we dare to allow ourselves such competitive drives.

Competitive impulses as well as the fear of competition are believed to arise from the oedipal situation. According to classical Freudian theory, the young girl desires the exclusive attention of Daddy, with the concurrent wish to eliminate Mother, who is perceived as a rival. However, psychoanalysts now believe that the girl's desire for her father is as much, if not more, symbolic of her desire for freedom from her mother's overwhelming grasp, for autonomy, than for her father's sexual attentions. Either way, competitive, jealous impulses are so threatening to the young girl that they are forced underground; the oedipal situation is believed to be resolved when she represses her unacceptable impulses and identifies with her mother out of fear of retaliation.

Although the original oedipal experience has its roots in the mother-daughter dyad, it is later reexperienced with our friends. The competition for men, the need to excel, to be noticed, to be recognized as someone special and important, is transferred from Mother to other women throughout the course of the life cycle, as are our fears of rejection and abandonment. As a result, competitive feelings between women are often resolved by the identical mechanisms of repression and identification we used in relationship to mother. The little girl who denies her desire for the boy her best friend has a crush on, the woman who dresses "down" because her friend is less attractive, and the professional woman who feels ambivalent about utilizing her full capabilities are but a few examples of how our competitive desires continue to be thwarted, repressed. To our strivings for achievement in the work world we bring all this baggage, as well as a gunny sack of competitive urges that have been repressed in our earlier relationships with one another. We say we want success, but underneath our competitive veneer there is still the young girl who wonders, can you beat out other women and still maintain their love?

WOMEN AND COMPETITION: THE DEADLY DUO

What precedents do women have for competing successfully in the working world? Lamentably few. Our life experiences leave us groping in the dark. We have a dearth of role models to look up to. And those models that do exist often portray a coldness, even ruthlessness which is enough to hurl almost any woman back into the safety of the symbiotic womb.

Women who feel unconflicted about competition are about as hard to find as diamonds in a coal heap. From the early sixties on, research has consistently shown that women experience far greater anxiety about competition than men. Not only are women uncomfortable with competition—it tends to make them ill, with competitive women suffering from many more mental and physical health problems than competitive males.[2]

Even competent women with impressive titles and all the trappings of power choke on the words "I am competitive." In Jane Adams' *Women on Top,* for example, she found that while successful women had no trouble accepting their ambitiousness, most could not accept their competitive instincts without feeling they had compromised their femininity. These women included company presidents, presidential advisers, doctors, lawyers, creative directors, deans of universities. Their salaries ranged from $25,000 to $750,000 a year.[3] Another study yielded similar results, with women across the board describing themselves as more sensitive and less competitive than their male counterparts. The authors of one study of competitiveness in women concluded, "There are several signs that competitiveness is undesirable and costly for female subjects, even if they are masculine in other ways." The paradox is that masculine traits were also found to be associated with higher levels of mastery and lower levels of stress related to achievement, while feminine characteristics like sensitivity and emotionality were detrimental to performance.[4]

In short, while we might like to think things have changed, competitiveness for a woman still carries a high price tag.

COMPETING WITH WOMEN, COMPETING WITH MEN

A recurring theme in these studies, however, is that women's fear of competition arises from the fear of being rejected by the opposite sex. Viewing aggressive, competitive urges as "unfeminine," women fear that they will threaten the delicate egos of the men in their lives. Hence, they develop what Martina Horner called the "fear of success." Says Dr. Horner, "Most women have a motive to avoid success, that is, a disposition to become anxious about achieving success because they expect negative consequences (such as social rejection and/or feelings of being unfeminine) as a result of succeeding."[5]

While Dr. Horner's findings explain some of the ambivalence about competing with *men,* they fall short in explaining how women feel about competing with other *women.* Given, women aren't groomed to compete. Also given is that competition is inherent in the mother-daughter situation. And while competing with a man may arouse conflicts about our femininity, common sense tells us that competing with a woman assumes far greater psychic costs.[6]

Psychiatrist Allan Mallinger lays it out flat. To succeed in beating out the same-sex parent results in tremendous fears of retaliation that cover "a wide range from fear of loss of the same parent's love to fear of desertion, physical injury or even murder by that parent."[7] In a nutshell, the person who is inhibited about competition unconsciously experiences competitive situations with individuals of the same sex as a recapitulation of old oedipal rivalries, with the underlying threat and fear of retaliation. Something about such situations rearouses the danger associated with competition with our most powerful competitor: Mother. The psychic resolution for women is to remove themselves from the competitive arena completely. "To defend against this danger, or the anxiety connected with it," says Dr. Mallinger, the woman "unconsciously sabotages success in that pursuit. With time, this defense can become part of [her] autonomic style."[8]

That doesn't mean that women nonchalantly skip through the cornfields when pitted against a man. In fact, women whose fathers never reached their career ambitions may very well feel guilty about showing their fathers up. But given women's relative position in the work force, only a handful of women are in direct competition with men. And by the time the potential for outdoing their fathers becomes an issue, they have already had to grapple with a far more deadly game —beating out their mothers. The woman who dares to do so pays the piper in spades.

CRIME AND PUNISHMENT

When Jill DeCosta, a twenty-seven-year-old buyer who purchases antiques, began working in Soho, her attitude toward her two peers was one of cooperation. She believed that what was good for one was good for all, and generously shared ideas and contacts. "It's always been my idea that a cooperative strategy was better than a competitive one."

Hardworking and talented, and with a knack for seeking out "interesting eccentric types" whose homes overflowed with the kind of merchandise the store's clientele begged for, Jill's talents were quickly recognized. Unfortunately, she quickly learned that the two other buyers seemed to prefer riding on her coattails than getting in the trenches themselves. "Whenever I'd make a really good connection, they'd come into my office and ask, 'Where did you get this?' or 'How did you find that?' At first, I told them, figuring that in the spirit of cooperation they would give me some leads in return." But the fair exchange never came to pass. "I felt as if I was doing my work and their work, too. What was even worse was that they were getting as much recognition from the boss as I was. They never once mentioned that it was because of me they were doing so well."

Uncomfortable with the lack of trade-offs, Jill began hoarding her contacts. Why be magnanimous, she thought, if no one was willing to reciprocate? Not surprisingly, her peers were distressed, and attempted to cajole information out of her by taking her into their confidence. When that ploy did not work, they simply ignored her.

The situation came to a head on a buying trip to London. Firming up a deal she had worked long and hard to solidify, Jill privately asked one vendor for exclusive rights to his merchandise. The vendor agreed. Unfortunately, he did not have the foresight to communicate the arrangement to his assistant. It proved to be a deadly mistake.

At lunchtime two days after Jill had pulled off her "coup of coups," the two other antique buyers approached the vendor's assistant. Oblivious to her boss's alliance with Jill, she proceeded to show them what she viewed as her most saleable merchandise, the same merchandise Jill had staked claim to.

"We'll take it," said the buyers, patting themselves on the back for having had the fortitude to have rummaged through Jill's Rolodex before leaving the States.

"Miss Jones, may I speak to you for a moment," said the vendor, who interrupted the coup propitiously returning from lunch. The assistant followed her boss into his office. Reemerging from behind the closed doors, she approached her clients directly.

"I'm sorry to have wasted your time," she apologized, "but the merchandise you've selected has already been spoken for."

"What else can you show us?" snarled the more brazen of the two.

"I'm sorry," responded the assistant in her most charming British accent. "I've just been informed that we've signed an exclusive agreement with a buyer from New York City. I'm afraid I am unable to show you anything further."

It did not take a computer to add up the pieces. "Was it or wasn't it you who told that vendor not to show us any merchandise," they demanded once back at the hotel.

"I did not want to lie," Jill recalls. "So I told them that yes, I had. I also told them that I felt that I had been ripped off and that they were getting credit that I deserved."

The women have exchanged fewer than a handful of words with Jill since.

Large Japanese companies such as Mitsubishi are rooted in the philosophy of patriotic allegiance to the company: All for one and one for all. Personal glory is frowned upon. While it might be argued that this model is the best for everyone concerned, it is not the American way; that is, at least for men. "You wouldn't expect a man to hand over his trade secrets on a silver platter, would you?" says Jill in retrospect.

But while women may consciously laud women's rights to get ahead, beating another woman out is perceived as a kind of oedipal crime that deserves due punishment.

"Ever since that incident, I dread going to work," she tells me. "It's just a bad feeling between us."

The dilemma is painfully obvious: Survival or not, "being out for yourself" is a notion that is diametrically opposed to everything we have come to view as feminine. Didn't Mother say that a woman's raison d'être was to serve others, that to consider one's own desires foremost was a breach of woman's first commandment: "Thou shall take for oneself only after giving to everyone else?" In noncompetitive situations, our feelings of alliance to other women allows for the squelching of rivalrous impulses. But in the dog-eat-dog world of professional stirrings, the inability to compete can spell disaster; where there is only limited room at the top, it is each woman for herself. In a world that defines success by the ability to compete, the price paid for our internal conflict is professional suicide.

COMPETITION, ACHIEVEMENT AND MOTHER-DAUGHTER REPLAY

Of course, some women are more allergic to competing with another woman than others. In fact, in my interviews I found that women's feelings about competition covered the gamut. Some appeared to have no difficulty competing at all, viewing competition as a kind of professional fact of life. Others despised the idea so thoroughly that they kept themselves as far from potentially competitive situations as possible. Still others wanted very much to achieve, yet had difficulty carrying those drives to fruition because they choked in competitive situations.

What accounted for the differences?

The answer rests in the young girl's earliest and often incongruous feelings about both *achievement* and *competition*.

While achievement and competition appear to be plotted on the same plane, in truth, women's desire to achieve and their ability to carry out that motivation to competition are generally derived from two different sources.

While every normal, healthy girl has a desire to master, the motive to achieve in the outside world, to place one's stamp on what has traditionally been thought of as a man's domain, is largely fueled by a strong, positive identification with Dad. Somewhere in the oedipal transition, the little girl who later grows up wanting more than the happy homemaker's life aligns herself with her father. She admires him. She sees his achievements as a good thing. In short, he becomes a role model for her: "When I grow up, I want to be like him."

Her ability to successfully compete, however, to actualize her desire to achieve "in a man's world," is largely determined by her relationship with her mother. Dad may give his little girl all the strokes in the world for exhibiting independent, "masculine" behavior. But what if Mom scorns her for it; worse yet, rejects her for her moves toward autonomy? What if she feels she has to choose between her identification with Dad and her mother's love? It is not difficult to see that such a little girl will have more than an ounce of conflict about competition, that will always feel like some kind of trade-off between her own desires and her mother's approval.[9]

It helps to think of the motive to achieve as the underlying drive, and competition as the vehicle to funnel it. A car may have the potential to cruise at 110 miles per hour, but without putting one's foot on the accelerator pedal, it will remain at a standstill. Similarly, a woman may have all the drive in the world to achieve, but unless she is willing to compete, her ambitions will forever remain stagnant.

In my interviews four distinct patterns of achievement and competitive motives emerged:

(1) *Achievement-oriented Competitors*

These are women who have the best of both worlds—a high motivation to achieve combined with a relatively unambivalent relationship to competition.

(2) *Achievement-oriented Noncompetitors*

The strong desire of these women to excel is often impeded by an even stronger desire to avoid competition, particularly with other women.

(3) *Supercompetitors*

The underlying force motivating these women is not merely the desire to get ahead on their own terms, but to crush their opponent.

(4) *Nonachievement-oriented Women*

With few professional aspirations of their own, these women nevertheless feel highly competitive with other women, a drama that is acted out in typical female fashion, such as gossip.

Since women who do not experience an innate push to accomplish in the business world do not have to consider the negative ramifications of competition on their professional standing, the discussion on the following pages will be limited to the first three.

ACHIEVEMENT-ORIENTED COMPETITORS

These are the most ambitious and least conflicted of all achievers. Frequently, they are found in upper-management positions or in occupations that tend to be dominated by men. Some of them forfeit family for the sake of career, but many more of them tend to simply postpone marriage and children until their mid to late thirties.

What these women have most in common is not their choice of career, but their intrapsychic histories. Tracing the life stories of twenty-five highly successful women, authors Margaret Hennig and Anne Jardim cited certain common threads throughout. All the women in their sample developed a desire for independence and autonomy early on. All of them had special relationships with their fathers and strongly identified with them. All of them remember having reasonably good but noncompetitive relationships with their mothers. In other words, while mother may not have been an achiever herself, or perhaps did not encourge her daughter's autonomy directly, neither did she punish her for it. Basically, she simply stayed out of her daughter's way.[10]

WHEN CINDY SHOWS UP at the office, people are surprised to see her. In her eight-year career, she has moved from junior analyst to vice president, from an office worker to a woman who spends most of her time traveling around the world. Her latest assignment is handling a crumbling Chilean engineering firm, and these days her Central Park West apartment is occupied only a few months a year. She makes her own hours, calls her own shots, decides which accounts she will or will not handle. If and when she tires of her high-powered career, she will retire and have children—another life "project" as she sees it. Or perhaps she will move to Hollywood and learn how to make movies.

"It has never occurred to me that I can't have whatever I want," she will tell you. "A lot of women I know doubt their capacities, or doubt whether they can make it within the system. They're afraid to take chances. They just don't have much confidence in themselves."

Not Cindy. For as long as she can remember, she has believed that all you need to do to get what you want is to go after it. "When everything's been possible in your life before, it's not unreasonable to think whatever obstacles are in your way, can be removed. You haven't developed a fear that you can't get what you want. You just don't have that way of thinking."

Her "thinking," as she put it, arose very early on in her relationship with her father. A bright, energetic man who owned his own manufacturing business, Cindy was supported in her ambitions from the outset. She would be everything he was, and more, he would tell her. By the time she was five, she and Dad would spend endless hours in intellectual discussions, bantering back and forth in a playful, competitive way. It never occurred to her that there were things that girls couldn't do. "We made quite a pair," she says, adding, "I absolutely loved that man."

Mother, Cindy recalls, was quite the opposite of Dad: a quiet woman who, at the time, harbored no more ambition than staying home and raising a large family. She was more pleased by Cindy's attractiveness than her intellectual potential. "I was a very pretty, seductive child, and she really loved to show me off." At the same time, she did not interfere with the burgeoning relationship between Cindy and her father. Rather, she let it flourish. "Women always tell me about mothers being jealous of their daughter's relationships with the father, but my mother was really pretty good about it. She just seemed to accept that we had something special, and wasn't threatened by it. As far as developing my intellectual capacity, she wasn't as active as Dad but was supportive in her own way. In fact, she was always the first to stress independence, that it was important for everyone to be able to take care of themselves."

With Dad to provide the achievement ammunition, coupled with Mom's blessings, women like these are likely to have the least amount of difficulty competing with women. Why should they? If all mothers were able to share their daughters with Dad, to give them a fair piece of the cake without resenting them for it, we might have to rewrite the whole oedipal story.

How does Cindy feel about competition today? "I like to compete. I'm constantly strategizing—it's kind of a game with me. I'm very goal-oriented and competing is the only way to get where you want. The idea for me is not to crush my opponents—just to be better at whatever it is than they are.

"What's so interesting," she adds, "is that I usually don't have to compete with women at all. When I want to get somewhere professionally, I get like a laser beam. I'm indomitable. That scares women off, so much so that I often find I don't have to compete with them at all. They simply move out of my way."

Where the sting of competition has bitten is in relationship to her lithe body, long auburn hair, and green eyes. "The same women who won't compete with me professionally become vicious when it comes to my looks. If women I work with talk about me, it generally has nothing to do with my work, but with what I wear, or who I might be sleeping with, or what I did to get as far as I got. I've never slept with anybody I've worked with, but still, there's the gossip."

ACHIEVEMENT-ORIENTED NONCOMPETITORS

Most likely to feel in a double bind about competition with women are women who have strong motives to achieve, yet at the same time fear the ramifications of beating the other woman out. Like the woman who competes with relative ease, conflict-ridden women develop a strong identification with their fathers early on. They aspire to achieve in traditionally "male" terms. Unlike their less conflicted counterparts, however, their relationships with their mothers tend to have a hostile edge. Contrary to the mothers of achievement-oriented, competitive women, if not encouraging autonomy directly, at least do not stand in the way of it; the mothers of achievement-oriented, noncompetitive women tend to be, in Dr. Mallinger's words, "nonnurturing, competitive, powerful, erratic, and sometimes childish."[11]

"To the degree that the mother is critical of her daughter's identification with the father, of her autonomy, the girl herself will feel conflicted," Angela Fox told me. "The mother may express the criticism by expressing jealousy or by saying things that minimize the girl's efforts. The mother wants her daughter to be the way *she* is. For the girl to be different is a direct threat to her own identity. It's a dilemma: the girl identifies with her father but is rejected for that identification with the mother. She will, therefore, maintain an ambivalent feeling about competition."

A traditional, unseparated mother is not the only type of mother who may arouse competition anxiety. Just as devastating is the mother who herself is oriented toward achievement yet who is highly competitive with her daughter. In this case the daughter is given some initial push toward autonomy—that is, until it looks as if she may beat her mother at her own game.

Either way, the deadly message remains the same: Separate from me, be different, be better than I am, and I will reject you.

Looking at her, no one would guess Sonia Berman has difficulties competing with women. An architect in her early forties whose salary sails about the $35,000 figure, she appears the epitome of the successful woman: well coiffed, stylishly dressed, and living in a fashionable New York co-op surrounded by valuable African artifacts. And yet success scared the hell out of her.

Books, typewriters, and the New York *Times* . . . she had been raised in an intellectual atmosphere in San Francisco, where she was an only child. Her father was an architect of professional acclaim. Her mother was a brilliant woman who had temporarily given up her aspirations to stay home with Sonia. Their courtship had been a sweep-me-off-my-feet love story, luring Sonia's mother into marriage before she was twenty, followed by motherhood at twenty-two. "I can always go back to school," Sonia remembers her mother saying to her as a child, "but I'll never have the chance again to see you grow up."

Her mother's love, however, was intermixed with more than a twinge of envy. "From the start I was the apple of Dad's eye," Sonia recalled. "I can remember him taking me into his studio from the time I was very young and showing me how he would turn an idea into a picture. I'd spend hours in there, just watching him draw, or talking about all kinds of things. It made me feel very special. His studio was his private place that was off limits to everyone when he was working, including my mother."

The seductive father-daughter relationship became the focus of intense conflict.

"You spend more time with that child than you do with me," Sonia remembers hearing her mother say.

"Maybe that's because she's more interesting than you are," her dad had retorted.

At which point Sonia's mother applied to medical school. Finances would be tight, she knew, but anything was better than losing her husband to a precocious seven-year-old child.

During her second year of medical school, tragedy struck when Sonia's dad died suddenly of a stroke. Sonia's mom was forced to quit school and accept a moderate-paying but professionally unsatisfying job as a civil servant. Her mother tried to remain even-keeled, but underneath the facade, a volcano brewed. It all came to a head during an argument when Sonia's mother refused to give her money to buy a ten-speed bike.

"I'm the only kid on the block without a bicycle," Sonia wailed.

"I'm the only mother on the block who had to give up medical school to support her child," was the scathing reply.

The assault threw Sonia into her artwork. Every free moment she drew prodigiously, coming up with extraordinary designs. Recognizing her talent, teachers began writing home, suggesting Sonia receive special lessons. Sonia's mother refused. "There's not enough money," was the repeated reply. Privately, Sonia felt there were other reasons. "It was beginning to look as if I could have a very successful career as an architect. I was getting all this reinforcement from the outside. And here was my mother stuck in what she thought was a menial job. She couldn't stand the thought that someday I might be more successful than she."

It was not an unrealistic possibility. At fifteen Sonia was accepted into a special program for artistically gifted children. At eighteen she received a partial scholarship to one of the best architectural programs in the country. The rest of her tuition was paid for by numerous freelance assignments. She was on her way.

If Sonia manifested few problems with achieving, it was because she had not, at that point, ever considered herself in competition with anybody else. As long as she was in school, she could convince herself that she was only in competition with herself. And the freelance assignments just seemed to come her way, with no active hustling involved. The only indication of potential trouble was Sonia's unrelenting attitude toward entering contests. "I just wouldn't do it. I rationalized it by saying that

I was the only true judge of my art, that I didn't need outsiders to tell me whether I was number one or not. My friends used to tell me that I was afraid of losing. The truth is, what I was really afraid of was winning."

After graduation Sonia was offered a prestigious job with a major New York City architectural firm. She loved her work, but could not help but recognize the condescending attitude of the three other men in the department. "Even though they were very different people, they were all of like mind when it came to women. We used to work together on strategies for a building design, and if there was a dispute, usually the men agreed and I didn't. The proof of the pudding was that the three of them agreed. My reasoning was always wrong; it was fallacious. At times I felt like I was going crazy. It was very difficult and I was very unhappy and constantly nervous."

Indeed, she was beginning to believe that she was misperceiving everything until Harriet, an architect twenty years her senior, was brought into the department. The two women became instant friends. "She saw what was going on immediately. After being there only three weeks, she pulled me aside and said, 'How do you stand this. You don't have to put up with this crap.' Validation at last."

Harriet became a kind of mentor for Sonia, the supportive, encouraging mother she had never had. Like Sonia's father, Harriet told her the sky was the limit. Unlike Sonia's mother, she did not sabotage Sonia's efforts to be all that she could, but encouraged them.

That is, until the firm lost one of its largest clients.

"It was a bloodbath. A lot of people were canned and everyone was afraid of losing their hides. We also heard through the grapevine that in all likelihood, either Harriet or I would be the first to get the shaft—you know, affirmative action and all that. The department already had two women, which was 40 percent of the entire staff, a much higher percentage than the percentage of women architects in general.

Suddenly, Sonia and Harriet were thrust from a cooperative mode into a competitive one. Harriet's response was to work doubly hard. She became cool toward Sonia. Their collaborative style became a thing of the past. It was each woman out for herself.

While recognizing that Harriet was merely looking out for her own professional interests, the loss of the friendship was a hard blow to absorb. To boot, while Harriet was playing it to the hilt, Sonia's own competitive impulses stood at a standstill. It was almost as if the harder

Harriet worked, the more lax Sonia became. Her creativity squelched by a force she could not explain, her productivity gradually dwindled. Her work was mundane and unexciting. It was as if she had lost all her creative juices.

The potential for obtaining a multimillion-dollar shopping center deal did not lift her spirits. "I choked. They could not get an interesting design out of me. Meanwhile, Harriet was producing some of the best concepts she had ever come up with. Eventually, I just gave up trying."

The firm did not receive the shopping mall contract. Sonia received the ax.

Five years later, and after extensive therapy, Sonia understands what went wrong but even now seems somewhat dumbstruck by the power of the unconscious. "It seems so simple that it's almost hard to believe. Competing with Harriet was like competing with my mother all over again. I had already beaten my mother out twice—first, in terms of my father's love, then in terms of professional success. The cost of that was rejection—I lost my mother's love."

Her fear had been that to beat Harriet out would cause a similar rejection. And indeed, the waning of their relationship indicated that her instincts were not completely off base. "I had been punished once, and I didn't want to be punished again. It was just easier to drop out."

SUPERCOMPETITORS

Every once in a while, one comes across a woman whose need to make her mark is so all-encompassing that nothing, absolutely nothing, stands in her way. It matters little whose toes she steps on, whose feelings are hurt in the process. To the contrary, a lot of the pleasure she derives arises from stamping out her opponent.

Similar to other high achievers, the supercompetitor develops a desire for autonomy early on. Unlike other achievers, she is spurred by a host of aggressive, ugly feelings—a motivation that generally develops when a person has two parents who are nonnurturing, rejecting, and hostile.

"There are two ways to develop an autonomous ego," says Angela Fox. "The first is within a nurturing, nonsymbiotic relationship. The second is within a rejecting parental relationship. What happens is that the girl is pushed into separation because her parents feel isolated from her. So, yes, she is propelled to achieve when she grows up. But at the same time, she has all this hostility which she couldn't really express toward her parents, and which eventually gets directed toward those with whom she works."

Samantha was such a woman. The youngest of four children, separated by twelve years from the sibling closest in age, she always remembers feeling she was an "accident." Her parents were poor immigrants, barely getting by on her father's laborer's salary before she was born. Her mother was arthritic, a condition Samantha's birth exacerbated. When she was born, her mother was forty-five, her father fifty-four.

"For as long as I can remember, I was always in the way," Samantha, forty-one and a bank vice president, recalls. "My parents simply did not have time for me. My father was always working and my mother was constantly in pain. My sister and brothers were already in adolescence, so they weren't too interested in playing baby-sitter either. So I was pretty much left to my own devices from a very young age. I was fairly independent by the time I was five years old. I was the type of child one typically calls 'mature.' "

There is some indication that a somewhat hostile attitude on the part of the mother during the preschool years precipitates a high motive to achieve.[12] The explanation for this phenomenon is that a less than nurturing relationship between mother and daughter precipitates separation from the mother. The drawback is that a lack of love is damaging to the ego. And Samantha not only had a dearth of affection from her mother, but from her father as well. It is these early scars that she is harnessed with to this day.

"I was a very angry child," she tells me, "highly aggressive. I know it's unusual for a girl to be physical, but I was, always finding a smaller kid to beat up on. Looking back, I think there was so much pent-up anger that I was propelled by this feeling that I wanted to destroy someone."

Her first "destruction" was directed toward a girl in high school. Her name was Kathy Brooks, and she was blond, pretty, and popular. She was also president of her sorority, a group that Samantha longed to be a part of, but from which she had been rejected on Kathy's say-so. "She's too much of a bookworm," Kathy had said.

"I hated her," says Samantha with an urgency that would lead one to believe it had happened only yesterday.

Propelled by a neurotic need for vengeance, Samatha spent her senior year plotting, looking for a way she might "do in" her archrival. Three weeks before the senior prom, her opportunity presented itself. Kathy was the steady of a tall, lanky boy named Gary Rollins, who was captain of the basketball team. Samantha herself never had any interest in the boy, who, in her opinion, had "nothing upstairs." He, however, had begun eyeing her lasciviously in the lunchroom. Rumor had it that pretty Kathy was also pretty much the prude, and at eighteen Gary was looking for the kind of excitement one expects from the captain of the basketball team. A virgin herself, Samantha, nevertheless portrayed the image of a seductress—well built, dark, with blue eyes that could melt an ice cube. It was that image she began cultivating to the hilt.

"I remember feeling what a coup it would be if Gary dropped Kathy, if he went with me to the prom. And here he was expressing interest. It seemed the perfect opportunity."

Gary and Samantha began seeing each other on the sly, her physical repulsion kept in check by her driving need to beat Kathy out. Yet he did not ask her to the prom. After all, "Gary and Kathy" had become household words. And as virginal as she was, Kathy was gorgeous.

There's only one way, Samantha thought.

The night of the prom Kathy stayed at home, devastated by Gary's sudden announcement that he was going with Samantha. Samantha, on the other hand, dressed in peach organdy, beamed with satanic glee. She had conquered—and destroyed.

Of course, there had been a price. That price had been her virginity.

Samantha's mercilessness, her unyielding tactics, have followed her into the working world. She has, by her own admission, slept with the boss, destroyed marriages, sabotaged a competitor's reputation through unfounded rumor. She has drawn people into her confidence, only to breach that confidence when professionally propitious. In the same breath she has initiated banking programs which have saved millions of dollars, and has developed worldwide alliances with a calculating shrewdness that allows her to write her own ticket.

She is, in a word, ruthless.

How do those who work with her view her? I asked.

"There's no doubt that they see me as someone who's very competent, but also very cutthroat. I'm not exactly the most popular woman around. There are a lot of men who see me as calculating and manipulative, and don't like me for that. But there have been others who admire me for those same traits."

And the women?

"Most women despise me," she answered with a crooked smile. "What's interesting about that is the fact that they tend to look up to a man who possesses the kinds of traits I do. There really does seem to be a double standard."

Samantha is raising an important point. There is little doubt that the kind of manipulative behavior and disregard for the other that Samantha exhibits are symptoms of an angry, damaged personality. At the same time, the cutthroat characteristics she exhibits are more acceptable in a man. A lot of the angry and aggressive feelings that are produced by an unloving mother and father and get worked into one's character yield a positive outcome for a man. He's a good businessman, we say, when hearing such an autobiography. The woman who possesses the same traits, however, is viewed as something little short of disgusting—aggressiveness and ruthlessness are simply more appropriate for men. So while a man who has accomplished through ruthless means is on some level applauded, the woman who secures what she wants via the same strategy is viewed as "sick." And they are most often despised.

Given the cost in interpersonal relationships that results when a woman utilizes hard-nosed tactics to get ahead, can we say that women such as these are conflicted about competition? Not really. "I've always been used to being a loner. I'm used to getting along without too many friends. When you've never had something, you don't miss it when it's not there." For women like Samantha, who never had either a mother's or a father's love, evoking the ill-will of others is a moot threat. As Janis Joplin put it, "Freedom's just another word for nothing left to lose."

CORPORATE GAMES

Of course, not all of the conflict about competition can be directly traced to the early mother-daughter relationship. Other factors, including siblings and societal attitudes, do their share to contribute to the problem. Not least among these is the specific work structure in which women in the labor force find themselves.

"I haven't found a lot of competition at this office," says Bobbi Rabinowitz, chief of public relations for a women's union. "A lot of that has to do with the fact that this office is not hierarchically organized. Women are more or less peers, and there are no men on top. If there's not a lot of competition, it's because there's simply nothing to compete for."

If settings as the one just described tend to ameliorate competition between women, corporate bureaucracies are breeding grounds for it to fester. First, the division of labor at most companies symbolically replays a time long past. One of the reasons that competition between women is so emotionally loaded, so hot, is because we have been raised to feel that winning comes always at someone else's expense. With only so much of Dad to go around, anything we take from him means there is less of him to be had by Mom. The achievement-oriented woman finds herself plunged into a replica of the same dilemma in a world in which there is only so much achievement, so many places on the top for a woman, to go around. Vying for that promotion, landing that job, leaves that much less of an opening in which other women can squeeze. Companies also do their share by subtly encouraging competition as a way of getting their employees to work harder. If we have the feeling that, like Dad's love, getting what we want cuts into someone else's piece of the pie, it is because that's really the way it is.

In addition, the patriarchal organization of many companies symbolically sets up the oedipal situation with stunning exactness. Think, for a moment, about the typical bureaucratic setting. You have, at the pinnacle, the big-daddy boss. Underneath him there is the mommy boss, who wields considerable power of her own, but nevertheless remains subservient to the omnipotent father. And then, of course, are all the sisters (secretaries, bookkeepers, assistants, etc.) on the lower rung.

Naturally, the larger the company, the more the themes and variations. Perhaps there are more mommy bosses, separated by yet another caste of older-brother bosses who reign above the little sisters. Or maybe the set up is more obviously discriminatory, with men running the show, women running to follow the men's orders, and a token woman manager thrown in for show. Whatever the configuration, however, the dynamics remain identical: men predominantly at the top, women predominantly underneath them. Says Jane Flax, "It's like being in your oedipal family all over again."

Now imagine for a moment that this was a real family. From where would the competition arise and toward whom would it be directed? Obviously, it would start with the daughters who by definition are rivals with Mother for Daddy's love, symbolically the desire for recognition.

The bottom line in almost every mother-daughter relationship, however, is power, and in almost every case it is the mother who has it, and the daughter who doesn't. A daughter is virtually powerless against her mother from both a psychological and economic point of view. She may desire Daddy's attention, but she is in no position to compete with her mother directly. She is simply too dependent upon her. So where do all these nasty, competitive impulses get directed, if not at mother herself? If she has one, to her sister. In fact, rivalry between sisters is generally believed to be a more benign form of competition with the mother. Says Elizabeth Fishel in her book *Sisters*, "Again and again, the rivalry we will see between sisters is, at least in part, an expression of the rivalry girls experience with their mothers in a more manageable, less threatening form."[13]

This explains why so many stories of competition between women who work in corporate settings are directed at women who are in similar capacities, who wield similar amounts of power. It is, in most cases, the only safe target toward whom such feelings can be vented.

The deadly impulses emerge in deadly sister-sister rivalry, corporate style.

THE TATTLETALE GAME

One of the most popular competitive games played by these working "sisters" is the tattletale game—telling the mommy (or when possible, the daddy) the wrongdoings of the other. The purpose behind the game is obvious; make the other sister look bad while you make yourself look good. The better "girl" you are, the more Mommy, and hence Daddy, will love you.

The game is played among women of all ages. "I see it all the time," says a thirty-three-year-old manager, "between the women who work for me. One will come in and tell me one of the others came in late yesterday. Then the one who has been tattled on will come in and accuse the tattler of making trouble or not doing an assignment completely. It's obvious how they're competing for my approval. What's so amazing is that the average age of the women who work for me is forty-five! Think about it—here are these grown women acting just like kids."

LET'S SPREAD A RUMOR

Closely aligned to the tattletale game is the rumor game. Here the idea is not only to make a woman look bad in the eyes of her boss, but to make her feel worthless and uncomfortable with her coworkers, her "siblings" as well.

Take, for instance, what I found to be a relatively common pattern in bureaucratically structured organizations. One woman in clique A starts a rumor about another woman in clique B—she's pregnant, she just had an abortion, her husband left her—a way of discrediting her without directly challenging her work performance. The woman starting the rumor, of course, knows that the rumor will get back to the person who is the subject of the rumor in lightning time. Then, of course, all those involved in starting the rumor deny knowing anything about the origins of the rumor, leaving the poor victim to feel she's been abused.

VERBAL DAGGERS

Also popular among women is the put-down, the kind of derogatory remark that is often said with a smile but meant to kill. Unlike other games, the put-down is a more direct expression of seething jealousy and aggression.

The specific remark can be about anything, but it is generally directed at the jugular. One woman, for example, who is the youngest middle-management woman on staff—in fact has a ten-year youth edge on any of the other women who are her peers—finds condescending remarks being directed at her constantly. A small woman, who looks far younger than her twenty-six years, the asides are inevitably directed at her appearance. She has been called the "kid," the "girl on the block," and, of course, the inevitable "dear."

"These women are so damn jealous and competitive that they can't see straight," she tells me. "Not only do they resent the fact that I'm young and attractive; they're afraid that it won't be too long before I'm in a higher position than they are. It usually comes out in derogatory ways. Sometimes they ignore me completely. Other times they demean me by trying to treat me like a child. For instance, yesterday I came into my office wearing a sophisticated suit. I had also put my hair up. That's unusual for me—usually, I dress a little more casually. Anyway, one of the women came up to me and said, 'My dear, you look almost grown up today.'"

THE GUILT TRIP

Perhaps the most popular device used to express hostile, angry feelings is the instillation of guilt, that is, making a peer feel as if she has done something inherently wrong by doing well.

The most poignant story I've heard concerns a twenty-four-year-old marketing assistant who was passed up for a promotion while the two other departmental assistants she worked with were promoted.

Susan, Debra, and Kelly had all been in their present positions for approximately three years. The structure of their department was a replica of the early oedipal family—their immediate boss was a woman, and her immediate boss was a man. The assistants had not considered themselves in direct competition with one another, as each assumed completely different responsibilities: Kelly was involved with sales, Debra with research, and Susan with advertising. Hence, they became good friends and cooperative workers, helping one another in any way they could.

The feeling of cohesiveness was destroyed when Susan and Debra received promotions and Kelly did not. Suddenly, without actually competing against each other, they had become rivals. Feeling like a child who is fed gruel when her other sisters are given ice-cream sundaes, Kelly began lashing out at her "siblings."

"She became a different person," Susan recalls. "She accused us of brownnosing the boss, of speaking badly about her behind her back. Debbie and I got her a bottle of wine for Christmas to make amends, and she wouldn't accept it. It was as if she was holding us responsible for what had happened.

"If you ask me," she continued, "I think that Kelly should have received a promotion. When Debra and I spoke about it privately, neither of us could understand why she hadn't. But the injustice that was done to her was not our fault, even though she was acting as if it were."

Kelly's response is not unusual. In fact, it is the norm. When a woman feels slighted by her boss in this way, she cannot express her aggression toward her boss. She cannot say, "Who the hell are you to deny me, when you give to them?" Not surprisingly, she expresses them to the only target available—the other women with whom she works.

ON YOUR GUARD

Competition is not always expressed overtly, of course. In fact, in many instances competition between peers is more a matter of omission—for instance, withholding critical information that is potentially damaging or helpful to someone else's career.

"In my office women are more competitive than the worst men," a woman who works for American Express tells me. "They are all these MBA types and they have nothing on their minds besides getting ahead."

How, I wondered, does she know?

"There's no camaraderie, no feeling that you're all working toward the same goal. A woman will have some information, say, that might be helpful to you, but she'll never let you know it. It could be something as simple as knowing that the computer system is going to be shut down during the afternoon. I can remember a few months ago speaking to a woman from another department, telling her about all the programming I had to get done that afternoon. She didn't respond at all. Later, when I got back from lunch, I found the system down. I walked into her office bitching and moaning about how my whole day had been thrown off, and there she was sitting cool as a cucumber. 'Oh yeah,' she told me, 'I heard about it this morning. I guess I just *forgot* to mention it to you.' I was really furious. But that kind of thing goes on all the time."

The sad truth is that not only does such withholding happen regularly, but it is frequently encouraged by the supervisor. While we might like to think that women in charge have a monopoly on fairness, many women have accused their bosses of playing favorites, a ploy which only aggravates an already competitive climate. As the mother who overtly favors one child, the effect is to play one off against the other.

One woman, for example, who is a supervisor for a large conglomerate, tells me that there is no doubt that she is treated differently than her peers. "There are eight supervisors working for my boss. Of all of them, I'm the favorite. I don't know why, but that's the way it is. It's as if she's keeping a special eye out for me. For instance, if she knows that there's a budget meeting coming up, she'll call me and tell me about it a few days before the interoffice memos are sent out. That gives me a head start over all the rest. It is very helpful professionally, but it also puts me in an uncomfortable position. I can't tell anybody else because that would be like betraying my boss. At the same time, I can't really develop relationships with these other women because they're constantly complaining how much they don't like her. Obviously, they don't know about our little covenant. If they did, I would really be a convenient scapegoat. In a way, I feel bad about it, but business is business, and it's always better to align yourself with someone who holds the power."

THE QUEEN BEE SYNDROME

Up until now we have been assuming that mother (the boss) perceives herself as more powerful than her "children," that she is secure in herself and her place in Daddy's heart, and therefore does not feel particularly threatened by her daughters' desires to get some of Daddy's attention. In the ideal case, she will even encourage it. What happens, however, if the daughter is too seductive and the father too interested, if that little tyke of a girl threatens to outdo mother herself? In all likelihood she will use her superior power to steer the girl away from the limelight.

In recent years there has been some evidence to suggest that one of the reasons women are dissatisfied with female bosses is because they squelch potential in their underlings. The situation arises when a boss feels tenuous about her own position. Calling it the "queen bee syndrome," it is characterized by "a successful female manager who sees female subordinates as potential competitors for her position and thus may treat them differently than male subordinates."[14]

Or as one executive put it, "In my office, I'm afraid that if I take my shoes off, even for a moment, someone else is going to step into them."

If the fear of being outstripped is less acute in relationship to men, it is because there is more room in the system to accommodate the aspiring male. Out of every one hundred managers, only fifteen are likely to be women.[15] It's a throwback to the oedipal situation, where there is only room for one wife, when there is not enough of Dad's love to go around.

Given the real limitations on women's advancement, it is little surprise that so few mentors exist. Why give a subordinate the benefit of expertise if she is merely going to use it to steal your job?

The fear of being replaced prevails even among women who have made it. Take, for example, the following responses of Jane Adams' interviewees, who qualified as "women on top."

Asking my boss for that kind of help is the quickest way to get transferred to another division. She is not quite at the top yet, and she sees women who work for her as a threat.

I can't handle competing with a woman, or having her supervise my professional advancement. I know it's an archaic, premovement attitude, but I can't shake it. I may have to deal with the sexual angle with a male mentor, but that I can handle.

In the mentor relationship, women are very competitive. While they want you to succeed, it's only up to a certain point. With so few women near the top, you are readily identifiable as a threat, because chances are only one of you will make it.[16]

If women such as these are threatened by other women, what might we expect from women who on some level doubt their own capabilities? That jealousy would exist is obvious. And having a boss's power in the organization gives her a perfect battleground in which to crush her opponent.

CINDERELLA IN THE WORLD OF HIGH FASHION

By far the most notorious story of the oedipal drama is the story of Cinderella. While hundreds of versions of the popular fairy tale exist, and at least as many psychoanalytic interpretations, at the most basic level Cinderella is the story of mother-daughter competition which arises from both Cinderella's desire for her father's attention and her stepmother's deadly impulses to get rid of her more beautiful, seductive daughter. In the end, Cinderella is rescued by her fairy godmother, who allows her to break free of the oedipal rivalry by finding her own prize, the prince.

Unfortunately, not all Cinderellas are so fortunate.

Felicia Miran was such a Cinderella. Her career as a clothing buyer, which had started out three years ago with a bang thanks to the guidance of a talented and unthreatened good-mommy boss, was now in a state of cinders. She was stuck in a deadly game of competition in which she was relatively powerless, in which she could neither retaliate nor break free—a game controlled by her new boss, who was quite the wicked stepmother.

Three years ago, at age twenty-two, Felicia considered herself a lucky young woman. Having graduated from the Fashion Institute of Technology, she was immediately grabbed by a prestigious retailing firm in New York and placed under the wing of one of the most reputed buyers in the company. "She was everything one could hope for in a boss," Felicia recalled, "nurturing without being overly involved, directive while still allowing me considerable opportunity to take initiative. Most of all, Norma (her boss) was so successful in her own right that Felicia's talents in no way threatened her. "Your success is my success," she had told her, allowing Felicia to indulge her competitive impulses without fearing she might be punished for them.

Two years after working for her first boss, Felicia's company was bought out by a large conglomerate. Departments were consolidated; many employees were given the ax. But Felicia's reviews from her boss had been so extraordinary that Felicia not only averted the flash fire but received a promotion to buyer. She was thrilled.

Ripples of unease began gripping her when she was assigned to her new squadron. She enjoyed working hard, and the two buyers with whom she would now be in constant contact had earned themselves a less than glowing reputation. Lazy and disorganized, one of the women had had tremendous difficulty completing her catalog only six months before. The other, a young woman close to Felicia's age, was recognized, above all else, for her mediocrity. In fact, Felicia speculated how they had managed to retain their positions at all. Secretly, she wondered whom they had been sleeping with.

The announcement of the appointment of her new boss, a woman in her late forties named Mary McGee, was even more enigmatic. Having worked for the past twenty years in mail-order, it made no sense to promote her to district head of a retailing division. There had been others who in Felicia's mind had been far more qualified for the job. Felicia sniffed around looking for answers. What she got was a glimpse of what was to be the new corporate policy. "The president of the company is a firm believer in seniority," she was told. "Mary's been here twenty years. There's no way they're going to get rid of her."

Ascribed status aside, there were rumblings that Mary was not entirely comfortable with her position as head supervisor. For one thing, she was unfamiliar with the mechanical end of retailing. "I had just been promoted, so in her eye I was the new kid on the block. I think she thought she was going to show me the ropes, polish my star." But it did not take long before it became clear that if anyone was equipped to do the star polishing, it was Felicia. "This was a new facet of the business for her, and she simply didn't know the mechanics as well as I. So here she was the boss, yet she always had to come to me for advice as to how to go about doing things. That started us out on the wrong foot."

Another difficulty was the tension created by Felicia's and Mary's divergent ideologies. "She was the type of woman who believed a woman should exploit her sexual wiles—bat your eyelashes, look pretty, and the world is yours. Underneath it there was also the suggestion that if I had to sleep with someone to get a sale, I should do it. I was a militant feminist in college, and it was very hard for me to accept orders from someone whose philosophy was so directly in opposition to mine."

Most upsetting to Felicia was Mary McGee's insistence on developing "a little family" among the women in the department. "She kept saying that we were a baby nucleus, a team that was going to show the big-daddy boss how well we were all getting along. In her book it was 'All for one and one for all.' " The problem was that Felicia wasn't interested in being a musketeer.

Aspiring women like Felicia are right to feel uncomfortable in such little families. Adopting a nurturant, interpersonal mode is a way of downgrading competition, of sweeping it under the rug. It's a compensatory device women tend to use when working with women they perceive as more competent than they: Divert her from the task at hand, and maybe she won't notice you don't know what you're doing.[17]

Felicia couldn't help but notice. Nor was she oblivious to the growing fondness between Mary and the two women who were Felicia's peers. There were conversations that turned into hushed whispers when Felicia passed by; forgetful 'slips' that excluded Felicia from receiving important company information; the nightmare of going out into the market with them.

"When it was the three of them, I wasn't there. They only talked to me when they had to. Things were so bad that I actually had salespeople calling me up asking what the hell was going on."

Felicia sought the counsel of her ex-boss. "You're in a jam," she had said with genuine sympathy. "I'd suggest you speak to the vice president."

"But couldn't that just make things worse?" Felicia had countered, instinctively knowing that one does not go over Mother's head without dire consequences.

"How much worse could things be than they are now?"

Felicia decided to take the risk. The VP listened, even appeared to be concerned, but like the father in the story of Cinderella—indeed, like most fathers—his primary allegiance remained with Mary. When he called Felicia into his office the following week, he had little to report other than that he had spoken to Mary and she had denied the whole thing. "Why don't you just try a little harder to get along," he admonished.

Felicia fumed. "What it came down to was the fact that Mary had worked with him for twenty years; I was a relative newcomer. On top of that, I think there's always an unspoken alliance between those who hold the power. So who was he going to believe? Her or me?"

In her frustration Felicia began working harder and harder. She thought that if she could only prove her competence with the highest sales figures her department had ever seen, surely she would be recognized. But Mary had an agenda of her own. How dare that little Cinderella complain behind her back! What began as a low-intensity campaign blossomed into an all-out crusade. Felicia's paperwork doubled. She was handed all the departmental tasks that no one else wanted to bother with. She felt quite the Cinderella, scrubbing the floors, sweeping the cinders.

She would have quit had the job market not been so tight—this was in the early eighties when retail sales hit an all-time low. As it was, the whole company was teetering on a financial tightrope, and came dangerously close to shutting down half its departments. So Felicia continued to wear her rags, spending her weekends preparing a new fall line which she knew secretly was her ticket to recognition, her gown for the ball. All she needed now was a Prince Charming to rescue her.

A few months later Felicia received an interoffice memo announcing that the new president of the company would be attending the next sales presentation. She squealed with anticipation. Her presentations, she knew, were impressive; after all, she had been trained by the best. The fact that Mary had, in the past, publicly chastised her for overproducing and overrepresenting was just another ace in her pocket. She knew that she was not overproducing, but her peers were underproducing. Now, if only she could be heard, if only she could get to the ball, she knew she would be saved.

"You don't get to be the president of a multimillion dollar company unless you have one priority—making money," Felicia told herself.

The morning of the presentation Felicia was walking briskly down the long hall to the boardroom when she felt a cold hand on her shoulder.

"Well, don't you look nice today," Mary said in her most mellifluous voice.

A shiver went down Felicia's spine, as if she suspected there was a tarantula crawling up her back.

"Look, dear," continued Mary with an irritating coo, "I know we've had our differences, but we shouldn't let such things interfere with business. And today's presentation is critical to the department. So," she continued as Felicia waited for the ax to fall, "you're not going to do something silly like outshine your peers, are you? We're all one little family, and we can't afford to have one look better than the others?"

Felicia responded with an icy stare. If she could establish her credibility in the eyes of the president, she knew she would be saved. If the ploy backfired, however, she was in grave danger of losing her job. Risk aside, she knew she had only one option.

"If I did what Mary wanted me to do, I would have been throwing my whole career down the tube, and my self-respect along with it."

Legs crossed, hands in lap, she appeared the epitome of poise and composure. Inside, she quaked, although she had to admit her nerves were somewhat soothed as she viewed the slipshod presentations of her two peers. She also had to admit she derived more than an ounce of pleasure watching the president, as his expression slipped from boredom to an out-and-out grimace as he assessed what Felicia was now convinced was an unruly state of affairs.

"Felicia," Mary's voice echoed, interrupting Felicia's thoughts.

Walking to the front of the boardroom, her knees trembled, buckled for a split second, and then became steadfast, firmly planted on the ground. It was 11 A.M. Sixty minutes later, the same amount of time it had taken both of the other buyers combined, Felicia completed her presentation.

"Well done, well done," said the president with genuine approval.

So began the final deterioration of Felicia's relationship with the women in her department, a phase punctuated by a slew of razor-sharp remarks that bit like paper cuts. She had defied the mother and was paying for it dearly. She had dared to go to the ball dressed in a gown adorned with competence, shining like a crown jewel. As in the Cinderella story, her wicked stepmother and stepsisters hated her for it.

In the end, Felicia's courage won out. Sales figures in her department came crashing down, and Mary and both buyers were ousted from the company. And like the glass slipper, Felicia's abilities and the need of the department for a top-rate district head fit like a glove.

Even now, the story of Cinderella does not end. In the hundreds of versions of the tale, two endings have been most popular. The first is that Cinderella marries the prince and benevolently offers her stepmother and stepsisters a place by her side in the palace. The other version is that vicious crows pluck out the eyes of the villainous trium-virate.

Similarly, a woman like Felicia may use her negative experience as a jumping-off point to help other women, to make things better than it was for her. But the more troublesome ending is just as apt to occur. Ravaged by the tidal wave of competition at its worst, she may rightly desire to crush any opponent who stands in her way, to pluck her eyes out.

BANDING TOGETHER: THE EMERGING FEMALE COALITION

As difficult as these issues are to deal with, there is hope glimmering on the horizon. Women, both on the job and off it, are collectively pooling their resources for the purpose of making it easier for other women to make their way to the top. Stemming from the realization that a lot of our competitive feelings come from the fact that women today still aren't given a fair shake in the job market, women across the country are responding to the good-old-boys networks by forming good-old-girls networks of their own.

Some groups are forums for women who are having difficulty inte-grating their career life with their home life (and who doesn't?). Other women are jointly bringing lawsuits against employers that use discrim-inatory hiring and promotional techniques. Still others are geared to teach women how to network.

Whatever their surface differences, these groups share one common goal: to help women work with women, not against them, to give women the chance men might not give them. "When I started my business, my first accounts were almost entirely made up of women," one fashion photographer told me. "I had pitched myself to as many men, probably more, but they just didn't seem as willing to give a 'newcomer' a chance. Now that I'm on my feet, I do the same thing—if there's a man and woman who are equally qualified, I'll hire the woman every time. I don't like discriminating against anyone, but as long as men don't let women in, someone's got to."

Does working with all women ever create problems with competition? I wondered.

"Oh, sure. But a lot of those feelings can be sidestepped when you know you're working for the common good."

By showing that women can work cooperatively together, women like these are the mentors so many of us search for. Great progress will be made, I think, when many more of us learn to follow their example.

Chapter 12

OUR INDEPENDENCE, OUR FRIENDS

THE woman of the eighties has more options than ever before, but she is learning that there is a certain tyranny in those options. While women's ultimate goals may be independence and equality, there is still a lot of confusion about how to reach those goals—to say nothing of the struggle of knocking down the social barriers and our own psychological obstacles that stand in the way. And there will be times in every woman's life when she will wonder if she can meet the challenge, or whether the rewards of independence are really worth all the cost. More than at any other time in history, she needs supportive relationships with other women to help move her forward; yet she may find to her dismay that it is those very relationships with women that on some level are holding her back.

Support for independence is not going to come from men, at least in the near future, which is why we need it so desperately from other women. What, then, can we do to give that support? What are the most important ingredients in making our friendships work for growth and independence as opposed to against it? What can women reasonably expect from each other? And what kind of commitment do women need to make to each other?

COMMITMENT STARTS AT HOME

At its most basic level, commitment means that we take our women friends into account in the way we organize our lives. It's all well and good to talk about being supportive of women's struggle for independence, but the fact of the matter is that our sentiments need to be followed up by an active participation in relationships with other women if they are to have any real substance. If women are going to change their position in society, their efforts must begin at home: with their own relationships with one another.

Women who work and have families will have the most difficulty making time and reserving energy for their friends. Even women who truly relish the company of other women may occasionally feel that the ever present demands on their time make friendship feel like yet another obligation. "How can I make time for others?" she may ask, "when I can't find a minute for myself?"

While there are no easy answers, a good place for women like these to start is by asking some questions: Why is it that I've chosen to structure my life in a way that doesn't allow me the pleasure of female relationships? Is there something about intimacy at this point that's frightening? How much effort does it really take to pick up the phone, or fit friends in for an occasional lunch or dinner?

In answering these questions, more often than not a woman will discover that she simply hasn't applied the organizational skills that help her keep her household and career afloat to her friendships; that even within the busiest of schedules, friendship can have a place. One woman who had made a commitment to exercising regularly enlisted a close friend to join the local health spa with her. Instead of seeing each other once every six weeks, they now get together three times a week. "It's been great for my body and great for my soul," she told me. "I feel better because I'm exercising, and seeing someone that often gives you a chance to share all the details of your life. We play racquetball and talk a little between points, then take a sauna for twenty minutes, get dressed, and talk some more. It's totally relaxing and very therapeutic . . . and very intimate."

Another woman told me that she has learned to set aside the hour between 10 and 11 P.M. exclusively for her friends. "The kids are in bed and my husband is usually unwinding in front of the tube, so I don't feel as if I'm taking time away from anyone. And I can give my total attention to the person I'm talking to because I'm not being disturbed—my mind's not straying to the supper dishes or the laundry or the stack of papers on my office desk. Sometimes I wish my women friends and I could have more face-to-face contact," she laments, "but given our busy lives, this pretty much fills the gap."

And what about the woman who still insists she doesn't have time for friends? Almost always, she's experiencing a hidden fear of her own needs both to nurture and to be nurtured. "Women like these haven't reached the point where they are psychologically integrated," Jane Flax told me. "Unconsciously, they feel they have to eclipse half their personalities because if they give in to their nurturing side, their whole facade of being independent will crumble."

Linda was such a woman. A successful entrepreneur in her late forties, she decided early in her career that her energies would be devoted to work and to her husband. Period. Relationships with women, while pleasant, seemed somewhat frivolous—unnecessary to her well-being and certainly not linked to her professional goals.

"For a long time I told myself that women just weren't important. Most of them didn't have the kind of career I had, so I justified shunning them by saying they weren't on my level. I thought of them as trivial, or as having nothing more important to talk about than diapers and babies. As for the ones that worked, I just told myself that they weren't really serious about their jobs . . . which for me meant they weren't willing to dedicate themselves to their careers at the expense of almost everything else."

For fifteen years Linda's life progressed just as she had envisioned it. Her career blossomed and she became what she sees in retrospect as a "female workaholic." She was so involved with her work that she didn't even notice that her marriage was on the rocks. That is, until her husband announced that he was leaving.

The shock hit hard. "I'd always thought of myself as independent, but I really started to come undone. And when I looked around for someone to talk to, for another woman to share my experience, there was . . . no one. It was as if I'd become alienated from the world. Or more accurately, I had alienated myself."

Linda eventually pieced her life back together, and one of the bigger pieces was developing friendships with other women. And in the process she began to realize why she had denied herself the pleasure of female companionship for so long. "A lot of it, I discovered, went back to my mother. She was a real homebody, very subservient. She catered to my father's every whim, and because he was a tyrant, it made me sick. And so on an unconscious level I think I was doing my best to be as different from her as possible—which meant working like a man and cutting off anything that had to do with being like a woman—like feelings of wanting to take care of someone or wanting to be taken care of by someone. That's why I think I was so adamant about never having kids."

It's too late, she says, to make up for the kids, but fortunately she has been able to allow her "feminine" side to express itself in relationship to women friends. "A lot of young women who want careers have asked me for advice about how to make it. They expect me to tell them how to position themselves so they can move up the corporate ladder. They're surprised when I say, 'Find a balance. Don't make work your whole life. Make time for family, for friends.' That's really the best advice I have to offer."

A woman who does not make a concerted effort to make friendship with other women a central part of her life hurts not only herself but the whole struggle for female independence. That's because she's giving off a message that says for women to be independent they must sacrifice a basic part of their personalities—the part that's loving and caring and empathic. How much encouragement do we give other women to become their own people when we portray the price of independence as being so high? It is only by making the commitment to keep our friends an integral part of our lives, by striking a balance between the demands of work, family, and friendship, that we can view independence in positive terms, that we can truly be the best of friends.

A NEED FOR DIALOGUE

Besides setting aside time for women, it is also critical for us to make a commitment to communicate our expectations of one another in explicit terms.

Because women identify so strongly with each other, women's friendships often operate under the "because you're a woman you should instinctively know what I need" credo. We hint, beat around the bush, expecting our friends to read our minds. And while there are times that friends *do* accurately intuit our needs without our having to spell them out, all too often unspoken needs end up as unmet needs or feelings of hurt and anger.

A woman named Eleanor provides a good example of what can happen when needs aren't clearly articulated. Eleanor was the type of woman who enjoyed sharing something good or bad that happened in her life as soon as it happened. Not surprisingly, she found it frustrating when she would call her closest friend only to discover her friend was busy. "I'd always tell her to call me back as soon as she had a minute, but often that meant I wouldn't hear from her for a day or two. By then my enthusiasm or dismay about whatever I had wanted to talk about had died down."

Their relationship went on like that for years, with Eleanor viewing her friend as insensitive to her needs. Finally, during an argument, she spilled out her discontent. Her friend was shocked. "It never occurred to me that was bothering you. When I call my friends and they're busy at that moment, I expect it to be at least a few days before they return my call unless I tell them it's an emergency."

Today Eleanor's friend tries to return Eleanor's calls more promptly. And Eleanor has come to accept that when her friend doesn't call her back right away, it isn't because she isn't interested but because she's too preoccupied with her own schedule. She's come to see that while she's important to her friend, she is not the only thing in her friend's life. "It's amazing how many bad feelings can erupt for no other reason than the fact that things aren't communicated," she told me.

The word "communicate" is the key, because understanding does not just happen—it is a process that involves a continuous dialogue. We were not born mind readers. In addition, the terms of a relationship often change. What one person needs at any particular time may not be what the other person has to give, and that needs to be discussed.

In essence, we need to negotiate the terms of our friendships with the same kind of openness that we negotiate the terms of a marital agreement—even more so, because friendship is an unstructured arrangement unbound by explicit duties and obligations. What do we need from this friendship? What are we willing to give? It's also helpful to state our expectations not just for the short term but for the long term. That's because letting our friends know that we want them to be a part of our lives over the long haul gives the friendship a certain stability. If we have the feeling that our friends are going to be a part of the rest of our lives, we'll be far more committed to resolving the difficulties that come between us.

And what if we fail to communicate our expectations, our hurts, our angers? More often than not, the feelings come out in all sorts of insidious ways: inducing guilt; playing the hurt and helpless victim; complaining; verbal assault (particularly the behind-the-back style); rejection. Psychiatrist Martin Symonds calls this potent, indirect expression of anger "horizontal aggression." Not surprisingly, he finds it most prevalent in people who are dependent in nature, that is, mostly in women.

The dangers inherent in horizontal aggression, says Dr. Symonds, are twofold. First, it reinforces early learned behaviors about dependency, keeping "the individual who employs it feeling powerless and helpless." More important is that it is confusing, frequently leaving the receiver of the message uncertain and the sender frustrated.[1] In short, the outcome of anger gone underground is more anger, hurt, and rejection.

One of the saddest stories I've heard involves a woman who is friends with my only good friend in the community that I recently moved to. This woman—let's call her Molly—and I have been introduced on a couple of occasions, and we've bumped into one another on the street when she walks her baby and I walk my dog. A mother and a sculptor with considerable talent, she seemed like an interesting person—someone I'd like to get to know better.

"I'm thinking of inviting Molly over for lunch," I told my friend as we lay on the lounges in our exercise center enjoying our facials.

My friend cast me a pained glance.

"I don't want this to come off like gossip," my friend told me, "but Molly is a very difficult person to be around. She's very high-strung and talks about her kids incessantly. You never have the feeling that she's listening to you." She then proceeded to tell me that in the past six months Molly had alienated almost all her friends. "She thinks it's because she has a daughter who's hyperactive," my friend told me, "and while it's true that she's tough to be around, the real truth is that Molly is *impossible* to be around. I just don't feel like I can have an adult exchange with her." The sad part, she added, "is that she has a very big heart, and she's feeling very depressed because women who were once her friends are shying away from her."

"Have you ever thought about sitting Molly down and telling her how you're feeling, clueing her in to how the others are feeling?" I asked.

"I'm afraid to hurt her feelings."

"Do you really think you're hurting her any less by not telling her?" I wondered, reminding her how constructive it had been to our relationship when she had told me that my penchant for long telephone conversations was not a shared enthusiasm.

My friend thought for a minute, then nodded her head. "I guess I never thought of it from that perspective."

Which isn't to say that talking solves all problems. Molly might reject my friend's feedback, or might lack the desire or ability to change her ways. Individuals also have different tolerance levels, as well as different expectations of friendship. That's why finding a reasonable friendship match is as important as compatibility in marriage. Some women, for example, prefer a myriad of friends, sharing one or two common interests with each. Others want a few close friends with whom they can relate on many levels. Some women feel most comfortable when they see or talk to their friends a few times a week. Others feel close to their friends with less frequent contact. "Between friends there's really no such thing as the right or wrong arrangement," said Dr. Flax. "There are just jointly agreed upon terms. What works for one woman may not work for another. That's why bringing things out into the open is so important."

About her own expectations, however, she has this to say: "If I have a friend and something major happens in my life, I expect my friend, withstanding hospitalization or imminent bankruptcy, to respond. I expect to know that she is emotionally accessible to me within any twenty-four hour period. That's what I need and that's what I expect. And that's what I am willing to do in return. But," she adds, "every woman has to negotiate the parameters of her friendships individually —to assess what she wants and go about getting it."

THE FANTASY OF THE PERFECT MOTHER

And what if we still find that the women in our life are not meeting our needs? One possibility is that we're choosing the wrong friends. But a far more likely scenario for the woman who experiences her needs as being continuously thwarted in her friendships is that she is unconsciously expecting the women in her life to make up for what she never got from her mother—that she is searching for the perfect mother in her friends.

Who wants a perfect mother? Who doesn't? The problem is not the desire, but allowing that desire to rule our lives. That's because the search for perfection stands in the way of healthy relationships between women. For one thing, if you're looking for a fantasy, you're bound to end up feeling disappointed. As Nancy Friday wrote, "Sometimes we are so hurt by mother's ambivalences that we reject the entire package, throwing out the good, positive aspects mother presented us, along with the painful ones."[2] So it is when the search for perfection is carried on through our friends. We keep looking, flitting from woman to woman, in pursuit of the one who will fill all our needs, who will fit the mode of our idealizations. Disappointed, we give up what might otherwise be constructive, joyful relationships, ultimately drawing the deadly conclusion that women cannot be trusted.

When I first met Jo Ann Brennan, for example, she said she had had it with women friends. They simply weren't dependable. She was sick and tired of giving more than she was getting and of not getting what she needed. If I wanted to hear about the virtues of women's friendships, she said, I had come to the wrong place.

Propelled by disillusionment, she had done a psychological spring cleaning, throwing away old friendships the way some people get rid of old clothing. For one reason or another, out they went, one by one—the disappointments, the hurts, the friends in whom she had invested many years of her life.

When I interviewed her two years later, however, her attitude had undergone an about-face. Triggered by the death of her mother, Jo Ann had entered therapy. It was there that her therapist helped her make the connection between Jo Ann's inability to find a true friend and her desire for the kind of all-giving, all-loving relationship she felt she never had with her mother. Setting herself up as the victim in her friendships, she was able to convince herself that she had no responsibility for the problems she was having with her friends. The idea that her expectations might have been unreasonable never crossed her mind—that is, until her therapist asked her to begin making checklists, writing down all the times her friends had come through for her on one side and all the times they had failed her on the other. "The results were a revelation," she confessed. "By far, the good things outweighed the disappointments. And that's when I began to realize that perhaps I was the cause of the problem, that I was simply looking for too much."

The idealization of friendship can lead to other problems, too. Women who unconsciously look for the perfect mother in their friends are women who are often looking for a feeling of fusion—of being totally enmeshed in someone else's life. They confuse the idea of nurturance with symbiosis, and while symbiosis might feel good, it does very little to foster growth. In fact, psychologists are increasingly beginning to feel that what a baby needs to develop a healthy sense of individuality is not fusion with the mother, but a "holding environment"—that is, a context in which she can feel dependent and cared for while still being viewed as a separate person. The result is that women who look for intensely meshed relationships with other women, even if they occasionally find them, are women who cannot possibly become independent, because in symbiotic relationships there is no acknowledgment of the other person's separateness.

Another consequence of looking for the perfect mother via our friends is that we endow our friend with an enormous amount of destructive psychological power. The relationship comes to exist on a fantasy plane in which our friend becomes the symbolic mother and we the child, leaving us open to psychological devastation if our needs aren't met. Reacting from the standpoint of the child, the woman who turns to her friends as the mother she never had may also be so fearful of rejection (what child isn't terrified of rejection from Mother?) that she will be unable to be herself. Instead, she will behave in a way to earn her friend's approval, which is not exactly a step toward self-development.

On the other side of the fence, the woman who's been put in the position of "perfect mother" may feel that she cannot relate honestly to her friend for fear of crushing her. She will also begin seeing her friend's needs as so insatiable and childlike that she will eventually abandon her friend completely . . . the exact thing her friend fears most.

For all these reasons it's critical that women begin identifying and dealing with these unconscious scripts and relinquishing idealized notions of friendship. But how? The first step, obviously, is to acknowledge the problem, to come to realize that you may be looking for the impossible dream. We need to recognize that as adults, there is no way to make up for what we missed as babies, that not getting what we perceived we needed from our mothers may always be a psychological scar. It's at the point that we can mourn the loss of what we never got and of our childish selves that we can begin the process of resolution.

Working to develop a sense of our own separateness, our own competency, is also a requisite to working through our desire for perfection. "In order for women to have reasonably healthy relationships, they must be reasonably healthy themselves," Angela Fox told me. "And sometimes that takes therapy, because you can't expect friends to do for you what a therapist can. What usually happens is that many patients start out with these strong needs to be totally merged with the therapist. They equate being loved with the feeling of fusion. But over time, as they gain confidence in their own strengths, they begin to realize that they are not the therapist, they are not their mothers—they are themselves."

It's that sense of separateness, she told me, that gets the developmental ball rolling. "When you're a separate individual, when you've developed a feeling of security in yourself, you begin to realize that you're in control of your own life." Which means that we can take care of many needs on our own, and that our psychological well-being is not totally contingent on the reactions of others.

In a nutshell, we will have to come to grips with what friends, even the best of friends, can and cannot do. Friends can't compensate for the feeling of fusion or give us the infantile security we may not have gotten when we were young. Friends can't be the totally available mother we may have desperately wanted. But friends *can* give us nourishment and intimacy. They can help us grow. And while not offering the same thing as therapy, they can be therapeutic.

Most of all, friendships between women can help reverse the message that being loved is at the expense of being independent.

LOVE AND INDEPENDENCE REVISITED

Perhaps the most important commitment women need to make to one another is to encourage one another to grow and succeed, to provide the assurance that we can be independent without rejection.

For women to trust one another, we need to believe that our friends are looking out for our interests. We need them to rejoice in our achievements, not to be resentful of them. We need to feel that we can grow without risking the loss of their love.

Getting past the feeling of jealousy or envy which may be triggered when a friend reaches a plateau we as yet have not (whether it be breaking out of an unhappy marriage, or reaching a higher level of professional success) requires more than covering up our feelings with psychic Band-Aids. To the contrary, women need to develop a new consciousness of their unresolved feelings toward women. "Getting in touch with one's negative feelings can be very useful in the sense that they clue you that it's time to become aware of the way you're acting or reacting to your friends," Angela Fox told me. "It does no good to be ashamed or to try and force those feelings underground because chances are they'll seep out in destructive ways." In other words, by acknowledging our difficulties with other women's growth and success, we take the first step in overcoming them.

Of course, as the popular saying about the therapeutic process goes, "insight is not enough." There were times during the course of writing this book, for instance, when I noticed that I shuttled between being supportive and being rejecting of certain friends whose success seemed more impressive than my own. And not surprisingly, there were periods of distance between us, usually triggered by my own less than accepting attitude of them. How did I work through those feelings? First, by recognizing and owning up to them. Second, by doing my best to be supportive in spite of those feelings; by realizing that I was creating a vicious circle in which my support was based on their failure to grow, and which would ultimately lead to the demise of the friendship. Finally, it was helpful to think of myself as being involved in something bigger than myself—the struggle for women's equality. And I knew that my feelings of envy did not speak well for that struggle.

The results were remarkable. With one friend of whom I had been particularly critical, I was able to turn a failing relationship into one that is supportive and constructive. She noticed my new attitude almost immediately and responded with increasing support of her own. She admitted that she had begun to have her doubts about our friendship because I reminded her of her critical mother, and that she was glad I had changed. Her assumption, however, was that my approach had altered because the circumstances of my own life had noticeably improved. Actually, they hadn't. What had changed was that I no longer saw her achievements as a threat to our relationship, but as a help to reaching my own potential. I also knew that by supporting her now I would be in a much better position to get her support in the future.

PARADOXICAL AS IT MIGHT at first appear, part of helping women grow is allowing for our friends' occasional bouts of dependence. Unless a woman is constantly a clinging vine, allowing her to "regress" from time to time helps her take a critical step toward independence. That's because separation and growth are frightening at any age. And only by having a firm hand and a loving heart behind us do we get the security we need to feel it's safe to take the risks so necessary for growth. We need to know that it's okay to need to be taken care of sometimes, and that our friends will not reject us for it.

"Independence develops from prior dependence and is probably related to self-confidence," writes psychologist Judith Bardwick. ". . . healthy interdependent interpersonal relationships seem to call upon the ability to trust the other person and upon the confidence that allows one to permit the other person to come close, to be dependent, to love . . ."[3]

The experience of Judith Stone provides a good example. A single woman in her thirties, she had gone through a crisis when she lost both her boyfriend and her job during the same four-week period. "I fell apart. I sank into a terrible depression. All I wanted was for someone to take care of me." Her closest friend had trouble providing that caretaking. "About two days of my wailing was all that she could take. Then she said it was time I get on my feet and pull myself together."

The problem was, Judith wasn't ready to care for herself. For the next six months she hopped from man to man looking for someone to hold her up. But when the last man in her life made his exit, she fell apart again. Fortunately, Judith had recently become close to a woman at her office who didn't seem to object to Judith's falling apart at the seams. "She acted like a temporary mother. She didn't criticize me for the way I was feeling. She allowed the child in me to come out full force." Miraculously, after a few weeks, that "child" seemed to take the backseat. "It was as if by giving me permission to fall apart and not rejecting me, I found my own strength. I guess that I got bored with being dependent after a while."

Most children, if left to their own devices, and if given the cushion of security to fall back on, do.

And what if a woman runs away from a friend in need? Almost always, she's struggling with some unresolved feelings about her own dependence. Women who have a sense of their individuality, their own separateness, aren't frightened off when their friends have a psychological downslide. They don't run away because they're sure of their own boundaries. The woman who can't be supportive under these circumstances flees because her friend's dependency triggers the fear of her own. She is, in essence, a woman who is running away from herself.

In the end, women who let their friends down when they need them most do them and women in general a grave disservice. To dissuade other women from chronic dependency is one thing. To not allow for the humanness of their fears only magnifies the fear, making it that much more difficult to overcome.

REAPING THE REWARDS

Ultimately, then, the commitment to women's friendships means establishing relationships which are supportive of our total personhood, relationships in which we can be loved and independent. It is a commitment to bolstering each other within a context of being accessible to one another. It is, at its taproot, a commitment to our own self-development, to reaching what psychiatrist Erik Erikson calls a stage of "integrity"—a point at which we take responsibility for our own lives and our own actions.[4]

And once we reach this stage, then what? Thinking about the women I have interviewed who have, there was no doubt that they were able to slough off the few disappointments of their friendships and respond to the overwhelmingly positive aspects. One woman expressed the renewed vigor in her friendships after setting realistic expectations of them: "For a long time I had taken the women in my life for granted—too much so. My feeling about it was that whatever I would do, no matter how I'd treat them, they'd forgive me. It took me a long time to accept that friends have limits, that they don't love you in the way you expect your mother to love you—unconditionally—that you will not be granted forgiveness no matter what slights you dish out, even unintentionally. Now I take it for granted that my friends will be there most of the time, but not always. I don't expect them to be a better friend to me than I am to them. And what's happened is that I've become more responsible to my friends, experience them more as an integral part of my life that I could not live without."

Another woman expressed a similar sentiment. For ten years she had been a homemaker, and while loving the role, she often questioned her ability to make it on her own in the world. Finally, after much procrastination, she took a job as a clerk-typist for a small manufacturing firm. The organizational skills she had mastered at home were quickly recognized and within six months she was promoted to administrative assistant. Today, five years later, she is head of quality control.

Her feelings about women followed along a similar upward curve. "When I was at home, I valued my relationships with women, but on some level I saw women as less interesting than men. I guess that's because there was a part of me that viewed what I was doing as less noteworthy than what my husband did. As soon as I went to work, though, my attitude changed. Some of my friends were working, others weren't, but somehow, maybe because I felt more confident in myself, I felt better about other women, too. It doesn't seem to matter so much what you do," she added, "as much as how you *feel* about what you're doing."

A woman is committed to her own growth and the growth of other women finds that she is able to accept her friend's "difference." She is not threatened when a friend chooses a different route, and is able to give wholehearted support for her friend's decisions. And usually, she discovers, that enthusiasm is reciprocated.

A Los Angeles woman who had developed a lucrative career as an attorney decided after much thought to take some time off to raise a family. Her closest friend, a lawyer who was also thinking about having a baby, could not conceive of leaving her job to stay at home full-time. Their different viewpoints could have created friction in their relationship if both women had not had such a strong sense of their own identity. "If I hadn't been clear in my own mind about staying at home, I think I might have felt a little intimidated by my friend who firmly believed she could be a fine mother and hold down her job. But I was so sure about what I was doing that I could hold my ground while still encouraging my friend to do what was best for her." Still, she had to admit there were times when she wondered if her friend frowned on her decision to temporarily give up her financial self-sufficiency. She learned that she was dead wrong. "About a month before I was due to have the baby, my friend insisted we go shopping for the day. Anyway, when we got back to my house, there were all my friends, and a beautiful spread of food. Having her give me a surprise shower like that made me feel terrific. But the thing that struck me most was this big poster she had made that said, 'To the woman who is a #1 friend and who will be a #1 mother.' I was so touched, felt so accepted that I could do what I wanted to do and still have her approval, that I cried."

The woman who has a clear sense of self is a woman who also has friendship flexibility. She is able to be open to varying kinds of relationships with other women without feeling cheated. Her openness arises from her ability to tolerate getting less than everything from a relationship. At the same time, she does not experience acquaintanceship as a second-rate form of friendship, because she does not look to all women as mother surrogates who are supposed to provide for all her needs. "It's the sum total of all my relationships with women that gives me what I need," one woman explained. "There are some women, those at work, for instance, from whom I get advice about my career. There are others that I go to museums or concerts with. There are the women in my child's play group that I naturally discuss children with. And of course, there are my two closest friends that I confide my innermost thoughts and feelings to." What this adds up to, she said, is a "rich and rewarding experience with women in which all of my friendship needs are taken care of."

One of the biggest pluses of all is a feeling of ease, security, and just plain fun that comes when you know that you are loved in the fullest sense of the word. I have never been one for multitudes of friends, but my relationship with my closest friend has progressed in leaps and bounds since I met her eight years ago. Much of that has come from having to deal with many of the tough issues discussed in this book—competition, disappointed expectations, the changing circumstances of our lives— issues which, over time, we've learned to confront honestly and directly. A lot of it has come from our shared history of having gone through important portions of our lives together. And naturally, there is the connection that we share of being women with women's problems in a man's world. But most of all, what I think has solidified our friendship is making time for sheer fun and nonsense. Because we feel accepted, we can let our guard down and do things that seem objectively ridiculous. We can tease each other about one another's shortcomings, knowing full well there is some truth to our chidings, but without feeling slighted by them. We have made time to go out to dinner or to a show or for a walk on the beach, and become antsy when the stretch of time between those outings is too long. We can find intimacy with each other and get pleasure from each other, perhaps because we have learned to laugh at ourselves.

Which isn't to say that all relationships between women will have a positive outcome. Once we've reached a plateau of integration, a closer inspection of some friendships may reveal some unpleasant truths. One woman, for example, was forced to reevaluate a relationship of twelve years when she learned that her "friend" had been bad-mouthing her. "She would tell me what a wonderful mother and a great cook I was—how I should think of going into the catering business. Meanwhile, I'd hear from a mutual friend that she was saying that I neglected my son and didn't have the vaguest idea about how to make a decent meal. It was a real slap in the face—I couldn't believe she was saying those things about me."

Still, it took this woman two years to finally end the relationship. "I was trying to hold on to something that had once been there. I had loved her so much, she had been so important to me, it was very difficult to let go."

Keeping women in our lives who continually hurt us, Angela Fox told me, is a detrimental, debilitating thing to do. "When a woman keeps clinging to a friendship that's very negative, she's acting out a neurotic theme. And it's almost always the woman who had less than adequate mothering who will do this. It's her way of replaying her negative relationship with her mother. It's a growth-stunting thing to do."

Why, then, is it so tough to give up friends like these? Angela Fox explains the dilemma in terms of the symbolic weight of some friendships. "If a woman meets another woman during an important period of her life and her friend gives her the kind of love and support she needs, it will be extremely difficult to end that relationship, no matter what happens to it later on. It's a lot like the woman who remembers the early relationship with her mother as positive but then finds her mother rejecting her when she begins making her own life. As lousy as that mother seems at the moment, there's still this earlier positive connection. To break off the relationship means to let go of that wonderful mothering and the fantasy that it lasts forever."

As hard as it might be to let go, women who've developed a healthy measure of autonomy do it, not out of callousness but out of self-preservation. And by not accepting relationships that are debilitating, they further their own growth and indirectly foster the growth of us all.

Similarly, some women may find they have to keep themselves physically or emotionally at bay from their mothers. The woman who's managed to break the fetters of dependency with her own mother may stand aside and, taking a good look, discover that her mother is not only far from perfect but a destructive force in her life—ever critical, ever thwarting her independence. There is no way to describe accurately the agonizing pain of the women who are forced to break off contact with their mothers: The process can take years and often requires therapeutic intervention. Even women who have been relatively successful told me that it's not something you ever completely resolve. Nor does one ever totally recover from the fact that one's mother was unloving. As one woman put it, "I'll never stop wishing on some level that things between me and my mother were different—never. And even with therapy I didn't give up the relationship with my mother without a tremendous struggle. I guess it boiled down to one thing: It was either her sanity or mine. What therapy did for me was to allow me to say that my psychological health was more important without punishing myself for having that feeling."

Luckily, once we stop looking for perfection and develop a secure sense of ourselves, chances are we'll discover that our mother, like most women, while not perfect, is "good enough." And we will be able to stop blaming her for all the injustices in the world, to understand that she, too, is a woman restricted, a woman in a man's world, a woman bound by a relationship to her own mother. True, my own mother is not the best person to turn to when I need someone to support my ambition. It is not that she wants to stand in the way, but that she sees my strivings as a slap in the face to the way she has lived her life. She cannot understand how it feels to need more than a husband and children. What my mother *can* do, however, is give me a sense of balance when I come precariously close to becoming a workaholic. And she will still take care of me at those moments when I'm feeling depressed, or just need to be a child, in the way that only a mother can. It no longer seems to matter so much if she can't be everything I need. The fact is, she's more than enough.

Besides, when I think about it, having a mother who is less than perfect has its advantages. After all, if she had been the perfect, all-encompassing person of my fantasies, what incentive would I ever have had to become independent from her?

NOTES

Chapter 1:   COMFORT AND CONFLICT

1. Jane Flax, "The Conflict Between Nurturance and Autonomy in Mother-Daughter Relationships and Within Feminism," *Feminist Studies* 4, no. 2 (June 1978): 171–91.
2. D. F. Hultsch and J. Plemons, "Life Events and Life-span Development," in *Life-span Development and Behavior,* ed. Paul Baltes and O. G. Brim, Jr., vol. 2 (New York: Academic Press, 1979).

Chapter 2:   EARLY DRAMAS

1. Zick Rubin, *Children's Friendships* (Cambridge, Mass.: Harvard University Press, 1980), p. 108.
2. Robert R. Bell, *Worlds of Friendship* (Beverly Hills, Calif.: Sage Publications, 1981), p. 41.
3. Janet Lever, "Sex Differences in the Games Children Play," *Social Problems* 23 (1976): 478–87.
4. Rubin, loc. cit.
5. Bell, op. cit., p. 43.
6. Detroit *Free Press,* March 3, 1966.

7. Judith M. Bardwick, *Psychology of Women* (New York: Harper & Row Publishers, 1971), pp. 126–27.

8. Judith M. Bardwick, *In Transition* (New York: Holt, Rinehart and Winston, 1979), p. 138.

9. Bell, loc. cit.

10. For a full discussion of preoedipal gender differences see Nancy Chodorow, *The Reproduction of Mothering: Psychoanalysis and the Sociology of Gender* (Berkeley and Los Angeles: University of California Press, 1978), pp. 92–110.

11. Ibid.

12. Helene Deutsch, *The Psychology of Women,* vol. 1 (New York: Grune & Stratton, 1944), pp. 13–14.

13. Chodorow, op. cit., p. 167.

14. Bardwick, *In Transition,* p. 137.

15. Lever, loc. cit.

16. Georgia Sassen, "Success Anxiety in Women: A Constructivist Interpretation of its Sources and Its Significance," *Harvard Educational Review* 50 (1980): 15.

17. Barbara E. Moely, Kurt Skarin, and Sandra Weil, "Sex Differences in Competition-Cooperation Behavior of Children at Two Levels," *Sex Roles* 5, no. 3 (1979): 329–42.

18. Martin Symonds, "Psychodynamics of Aggression in Women," *American Journal of Psychoanalysis* 36 (1976): 195–203.

Chapter 3: BEST OF FRIENDS

1. Elizabeth Douvan and J. Adelson, *The Adolescent Experience* (New York: John Wiley & Sons, 1966), pp. 203–14. In their discussion of dating, the authors claim that alleviating anxiety about sex is one of the primary functions of girls' adolescent friendships.

2. Chodorow, *Reproduction of Mothering,* p. 136–37.

3. Marjorie and Harold Richey, "The Significance of Best Friend Relationships in Adolescence," *Psychology in the Schools* 17, no. 4 (October 1980): 536–40.

4. Joseph H. Pleck, "Man to Man: Is Brotherhood Possible?" in *Old Family/New Family: Interpersonal Relationships,* ed. Nona Glazer-Malbin (New York: D. Van Nostrand Co., 1975), p. 236. A similar tendency can be noted for boys who assert their independence by selecting girlfriends their parents will disapprove of.

5. Deutsch, *Psychology of Women,* p. 116.

6. Igor S. Kon and Vladimir A. Losenkov, "Friendship in Adoles-

cence: Values and Behavior," *Journal of Marriage and the Family,* February 1975, pp. 150–51.

7. Marie Richmond-Abbott, *The American Woman* (New York: Holt, Rinehart & Winston, 1979), pp. 150–51. See also Richey, loc. cit., and Douvan and Adelson, the chapter "Friendship."

8. Aaron Hass, *Teenage Sexuality* (New York: Macmillan Publishing Co., 1978), p. 139. This statistic is somewhat biased. Many of these contacts, the respondents report, occurred in preadolescence. It is also possible that girls who have homosexual contacts in adolescence may be too embarrassed to report them.

9. Douvan and Adelson, op. cit., pp. 193, 216.

10. Chodorow, op. cit. For a complete psychoanalytic interpretation of the oedipal crisis, see pp. 111–40.

11. "Girl Love Test Gets Barbs," Sacramento *Bee,* May 15, 1973.

12. Douvan and Adelson, op. cit., p. 214.

13. Elizabeth Douvan, "New Sources of Conflict in Females at Adolescence," in *Feminine Personality and Conflict,* J. M. Bardwick, et al. (Belmont, Calif.: Brooks/Cole Publishing Co., 1970), p. 38.

14. Bell, *Worlds of Friendship,* p. 49.

15. Douvan and Adelson, op. cit., p. 201.

16. Douvan and Adelson, loc. cit.

17. Bardwick, *Psychology of Women,* pp. 177–78.

18. Douvan and Adelson, loc. cit.

19. Bardwick, op. cit., p. 149.

20. Richmond-Abbott, loc. cit., and Hass, op. cit., p. 10.

21. Hass, loc. cit.

Chapter 4: SINGLES: COMPANIONS, OR COMPANIONS IN LONELINESS?

1. Anne Hodge, "Loneliness: The Relation of Attribution Theory and Female Loneliness in the Female World," 1978, Draft of then unpublished paper.

2. J. L. Barkas, "Friendship Patterns Among Young Urban Single Women," (Ph.D. diss., City University of New York, 1983).

3. Judith Bardwick, for example, believes that women are inherently mistrustful of each other. See *In Transition,* chap. 8.

4. The 1980 Virginia Slims American Women's Opinion Poll. The Roper Organization, New York, 1980.

5. Erik H. Erikson, *Identity and the Life Cycle* (New York: W. W. Norton & Co., 1980), pp. 100–4.

6. J. L. Barkas, *Singles In America* (New York: Atheneum Publishers, 1980), p. 147.

7. Barkas, op. cit., p. 17.

8. Joel Block, *Friendship: How To Give It, How To Get It* (New York: Collier Books, 1980), p. 37.

9. Peter J. Stein, "Understanding Single Adulthood," in *Single Life: Unmarried Adults in Social Context,* ed. Peter J. Stein (New York: St. Martin's Press, 1981), p. 14.

10. Laura Bergquist, "How Come a Nice Girl Like You Isn't Married," in *Toward a Sociology of Women,* ed. Constantine Safilios-Rothschild (Lexington, Mass.: Xerox College Publishing, 1972), p. 107.

11. Barkas, *Friendship Patterns.*

12. Helen Hacker, "Blabbermouths and Clams: Sex Differences in Self-disclosure in Same-Sex and Cross-Sex Friendship Dyads," *Psychology of Women Quarterly* 5, no. 3 (Spring 1981), pp. 385–401. According to this study, 56 percent of married women were characterized as high self-disclosers to their female friends compared to only 29 percent of single women.

13. Barkas, *Friendship Patterns.*

14. Ibid.

15. For a complete discussion of this prototype see Douvan and Adelson, *The Adolescent Experience,* pp. 245–47.

16. Barkas, *Singles In America,* pp. 70–71.

17. A summary of studies leading to this conclusion can be found in Bardwick, *Psychology of Women,* pp. 175–76.

18. P. S. Rosenkrantz et al., "Sex-Role Stereotypes and Self-concepts in College Students," *Journal of Consulting and Clinical Psychology* 32 (1968): 287–95. Also see Bardwick, *Psychology of Women,* p. 19.

19. Bardwick, *Psychology of Women,* p. 153.

20. Barkas, *Singles In America,* pp. 138–39.

21. Lois W. Hoffman, "Effects of Maternal Employment on the Child," *Child Development* 32: 187–97.

22. For a discussion of transitional singles see Barkas, *Singles In America,* p. 15.

23. L. Janson et al., "Characteristics of Significant Dating Relationships: Male vs. Female Initiators," *Journal of Psychology* 109, no. 2 (November 1981): 185–90.

24. Jacqueline Simenauer and David Carroll, *Singles: The New Americans* (New York: Signet Books, 1983), p. 367.

25. Janet Harris, *The Priming of Ms. America* (New York: G. P. Putnam's Sons, 1975), pp. 146–47.

26. Linda Wolfe, "Friendship in the City," *New York Magazine,* July 18, 1983, p. 27.

27. Quoted in Christine Doudra with Fern McBride, "Where Are the Men for the Women at the Top?" in *Single Life: Unmarried Adults in Social Context,* p. 23.

28. Barkas, *Friendship Patterns,* p. 17.

29. Philip Blumstein and Pepper Schwartz, "Bisexuality: some psychological issues," *Journal of Social Issues,* 33(2), 1977, pp. 30–45.

30. Philip Blumstein and Pepper Schwartz, *American Couples* (New York: William Morrow & Co., 1983), pp. 53–54.

31. Madonna Kohlbenschlag, *Kiss Sleeping Beauty Goodbye* (New York: Bantam Books, 1979), p. 58.

32. Gerald Gurin, Joseph Veroff, and Sheila Feld, *Americans View Their Mental Health* (New York: Basic Books, 1960), pp. 42, 72, 110, 190, 234–35. Many other studies confirm these findings.

33. Sophie Lowenstein, "A Study of Satisfactions and Stresses of Single Women in Midlife," *Sex Roles* 7, no. 11 (November 1981): 1127–41.

Chapter 5: *MARITAL BLISS OR THE LONELY CROWD?*

1. Angus Campbell, "The American Way of Mating: Marriage Sí, Children Only Maybe," *Psychology Today,* May 1975, pp. 37–43. According to Dr. Campbell, women still view marriage as their greatest achievement, with newly married wives being the most euphoric. Husbands are happy, too, but at the same time they recognize that they have undertaken big responsibilities.

2. For an excellent summary of the changes in women's friendships precipitated by early marriage, see Bell, *Worlds of Friendship,* chaps. 6 and 7. Only when friendships are based on common interests do relationships remain relatively unaffected by a woman's change in marital status. (Barkas, *Friendship Patterns.*)

3. Hacker, "Blabbermouths and Clams."

4. Uta West, "Friends and Females," *Viva* 2 (1975): 37–38, 106–8.

5. Robert Bell, "Friendships of Women and of Men," *Psychology of Women's Quarterly* 5, no. 3 (Spring 1981).

6. Jessie Bernard, *The Female World* (New York: Free Press, 1981), p. 98.

7. Ibid., chap. 5.

8. Bell, *Worlds of Friendship,* p. 127.

9. Johanna Dobkin Gladieux, "Pregnancy—The Transition to Parenthood: Satisfaction with the Pregnancy Experience as a Function of

Sex Role Conceptions, Marital Relationship, and Social Network," in *The First Child and Family Formation,* ed. Warren B. Miller and Lucile F. Newman (Chapel Hill: University of North Carolina, Carolina Publication Center, 1978), p. 292.

10. Blumstein and Schwartz, *American Couples,* p. 273.

11. Ibid., pp. 275–77.

12. Quoted in Gail Sheehy, *Pathfinders* (New York: Bantam Books, 1982), p. 212.

13. Zena Blau, *Old Age in a Changing Society* (New York: Franklin Watts, 1973), p. 73. Also see Robert Bell's discussion of "Men and Friendship" in *Worlds of Friendship.*

14. Bell, "Friendships of Women and Men," op. cit. According to the author, "conventional" women were much more reticent about revealing problems in their marriages than were less conventional women.

15. Block, *Friendship,* pp. 112, 114.

16. Bell, *Worlds of Friendship,* p. 125.

17. Robert Bell, "Female and Male Friendship Patterns." Paper presented at Sociological Association of Australia and New Zealand, University of Waikato, Hamilton, New Zealand, 1975.

18. These findings are summarized in Block, op. cit., pp. 117–22.

19. Letty Cottin Pogrebin, "Hers," New York *Times,* October 6, 1983, sec. C.

20. Michele Barcus Warren, "The Work Role and Problem Coping: Sex Differentials in the Use of Helping Systems in Urban Communities." Paper presented at American Sociological Association, San Francisco, 1975.

21. R. O. Blood, Jr., and D. M. Wolfe, *Husbands and Wives: The Dynamics of Married Living* (New York: Free Press, 1960).

22. Lillian Rubin, *Worlds of Pain: Life in the Working-class Family* (New York: Basic Books, 1976), p. 117. While this finding pertains to working-class families only, my interviews indicate that a similar pattern occurs in many marriages.

23. Blau, op. cit., p. 73.

24. Block, op. cit., pp. 122–23. Also see Herb Goldberg, *The New Male-Female Relationship* (New York: William Morrow & Co., 1983).

25. In Jessie Bernard's article, "Homosociality and Female Depression," *Journal of Social Issues* 32, no. 4 (1971), pp. 213–38, she says that the "relational deficit that occurs when married women have no close women friends is a major source of depression in the fe-

male population, particularly among women at home with young children."

26. Chodorow, *Reproduction of Mothering,* p. 199.

27. Judith Bardwick, "The Dynamics of Successful People," *New Research on Women, and Sex Roles at the University of Michigan,* ed. Dorothy E. McGuigan (Ann Arbor: University of Michigan, Center for Continuing Education of Women, 1976).

28. Nancy Cott, *The Bonds of Womanhood* (New Haven, Conn.: Yale University Press, 1977), p. 193. The author points out that in the last century, female friendships were what made many marriages bearable.

29. An extensive discussion of difficulties faced in two-career families can be found in Caroline Bird, *The Two-Paycheck Marriage* (New York: Pocket Books, 1979).

30. This trend is discussed in Chodorow, op. cit., p. 197.

31. Block, op. cit., p. 123.

32. Jayne I. Gackenbach and Stephen M. Auerback, "Empirical Evidence for the Phenomenon of the Well-meaning Liberal Male," *Journal of Clinical Psychology* 31, no. 4 (October 1975): 632–35.

33. In Bird, op. cit., p. 237.

34. *Wall Street Journal,* September 29, 1980.

35. Annie Gottlieb, "What Men Need From Women," *Readers Digest,* January 1984, pp. 145–48.

36. Blumstein and Schwartz, op. cit., p. 162.

37. Quoted in Gottlieb, loc. cit.

38. Block, op. cit., pp. 109–12.

39. Pogrebin, loc. cit.

40. Blumstein and Schwartz, op. cit., p. 162. Say the authors: "He may not wish to do better than his wife, but he certainly does not want to do less well. Even most modern-day egalitarian husbands do not want to play a secondary role to their wives, either in their own eyes, their wives' eyes, or the eyes of the world. . . . Her husband encourages her to achieve great things, but he is likely to become competitive if she begins to surpass what he has done."

41. Block, op. cit., pp. 112–13.

42. Barbara L. Forisha, "Dual-Career Families: Intimacy or Productivity?" in *Outsiders on the Inside,* eds. Barbara L. Forisha and Barbara H. Goldman (Englewood Cliffs, N.J.: Prentice-Hall, 1981), p. 260.

Chapter 6: FULL-TIME MOTHERS, FULL-TIME FRIENDS:
A LIFESTYLE AT RISK

1. Helena Znaniecki Lopata, *Occupation Housewife* (New York: Oxford University Press, 1977), pp. 331–34.
2. Erik H. Erikson, *Identity: Youth and Crisis* (New York: W. W. Norton & Co., 1968), p. 266.
3. Ravenna Helsen, "The Changing Image of the Career Woman," *Journal of Social Issues* 28 (1972): 39.
4. Z. Lurie, "Women College Graduates." Presidential address, New England Psychological Society, 1972.
5. Cited in Bernard, *The Female World,* p. 244.
6. Commission on Population Growth and the American Future, *Population and the American Future* (New York: Signet Books, 1972), pp. 153–54.
7. Jessie Bernard, *The Future of Motherhood* (New York: Penguin Books, 1975), p. 205.
8. Mirra Komarovsky, *Blue-collar Marriage* (New York: Vintage Books, 1967), p. 61.
9. Bernard, op. cit., p. 201.
10. Joseph Katz, "Home Life of Women in Continuing Education," in *Some Action of Her Own: The Adult Woman and Higher Education* ed. Helen Astin, (Lexington, Mass.: Lexington Books, 1976), pp. 89–106.
11. Komarovsky, op. cit., p. 70.
12. Jean Curtis, *Working Mothers* (Garden City, N.Y.: Doubleday and Co., 1976), p. 42.
13. Joseph Veroff and Sheila Feld, *Marriage and Work in America* (New York: Van Nostrand Reinhold Co., 1970), p. 173. Also see Anne Russell and Patricia Fitzgibbons, "An Honest Appraisal of Children Who Lead a Life Free of Hang-ups *Because* Mommy Works Outside the Home," *New Woman,* June 1983, pp. 92–95.
14. Komarovsky, op. cit., p. 62.
15. Mirra Komarovsky, *Women in the Modern World: Their Education and Their Dilemmas* (Boston: Little, Brown & Company, 1953), chaps. 4 and 5. While this is an early study, my findings confirm that these attitudes have changed very little.
16. Curtis, op. cit., p. 37. The author found that women's disapproval of working mothers hurts more than male disapproval.
17. Bernard, op. cit., p. 200.
18. Curtis, op. cit., pp. 34–35.
19. New York *Times,* Friday, May 25, 1984, sec. A.

20. Louis Harris and others, The 1972 Virginia Slims American Women's Opinion Poll.
21. New York Times poll reported in the New York *Times,* December 4, 1983, section 1. It is important to note that while this is true of women as a whole, women in blue-collar professions were less likely to want to work—only 43 percent of these women said they'd rather be working than at home.
22. Bernard, op. cit., p. 204.
23. Simone de Beauvoir, *The Second Sex* (New York: Vintage Books, 1974), p. 777.
24. Judith Lynn Abelow Birnbaum, "Life Patterns, Personality Style and Self-esteem in Gifted Family-oriented and Career-committed Women" (doctoral diss., University of Michigan, 1971), pp. 244–45.
25. For an excellent discussion of money and power in the family, see Hilary M. Lips, *Women, Men and the Psychology of Power* (Englewood Cliffs, N.J.: Prentice-Hall, 1981), chap. 7.
26. Louise Bernikow, *Among Women* (New York: Harper Colophon Books, 1980), p. 207.
27. Bernard, op. cit., p. 192.
28. Judith Tolmack, "Crumbling Families and the Generation Factor," *Potomac Magazine,* June 25, 1972, p. 8.
29. Department of State, *Manpower Report of the President 1973,* (Washington, D.C.: GPO, 1973), p. 38.
30. Birnbaum, op. cit., p. 38.
31. Elizabeth Moen, "Women in Energy Boom Towns," *Psychology of Women Quarterly* 6, no. 1 (Fall 1981): 99–112.
32. Birnbaum, loc. cit.
33. Ibid., p. 246.

Chapter 7: THE NEW WOMAN, THE NEW FRIENDSHIP

1. New York *Times,* January 6, 1975.
2. Statistic from K. Walker and M. Woods, "Time Use: A Measure of Household Production of Family Goods and Services." Washington, D.C.: American Home Economics Association, 1976. For a discussion of "role overload" for women, see also J. Pleck, L. Lang, and M. Rustad, "Men's Family Work, Involvement and Satisfaction." Wellesley, Mass.: Wellesley College Center for Research on Women, 1980.
3. In Blumstein and Schwartz, *American Couples,* the authors con-

cluded that "working wives still bear almost all the responsibility for housework." For specific data see table on p. 144.

4. Pleck, Lang, and Rustad, loc. cit.

5. Joseph H. Pleck, "The Work-Family Problem: Overloading the System," in *Outsiders on the Inside,* eds. Barbara L. Forisha and Barbara H. Goldman (Englewood Cliffs, N.J.: Prentice-Hall, 1981), p. 243.

6. According to Blumstein and Schwartz (loc. cit.), this attitude is not just reflective of men but of the women themselves. See also "The Psychological Parent" in Jean Curtis, *Working Mothers.*

7. Linda Wolfe, "Friendship in the City," *New York Magazine,* July 18, 1983, pp. 20–28.

8. For a full discussion of men's friendships see Bell, *Worlds of Friendship,* chaps. 3 and 4, pp. 55–74. See also Block, *Friendship,* pp. 53–77.

9. Quoted in *Time,* March 12, 1984.

10. Sandra E. Candy, "Women, Work and Friendship: Personal Confirmation and Support," in *Outsiders on the Inside,* p. 193.

11. Robert Bell, "Friendships of Women and of Men," *Psychology of Women Quarterly* 3, no. 3 (Spring 1981).

12. Candy, "Women, Work and Friendship," loc. cit. See also Barbara Kaye Greenleaf, *Help: A Handbook for Working Mothers,* (New York: Thomas Y. Crowell, 1979), pp. 269–71.

13. Andrée Brooks, "Relationships," New York *Times,* February 27, 1984, sec. C.

14. Curtis, *Working Mothers,* p. 145.

15. David Gutmann, "Female Ego Styles and Generational Conflict," in *Feminine Personality and Conflict,* Bardwick et al., pp. 82–86.

16. This theory is presented in Abraham H. Maslow, *Motivation and Personality,* 2nd ed. (New York: Harper & Row Publishers, 1954).

17. Margaret Hennig and Anne Jardim, *The Managerial Woman* (New York: Pocket Books, 1977), pp. 153–54.

18. Quoted in Jane Adams, *Women on Top* (New York: Hawthorn Books, 1974).

19. For an excellent discussion of envy in women's relationships, see Madonna Kohlbenschlag, *Kiss Sleeping Beauty Goodbye* (New York: Bantam Books, 1981), pp. 48–52.

20. Diane F. Kravetz, "Sex Role Concepts of Women," *Journal of Consulting and Clinical Psychology* 44, no. 3 (1976): 437–43.

21. Nancy Sahli, "Smashing: Women's Relationships before the Fall," *Chrysalis,* no. 8 (1978): 17–27.

22. Carol Gilligan, *In a Different Voice* (Cambridge, Mass.: Harvard University Press, 1982), p. 124.

Chapter 8: *FRIENDS AND DIVORCE*

1. The finding that the resolution of the divorce crisis leads to more of an internal locus of control is discussed in William Doherty's article "Divorce and Belief in Internal vs. External Control of One's Life," *Journal of Divorce* 3, no. 4 (Summer 1980): 391–401.

2. Stan Albrecht, "Reactions and Adjustments to Divorce: Differences in the Experiences of Males and Females," *Family Coordinator,* January 1980, pp. 59–68. See also the classic study on women's reactions to divorce by William J. Goode entitled *Women in Divorce* (New York: Free Press, 1956).

3. In "The Relationship Between Sex Roles, Marital Status and Mental Illness" *(Social Forces* 51 (1972): 34–44), W. R. Gove notes that all unmarried men, including the never-married, the widowed, and the divorced, experience more mental health problems than women. One possible explanation for this finding is that men lack the support networks (i.e., friendships) available to women.

4. C. M. Parkes calls this the "separation distress" syndrome *(Bereavement* [New York: International Universities Press, 1972]). For a discussion of the similarities between divorce and loss of attachment figure in childhood, see Robert S. Weiss, "The Emotional Impact of Marital Separation," in *Single Life: Unmarried Adults in Social Context,* ed. Peter J. Stein, (New York: St. Martin's Press, 1981), pp. 69–79.

5. Albrecht, op. cit., p. 61. Goode (op. cit.) claims that close to one third of women do not view divorce as traumatic; however, his findings must be viewed with caution, as some of the responses were obtained as long as a few years after separation.

6. Paul Bohannan, "The Six Stations of Divorce," in *Divorce and After,* ed. Paul Bohannan (Garden City, N.Y.: Doubleday & Co., 1968), p. 53.

7. For an excellent discussion of problems specific to the divorced mother, see Janet A. Kohen, Carole A. Brown, and Roslyn Feldberg, "Divorced Mothers: The Costs and Benefits of Female Family Control," *Single Life: Unmarried Adults in Social Context,* pp. 288–305.

8. Jessie Bernard, "No News, but New Ideas," in *Divorce and After,* p. 8.

9. Parents, notes Robert Weiss, also tend to be more judgmental about divorce than friends. "Parents, especially, assume the right to comment on the separation, to criticize it, to disapprove or approve of it, perhaps going on until the separated individual is driven to exasperation" *(Marital Separation* [New York: Basic Books, 1975], p. 132). William Goode's observation that the most constructive response to divorce is one that is indifferent (as opposed to approving or disapproving) provides another argument against relying too heavily on parental support during the divorcing process (Goode, op. cit., p. 198).

10. Arthur A. Miller, "Reactions of Friends to Divorce," in *Divorce and After,* p. 62.

11. Helena Znaniecki Lopata, "Couple Companionate Relationships in Marriage and Widowhood," in *Old Family/New Family: Interpersonal Relationships,* ed. Nona Glazer-Malbin (New York: D. Van Nostrand Co., 1975), p. 143.

12. Arthur Miller proposes, "In some social cliques divorce may become 'contagious.' Once one of the circle of friends has divorced, shame about divorcing is diminished. The standard of behavior might, in fact, swing in the opposite direction, where divorcing takes on a positive significance" (Miller, op. cit., p. 59).

13. Miller, op. cit., p. 64.

14. Bernard, op. cit., p. 5.

15. Ibid., p. 6.

16. This figure is only an approximation, based on current statistics that 50–60 percent of women with school-aged children work. It is assumed that for married women without children, the percentage is even higher.

17. Kohen, Brown, and Feldberg observed: "From an average pre-divorce family income of $12,500, the women in our sample fell to a post-divorce average of $6,100, a drop of just over half. This overall average obscures an important class difference—the higher they start, the farther they fall. The eight highest income families dropped 60 percent, the nine lowest income families dropped only 19 percent. The less the husband had contributed, the less he could take away" (Kohen, Brown, and Feldberg, op. cit., p. 294).

18. See Carol Travris, "Divorce and Your Career—The Surprise Effects," *Vogue,* June 1983, p. 72.

19. Miller, op. cit., p. 61.

20. Miller, op. cit., p. 65.

21. Miller, op. cit., pp. 65–66.

22. Miller, op. cit., p. 61.

23. Miller, op. cit., pp. 66–67.
24. Miller, op. cit., p. 69.
25. Djuna Barnes, *Nightwood* (New York: New Directions Publishing Corp., 1961), p. 143.
26. The finding that nonsupportive friends make adjustment to separation more difficult is reported in, Graham B. Spanier and Robert F. Castro, "Adjustment to Separation and Divorce: A Qualitative Analysis," in *Close Relationships,* eds. G. L. Levinger and H. L. Rausch (Amherst: University of Massachusetts Press, 1977), p. 217.

Chapter 9: OFFICE HOURS

1. Chodorow, *Reproduction of Mothering,* p. 169.
2. These findings are summarized by Barbara Forisha in "The Inside and the Outsider: Women in Organizations," in *Outsiders on the Inside,* eds. Barbara L. Forisha and Barbara H. Goldman (Englewood Cliffs, N.J.: Prentice-Hall, 1981), pp. 9–30.
3. Ibid., p. 21.
4. Constantine Safilios-Rothschild, "Women and Work: Policy Implications and Prospects for the Future," in *Women Working: Theories and Facts in Perspective,* eds. A. Stromberg and S. Harkness (Palo Alto, Calif.: Mayfield Publishing Co., 1978), p. 429.
5. Quoted in Adams, *Women on Top,* p. 23.
6. For an extensive review of these studies see Bardwick, *Psychology of Women,* pp. 172–74.
7. Bell, *Worlds of Friendship,* pp. 71–72.
8. Hennig and Jardim, *Managerial Woman,* p. 52. See also R. Schuler, "Sex, Organizational Level and Outcome Importance: Where the Differences Are," *Personnel Psychology* 28 (1975): 365–75.
9. Faye J. Crosby, *Relative Deprivation and Working Women* (New York: Oxford University Press, 1982), pp. 56–57.
10. Barbara H. Goldman and Barbara L. Forisha, eds., "Women, Work and Friendship," *Outsiders on the Inside,* p. 151.
11. E. Spangler, M. Gordon, and R. Pipkin, "Token Women: An Empirical Test of Kanter's Hypothesis," *American Journal of Sociology* 84 (1978): 160–70.
12. Pat Rotter in preface to *Bitches and Sad Ladies* (New York: Dell Publishing Co., 1975), p. 9.
13. Adams, op. cit., p. 105.

14. Erich Fromm, *Escape from Freedom* (New York: Avon Books, 1965), p. 180.

Chapter 10: BOSS-EMPLOYEE CONFLICTS: THE SAGA OF ARLENE NIELSEN

1. Findings of a Gallup poll reported in the New York *Times,* Thursday, July 19, 1984, sec. A.
2. Quoted in "Women Now: The Open Doors," *Vogue,* a seminar edited by Lorraine Davis, June 1983, p. 191.
3. Joyce Brothers, "How to Be Unafraid of Success," *Harper's Bazaar,* January 1976, p. 47.
4. Hennig and Jardim, *Managerial Woman,* pp. 165–77.
5. These findings were cited in Carol Hymowitz, "Male Workers and Female Bosses Are Confronting Hard Challenges," *Wall Street Journal,* July 16, 1984, sec. 2.
6. Patricia Kosinar, "Socialization and Self Esteem: Women in Management," in *Outsiders on the Inside,* p. 36.
7. Bardwick, *In Transition,* p. 142.
8. K. Bartol and M. Wortman, Jr., "Male versus Female Leaders: Effects on Perceived Leader Behavior and Satisfaction in a Hospital," *Personnel Psychology* 28 (1975): 533–47.
9. Cited in "Labor Letter," *Wall Street Journal,* January 11, 1983.
10. M. G. Williams, *The New Executive Woman: A Guide to Business Success* (New York: New American Library, 1977).
11. Adams, *Women on Top,* p. 54.
12. Schuler, "Sex, Organizational Level and Outcome Importance," pp. 365–75.
13. Bardwick, *In Transition,* p. 143.
14. David Gutmann, "Female Ego Styles and Generational Conflict," in *Feminine Personality and Conflict,* Bardwick et al., p. 84.
15. Forisha and Goldman, eds., *Outsiders on the Inside,* p. xvii.
16. Hymowitz, loc. cit.
17. Barbara Forisha, "The Setting: Are Women Really Different from Men," in *Outsiders on the Inside,* p. 31.
18. G. I. Pheterson, S. B. Kiesler, and P. A. Goldberg, "Evaluation of the Performance of Women as a Function of Their Sex Achievement and Personal History," *Journal of Personality and Social Psychology* 19 (1971): 114–18.
19. Joan A. W. Linsenneir and Camille B. Wortman, "Attitude Toward Workers and Toward Their Work: More Evidence That Sex Makes

a Difference," *Journal of Applied Social Psychology* 9, no. 4 (July-August 1979): 226–34.

Chapter 11: *COMPETITION ON THE JOB*

1. New York *Times,* September 8, 1982, sec. A, p. 1.
2. Debra Eaton Olds and Philip Shaver, "Masculinity, Femininity, Academic Performance and Health: Further Evidence Concerning the 'Androgyny Controversy,' " *Journal of Personality* 48, no. 3 (September 1980): 323–41.
3. Adams, *Women on Top,* p. 54.
4. Olds and Shaver, op. cit., p. 333.
5. Martina S. Horner, "Sex Differences in Achievement Motivation and Performance in Competitive and Non-competitive Situations," (Doctoral dissertation, University of Michigan, 1968).
6. What little empirical data that exists also suggests this might be so. In L. Monohan, D. Kuhn, and P. Shaver, "Intrapsychic Versus Cultural Explanations of the 'Fear of Success' Motive," *(Journal of Personality* 29 [1974]: 60–64), the researchers found that girls in all-girls' schools exhibited a greater fear of success than girls in coeducational schools.
7. Allan E. Mallinger, "Fear of Success and Oedipal Experience," *Journal of Psychology,* 1978, pp. 91–106.
8. Ibid.
9. From an interview with Angela Fox, November 1983.
10. Hennig and Jardim, *Managerial Woman,* pp. 99–117.
11. Mallinger, op. cit., p. 103.
12. Joseph Verloff, "Social Comparison and the Development of Achievement Motivation," in *Achievement-related Motives in Children,* ed. Charles P. Smith (New York: Russell Sage Foundation, 1969).
13. Elizabeth Fishel, *Sisters* (New York: Bantam Books, 1980), p. 101.
14. Hilary Lips, *Women, Men and the Psychology of Power,* (Englewood Cliffs, N.J.: Prentice-Hall, 1971), p. 175.
15. Rosebeth Moss Kanter, *Men and Women of the Corporation* (New York: Basic Books, 1977).
16. Quoted in Adams, *Women on Top,* pp. 89–90.
17. Marcia Swanson, "The Effects of Unequal Competence and Sex on Achievement and Self-presentation," *Sex Roles* 5, no. 3 (June 1979): 279–85.

Chapter 12: OUR INDEPENDENCE, OUR FRIENDS

1. Martin Symonds, "Psychodynamics of Aggression in Women," *American Journal of Psychoanalysis* 36 (1976): 209.
2. Nancy Friday, *My Mother/My Self* (New York: Delacorte Press, 1977), p. 30.
3. Bardwick, *Psychology of Women,* p. 115.
4. Erik Erikson, *Identity: Youth and Crisis* (New York: W. W. Norton & Company, 1968), p. 139.

INDEX